COOL CARS

Quentin Willson

COOL
CARS

Quentin Willson

A DORLING KINDERSLEY BOOK

London, New York, Munich, Melbourne, Delhi

THIS EDITION

EDITOR: ALEXANDRA BEEDEN
PROJECT ART EDITOR: LAURA ROBERTS
SENIOR ART EDITOR: HELEN SPENCER
US EDITOR: ALLISON SINGER
MANAGING ART EDITOR: KAREN SELF
MANAGING EDITOR: ESTHER RIPLEY
PUBLISHER: SARAH LARTER
ART DIRECTOR: PHIL ORMEROD
ASSOCIATE PUBLISHING DIRECTOR:
LIZ WHEELER
PUBLISHING DIRECTOR: JONATHAN METCALF
PRE-PRODUCTION PRODUCER:
REBECCA FALLOWFIELD
SENIOR PRODUCER: GEMMA SHARPE
JACKET DESIGNER: NATALIE GODWIN
JACKET EDITOR: MANISHA MAJITHA
JACKET DESIGN DEVELOPMENT MANAGER:
SOPHIA TAMPAKOPOULOS

DK INDIA
SENIOR ART EDITORS: ANJANA NAIR,
RANJITA BHATTACHARJI
ART EDITOR: DEVAN DAS
ASSISTANT ART EDITORS: ANKITA MUKHERJEE,
NIYATI GOSAIN, PAYAL ROSALIND MALIK
MANAGING ART EDITOR: ARUNESH TALAPATRA
SENIOR EDITOR: SRESHTHA BHATTACHARYA
EDITOR: VIBHA MALHOTRA
MANAGING EDITOR: PAKSHALIKA JAYAPRAKASH
DTP DESIGNERS: VISHAL BHATIA,
SACHIN GUPTA, NEERAJ BHATIA
PRE-PRODUCTION MANAGER:
BALWANT SINGH
PRODUCTION MANAGER: PANKAJ SHARMA

PREVIOUS EDITION

PRODUCED FOR DORLING KINDERSLEY BY
PHIL HUNT (EDITORIAL), **MARK JOHNSON DAVIES** (DESIGN)

SENIOR EDITOR: EDWARD BUNTING
SENIOR ART EDITOR: KEVIN RYAN
MANAGING EDITOR: SHARON LUCAS
SENIOR MANAGING ART EDITOR: DEREK COOMBES
DTP DESIGNER: SONIA CHARBONNIER
PRODUCTION CONTROLLER: BETHAN BLASE
US EDITOR: GARY WERNER

REVISED AMERICAN EDITION, 2014
PUBLISHED IN THE UNITED STATES BY DK PUBLISHING
1450 BROADWAY, SUITE 801, NEW YORK, NY 10018

22 21 20 19 11 10 9 8
012 - 192885 - APR/14

Note on Specification Boxes: Unless otherwise indicated, all figures pertain to the particular
model in the specification box. A.F.C. is an abbreviation for average fuel consumption.

CONTENTS

INTRODUCTION

Some cars are cool and some have all the sexiness and desirability of an old shoe. Automotive history is littered with dismal failures that were ugly, slow, badly made, drove like donkey carts, or were just plain awful. Some of us are old enough to remember Morris Marinas, Austin Allegros, Ford Pintos, Trabants, Triumph TR7s, Toyota Cedrics, Volkswagen K70s, and Yugos. That such mediocre vehicles actually made it into production will always be a mystery, but the public wasn't fooled and proved it by buying these clunkers in tiny numbers. Cars like these will always stand as monuments to how the automotive industry occasionally gets things dramatically wrong. But mercifully, sometimes, they get it right and produce cars that become hugely desirable icons of cool. And that's what this little book is all about.

Between these pages you'll find a colorful selection of some of the world's greatest cars. Some are breathlessly fast, some are pinnacles of clever design, and some set new technological standards. But all possess that magical allure that makes us want to own and drive them. As I write, the world's appetite for cool cars has never been greater. The market for curvy classics is red-hot, and hardly a month goes past without another auction price record being broken for an elderly Ferrari or an Aston Martin. Old cars that a couple of decades ago were changing hands for tiny amounts of money have now increased in value as much as a thousand times and become a better investment than gold—literally.

When I first wrote this book I said that many classics were so cheap it seemed criminal. I was amazed that the selling prices of E-Type Jaguars *(see pages 306–09)* and Aston Martin DB4 *(see pages 32–35)* were so ridiculously low. Well, time has proved me right and a lot of the classics I recommended as bargain buys in the first edition of this book have since mushroomed in price to insanely stratospheric levels. I hate to say "I told you so," but if you'd done as I suggested and bought an Aston Martin DB4 and Ferrari Daytona *(see page 233)* for around $100,000 in 2001, the pair would now be worth more than a million and a half today. In a little over a decade the desire to own distinctive and rare classics has become an unstoppable market force worth many billions.

But our obsession with cool cars doesn't stop at the old stuff. The market for high-tab, glamorous new cars is red-hot, too. And the market is cooking all over the world. Modern Bentleys, Rolls Royces, Ferraris, Aston Martins, Maseratis, and McLarens have almost become celebrities in their own right. There are waiting lists for Jaguars and Range Rovers, over-list premiums being paid for Ferraris, and lines of desperate buyers chasing used luxury and sports cars. And given that the world is suffering under the worst recession since the Second World War, this simply should not be happening. Our desire for distinctive sexy wheels is probably the most powerful it's ever been in the history of the motor car, and many of us are willing to spend all the money we haven't got just to get behind the wheel of a cool ride.

What is even more surprising is that a blizzard of anti-car legislations, dire warnings about climate change, growing congestion, and pressure from environmentalists hasn't really changed our attitudes. Most people with a soul, when given the choice between a Toyota Prius hybrid and a BMW 3 Series, will always go for the BMW. The Prius may be an enormously smart car but it just can't tickle our hearts with the same delicate fingers as the BMW. And that's because a cool car defines who we are in the social pecking order. No other symbol in society changes other people's perceptions of us like cars—they're mobile, they're visible, and they're a currency that almost everybody understands. And if your ride is cool, onlookers just sigh in admiration. Being bland and predictable won't get you those coveted looks of warm approval. It doesn't matter if your cool car is ancient or modern; you'll be making that very important statement that you chose to be different from everybody else.

So let's sit back and relish this new golden age of motoring where there are so many wonderful cars to choose from. In all the years I've been writing and broadcasting about motoring, I can't remember a time when the choice of desirable and genuinely charismatic cars was so amazingly huge. The selection of cars in this book may be eclectic but I guarantee that all of them, without exception, will turn heads and disarm and charm in equal measure.

And remember this: Our love of cool cars isn't going to go away anytime soon so if you've got the cash, think about buying yourself a cool classic. There are very few things that you can buy in life that can offer the same level of enjoyment and fun as an old car that steadily increases in value over the years. It may be too late to buy that cheap Daytona or DB4 but there are plenty of other classics (and modern neoclassics) that are still affordable, still sexy, and still special. Go on, change your life and buy a cool car. I promise that you won't regret it and you'll be getting the keys to a new world of like-minded enthusiasts, all of whom refuse to drive something dreary, plain, or beige. Enjoy the ride.

AC *Ace-Bristol*

AGONIZINGLY PRETTY, THE AC ACE catapulted the homespun Thames Ditton company into the automotive limelight, instantly earning it a reputation as makers of svelte sports cars for the tweedy English middle classes. Timelessly elegant, swift, poised, and mechanically uncomplicated, the Ace went on to form the platform for the legendary AC Cobra *(see pages 16–19)*. Clothed in a light alloy body and powered by a choice of AC's own delicate UMB 2.0 unit, the hardier 2.0 Bristol 100D2 engine, or the lusty 2.6 Ford Zephyr power plant, the Ace drove as well as it looked. Its shape has guaranteed the Ace a place in automotive annals. Chaste, uncluttered, and simple, it makes a Ferrari look top-heavy and clumsy. Purists argue that the Bristol-powered version is the real thoroughbred Ace, closest to its original inspiration, the Bristol-powered Tojeiro prototype of 1953.

SIDE VIEW

The most handsome British roadster of its day, and as lovely as an Alfa Romeo Giulietta Sprint, the Ace had an Italianate simplicity. Proof of the dictum that less is more, the Ace's gently sweeping profile is a triumph of form over function.

SIDESCREEN

Folding Plexiglas sidescreens helped to prevent turbulence in the cockpit at high speed.

IMPRESSIVE SPEC
The Ace had triple Solex carbs, push-rod overhead valve gear, a light alloy head, and cast-iron crankcase.

BRASS PLATE
The firing order of the Ace's six cylinders was displayed on an engine plate.

FIRING ORDER
1 5 3 6 2 4
Bristol

HOOD LATCHES
Forward-hinged hood was locked by two chrome latches, opened by a small T-shaped key.

ENGINE
Shared by the BMW 328, the hemi-head 125 bhp 2-liter Bristol engine was offered as a performance conversion for the Ace.

SPECIFICATIONS

MODEL AC Ace-Bristol (1956–61)
PRODUCTION 463
BODY STYLE Two-door, two-seater sports roadster.
CONSTRUCTION Space-frame chassis, light alloy body.
ENGINE Six-cylinder push-rod 1971cc.
POWER OUTPUT 105 bhp at 5000 rpm (optional high-performance tune 125 bhp at 5750 rpm).
TRANSMISSION Four-speed manual Bristol gearbox (optional overdrive).
SUSPENSION Independent front and rear with transverse leaf spring and lower wishbones.
BRAKES Front and rear drums. Front discs from 1957.
MAXIMUM SPEED 117 mph (188 km/h)
0–60 MPH (0–96 KM/H) 9.1 sec
0–100 MPH (0–161 KM/H) 27.2 sec
A.F.C. 21.6 mpg (7.6 km/l)

BRAKES
Front discs were an option in 1957, but later standardized.

PROPORTIONS

The Ace was simplicity itself —a box for the engine, a box for the people, and a box for the luggage. On the handling side, production cars used Bishop cam-and-gear steering, which gave a turning circle of 36 ft (11 m) and required just two deft turns of the steering wheel lock-to-lock.

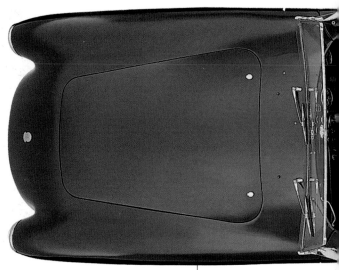

SHARED WHEEL

Steering wheel was shared with the Austin Healey (see pages 48–55) *and the Daimler SP Dart* (see pages 190–93).

CONSTRUCTION

Known as Superleggera *construction, a network of steel tubes was covered by aluminum panels, based on the outline of the 1949 Ferrari 122.*

EXPORT SUCCESS

The Ace became one of AC's most successful creations, with a huge proportion exported to America, where its character as an Englishman's girl-catcher justified its price tag of a small house.

COOLING

The Ace's wide, toothy grin fed air into the large radiator that was shared by the AC two-liter sedan.

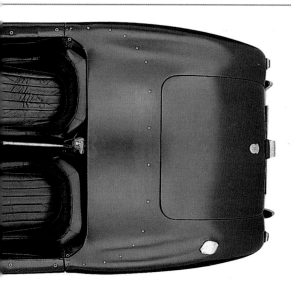

INTERIOR

In pure British tradition, the Ace's cockpit was stark, with gauges and switches haphazardly scattered across the dashboard. The two larger dials were a speedometer—with a clock inset into the dial—and a tachometer.

TONNEAU FASTENERS
For diehards who always drove with the top down, a tonneau cover could be attached which kept your feet warm while your face froze.

EAR-ENGINED GUSTO
ngines were placed well back
d gave an 18 percent rearward
as to the weight distribution.
rformance-wise, it helped—
 Ace recorded an average of
 mph (156 km/h) over 2,350
iles (3,781 km) at the 1957 Le
ans 24 Hours, the fastest ever
r a Bristol-engined car.

REVISED LIGHTS
Later Aces had a revised rear deck, with square taillights and a bigger trunk.

AC *Cobra 427*

AN UNLIKELY ALLIANCE BETWEEN AC CARS, a traditional British car-maker, and Carroll Shelby, a charismatic Texas racer, produced the legendary AC Cobra. AC's sports car, the Ace *(see pages 12–15)* was turned into the Cobra by shoehorning in a series of American Ford V8s, starting with 4.2 and 4.7 Mustang engines. In 1965 Shelby, always a man to take things to the limit, squeezed in a thunderous 7-liter Ford engine, in an attempt to realize his dream of winning Le Mans. Although the 427 was not fast enough to win and failed to sell in any quantity, it was soon known as one of the most aggressive and romantic cars ever built. GTM 777F at one time held the record as the world's fastest accelerating production car and in 1967 was driven by the British journalist John Bolster to record such Olympian figures as an all-out maximum of 165 mph (265 km/h) and a 0–60 (96 km/h) time of an unbelievable 4.2 seconds.

MUSCLY PROFILE
The 427 looked fast standing still. Gone was the lithe beauty of the original Ace, replaced by bulbous front and rear arches, fat 7½-in (19-cm) wheels, and rubber wide enough to climb walls.

WHEELS
Initially pin-drive Halibrand magnesium alloy, but changed for Starburst wheels (designed by Shelby employee Pete Brock) when supplies dried up.

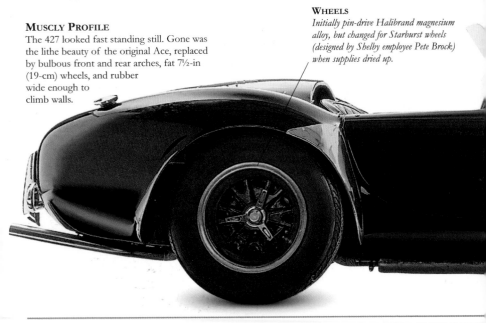

BODYWORK
The Cobra's body was constructed from hand-rolled aluminum wrapped around a tubular steel frame, which proved very light yet extremely strong.

BUMPERS
Bumpers were token chromed tubes, with the emphasis on saving weight.

EXHAUST
Racing Cobras usually had side exhausts, which increased power and noise.

SIDESCREENS
Small Plexiglas sidescreens helped cut down wind noise.

COOLING
Side vents helped reduce brake and engine temperatures.

EXTRA HORSEPOWER
Competition and semi-competition versions with fine-tuned engines could exceed 500 bhp.

ENGINE
The mighty 7-liter 427 block had years of NASCAR (National Association of Stock Car Automobile Racing) racing success and easily punched out power for hours. The street version output ranged from 300 to 425 bhp.

FRAME
The windshield frame was handmade and polished.

RADIATOR TANK
Radiator header tank kept things cool, helped by twin electric fans.

AIR FILTER
Under the massive air filter are two large four-barrel carburetors.

TIRES
Cobra tires were always Goodyear since Shelby was a long-time dealer.

UPGRADED CHASSIS
The chassis was virtually all new and three times stronger than the earlier Cobra 289's, with computer-designed anti-dive and anti-squat characteristics. Amazingly, the 289's original Salisbury differential proved more than capable of handling the 427's massive wall of torque.

POCKET DYNAMO

Even the "baby" 4.7 Cobras—as seen in this contemporary poster—were good for 138 mph (222 km/h) and could squeal up to 60 mph (96 km/h) in under six seconds.

ENGINE CHANGES
Early Cobras had 260cid engines. Later cars were fitted with Mustang 289 V8s.

SPECIFICATIONS

MODEL AC Cobra 427 (1965–68)

PRODUCTION 316

BODY STYLE Light alloy, two-door, two-seater, open sports.

CONSTRUCTION Separate tubular steel chassis with aluminum panels.

ENGINE V8, 6989cc.

POWER OUTPUT 425 bhp at 6000 rpm.

TRANSMISSION Four-speed all-synchromesh.

SUSPENSION All-around independent with coil springs.

BRAKES Four-wheel disc.

MAXIMUM SPEED 165 mph (265 km/h)

0–60 MPH (0–96 KM/H) 4.2 sec

0–100 MPH (0–161 KM/H) 10.3 sec

A.F.C. 15 mpg (5.3 km/l)

INTERIOR
The interior was basic, with traditional 1960s British sports car features of black-on-white gauges, small bucket seats, and wood rim steering wheel.

AC *428*

THE AC 428 NEEDS A NEW word of its very own—"brutiful" perhaps, for while its brute strength derives from its Cobra forebear, the 428 has a sculpted, stately beauty. This refined bruiser was born of a thoroughbred crossbreed of British engineering, American power, and Italian design. The convertible 428 was first seen at the London Motor Show in October 1965; the first fixed-head car—the so-called fastback—was ready in time for the Geneva Motor Show in March 1966. But production was beset by problems from the start; the first cars were not offered for sale until 1967, and as late as March 1969, only 50 had been built. Part of the problem was that the 428 was priced between the more expensive Italian Ferraris and Maseratis and the cheaper British Astons and Jensens. Small-scale production continued into the 1970s, but its days were numbered and it was finally done for by the fuel crisis of October 1973; the last 428—the 80th—was sold in 1974.

ITALIAN STYLING
Styled by Pietro Frua in Turin, the AC 428 was available in both convertible and fixed-head fastback form. It was based on an AC Cobra 427 chassis, virtually standard apart from a 6-in (15-cm) increase in wheelbase.

THIN SKINNED
Early cars had aluminum doors and hood; later models were all steel.

CONTEMPORARY LOOKS
The design contains subtle reminders of a number
of contemporary cars, not least the Maserati Mistral.
This is hardly surprising, since the Mistral was
also penned by Pietro Frua.

SPECIFICATIONS

MODEL AC 428 (1966–73)

PRODUCTION 80 (51 convertibles,
29 fastbacks)

BODY STYLES Two-seat convertible
or two-seat fastback coupe.

CONSTRUCTION Tubular-steel backbone
chassis/separate all-steel body.

ENGINES Ford V8, 6997cc or 7016cc.

POWER OUTPUT 345 bhp at 4600 rpm.

TRANSMISSION Ford four-speed manual
or three-speed auto; Salisbury rear axle
with limited-slip differential.

SUSPENSION Double wishbones and
combined coil spring/telescopic damper
units front and rear.

BRAKES Servo-assisted Girling discs front
and rear.

MAXIMUM SPEED 139.3 mph
(224 km/h) (auto)

0–60 MPH (0–96 KM/H) 5.9 sec (auto)

0–100 MPH (0–161 KM/H) 14.5 sec

A.F.C. 12–15 mpg (4.2–5.3 km/l)

AIR VENTS
*In an effort to combat engine
overheating, later cars have
air vents behind the wheels.*

ALL LACED UP
*Standard wheels were substantial triple-laced,
wired-up affairs, secured by a three-eared nut.*

WEATHER BEATER

The top was tucked under a cover which, in early models, was made of metal. When up, the hood made the cockpit feel somewhat claustrophobic, but the plastic rear "window" was generously proportioned.

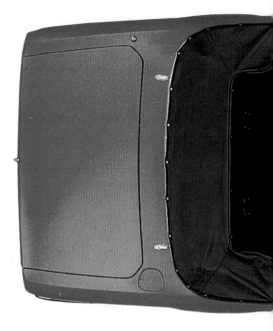

DASHBOARD

Switchgear may be scattered around like confetti, but the instruments are grouped clearly in front of the driver. The speedo *(far left)* reads to an optimistic 180 mph (290 km/h), while the tachometer *(far right)* reaches 8,000 rpm.

REAR VIEW

The 428 may have been a refined muscle car, but it was not totally unique; it featured parts from other manufacturers, such as rear lights from Fiat.

DESIGN CREDIT
Frua is credited with a "Creazione Frua" badge on each side.

POWER UNIT
Pre-1967, the car used the same 427 cubic inch (6998cc) V8 as the Cobra *(see pages 16–19)*, so was originally known as the AC 427.

ALFA ROMEO *1300 Junior Spider*

DRIVEN BY DUSTIN HOFFMAN TO THE strains of Simon and Garfunkel in the film *The Graduate*, the Alfa Spider has become one of the most accessible cult Italian cars. This is hardly surprising when you consider the little Alfa's considerable virtues: a wonderfully responsive all-alloy, twin-cam engine, accurate steering, sensitive brakes, a finely balanced chassis, plus movie idol looks. It hasn't been called the poor man's Ferrari for nothing. First launched at the Geneva Motor Show in 1966, Alfa held a worldwide competition to find a name for its new baby. After considering 140,000 entries, with suggestions like Lollobrigida, Bardot, Nuvolari, and even Stalin, they settled on Duetto, which neatly summed up the car's two's-company-three's-a-crowd image. Despite the same price tag as the much faster and more glamorous Jaguar E-Type *(see pages 306–09)*, the Spider sold over 100,000 units during its remarkable 26-year production run.

CONTEMPORARY CONTROVERSY
One of Pininfarina's last designs, the Spider's rounded front and rear and deep-channeled scallop running along the sides attracted plenty of criticism. One British car magazine dubbed it "compact and rather ugly."

TOP
The Spider's top was beautifully effective. It could be raised with only one arm without leaving the driver's seat.

LOGO
Pininfarina's credit indicated by his logo.

TRUNK
Spiders had huge trunks by sports car standards, with the spare wheel tucked neatly away under the trunk floor.

INTERIOR

The dashboard was painted metal up to 1970. Minor
controls were on fingertip levers, while the
windshield wipers had an ingenious foot
button positioned on the floor.

SPECIFICATIONS

MODEL Alfa Romeo 1300 Junior Spider
(1968–78)

PRODUCTION 7,237

BODY STYLE Two-door, two-seater.

CONSTRUCTION All-steel monocoque
body.

ENGINE All-alloy twin-cam 1290cc.

POWER OUTPUT 89 bhp at 6000 rpm.

TRANSMISSION Five-speed.

SUSPENSION *Front:* independent; *Rear:* live
axle with coil springs.

BRAKES Four-wheel disc.

MAXIMUM SPEED 106 mph (170 km/h)

0–60 MPH (0–96 KM/H) 11.2 sec

0–100 MPH (0–161 KM/H) 21.3 sec

A.F.C. 29 mpg (10.3 km/l)

RACING ALFA

*The later Alfa Romeo
Montreal had a race-bred 2.5
V8 that gave a top speed of
140 mph (225 km/h).*

HEADLIGHTS

*Plexiglas headlight covers were
banned in the US and were never
used on the 1300 Juniors.*

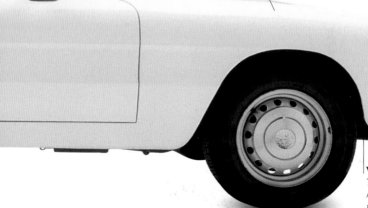

WHEEL ARCHES

*The lack of rustproofing
meant that the arches
were prone to decay.*

DRIVING POSITION
All Spider cockpits had the Italian apelike driving position—long arms and short legs.

QUALITY TAIL
The "boat-tail" rear was shared by all Spiders up to 1970 and is the styling favored by Alfa purists. It was replaced by a squared-off Kamm tail.

BODYWORK
The Spider's bodywork corroded alarmingly quickly due to the poor-quality steel.

STYLISH AND COOL
The Spider has to be one of Alfa's great postwar cars, not least because of its contemporary design. It was penned by Battista Pininfarina, the founder of the renowned Turin-based design house.

NOSE SECTION
Disappearing nose was very vulnerable to parking dents.

WMT 97G

ALFA'S BAMBINO
The 1300 Junior was the baby of the Spider family, introduced in 1968 to take advantage of Italian tax laws. As well as the "Duetto," which refers to 1600 Spiders, there was also a 1750cc model in the line. Large production numbers and high maintenance costs mean that prices of Spiders are invitingly low.

STYLISH GRILLE
This hides a twin-cam, energy-efficient engine with hemispherical combustion chambers. Some of the mid-'70s Spiders imported to the US, however, were overly restricted; the catalyzed 1750, for example, could only manage a miserly top speed of just 99 mph (159 km/h).

AMC *Pacer*

THE 1973 FUEL CRISIS HIT America's psyche harder than did the Russians beating them to space in the Fifties. Cheap and unrestricted personal transportation had been a way of life, and then America suddenly faced the horrifying prospect of paying more than forty cents a gallon. Overnight, stock in car manufacturers became as popular as Richard Nixon. Detroit's first response was to kill the muscle car. The second was to revive the "compact" and invent the "subcompact." AMC had first entered the subcompact market in 1970 with its immensely popular Gremlin model, but the 1975 Pacer was a different beast. Advertised as "the first wide small car," it had the passenger compartment of a sedan, the nose of a European commuter shuttle, and no back end at all. Ironically, it wasn't even that economical, but America didn't notice because it was on a guilt trip, buying over 70,000 of the things in '75 alone.

WINDSHIELD
The aerodynamic windshield aided fuel economy and reduced interior noise.

STYLING TO TALK ABOUT
In the mid-Seventies, the Pacer was sold as the last word; "the face of the car of the 21st century" bragged the ads. Happily, they were wrong. Pundits of the time called it a "football on wheels" and a "big frog."

GLASS COVERAGE

The Pacer had the largest glass area of any contemporary American sedan, making the $425 all season air-conditioning option almost obligatory. There was no doubt that outward vision, though, was quite superb.

INTERIOR

Inside was stock Detroit, with sporty front bucket seats and a cheesy polyurethane dash.

EXTRA GRIP

Twin-Grip differential was a $46 option.

MAX HEADROOM

There was more headroom and legroom than the contemporary Chevelle or Torino, making it feel spacious.

EXTRA WIDTH

The body was almost as wide as it was long, and though opinion was divided on the Pacer's looks, it did garner some hefty praise; *Motor Trend* magazine called the styling "the most innovative of all US small cars." Credit went to Richard Teague, who also penned the '84 Jeep Cherokee.

TRUNK SPACE
With rear seat folded, cargo area was an impressive 30 cubic feet.

FRONT RECLINERS
Adaptability even stretched to the front of the car; 26 percent of all Pacers had reclining front seats.

LATER LENGTH
In 1977 Pacers were stretched a further 4 in (10 cm) and offered as station wagons.

COSTLY EXTRAS

Surprisingly, the Pacer was never a cheap car. Add a few interior options and air-conditioning and you could easily have been presenting the dealer with a check for $5,000. De Luxe trim pack included wood effect side and rear panels, which made the Pacer about as tasteful as Liberace.

STEERING
The Pacer's rack-and-pinion steering was one of the first on a US car.

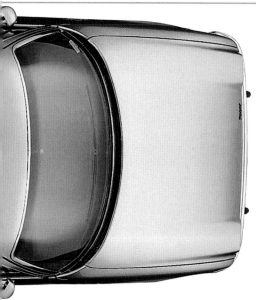

SPECIFICATIONS

MODEL AMC Pacer

PRODUCTION 72,158 (1975)

BODY STYLE Three-door sedan.

CONSTRUCTION Steel unitary body.

ENGINES 232cid, 258cid sixes.

POWER OUTPUT 90–95 bhp.

TRANSMISSION Three-speed manual with optional overdrive, optional three-speed Torque-Command automatic.

SUSPENSION *Front:* coil springs; *Rear:* semi-elliptic leaf springs.

BRAKES Front discs, rear drums.

MAXIMUM SPEED 105 mph (169 km/h)

0–60 MPH (0–96 KM/H) 14 sec

A.F.C. 6.4–8.5 km/l (18–24 mpg)

REAR INSPIRATION
Unbelievably, the Pacer's rear end inspired the comely rump of the Porsche 928.

ACER POWER
ock power was a none-too-rifty 258cid straight six unit. In dition, for all its eco pretensions, u could still specify a 304cid V8.

BUMPERS
Originally slated to use urethane bumpers, production Pacers were equipped with steel versions to save money.

SE 2345
19 colorado 75
centennial

ASTON MARTIN *DB4*

THE DEBUT OF THE DB4 IN 1958 heralded the beginning of the Aston Martin glory years, ushering in the breed of classic six-cylinder DB Astons that propelled Aston Martin onto the world stage. Earlier postwar Astons were fine sports enthusiasts' road cars, but with the DB4 Astons acquired a new grace, sophistication, and refinement that was, for many, the ultimate flowering of the grand tourer theme. The DB4 looked superb and went like the wind. The DB5, which followed, will forever be remembered as the James Bond Aston; and the final expression of the theme came with the bigger DB6. The cars were glorious, but the company was in trouble. David Brown, the millionaire industrialist owner of Aston Martin and the DB of the model name, had a dream. But, in the early Seventies, with losses of $1.5 million a year, he bailed out of the company, leaving a legacy of machines that are still talked about with reverence as the David Brown Astons.

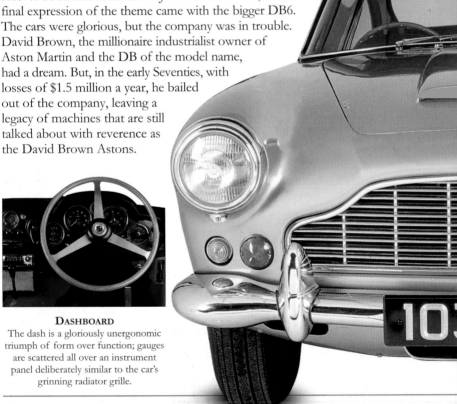

DASHBOARD
The dash is a gloriously unergonomic triumph of form over function; gauges are scattered all over an instrument panel deliberately similar to the car's grinning radiator grille.

Superleggera

BRITISH LIGHTWEIGHT
Superleggera, Italian for "super-lightweight," refers to the technique of body construction: aluminum panels rolled over a framework of steel tubes.

IN THE MIRROR
Dipping rearview mirror was also found in many Jaguars of the period.

UNHINGED
First generation DB4s had a rear-hinged hood.

SPECIFICATIONS

MODEL Aston Martin DB4 (1958–63)

PRODUCTION 1,040 (fixed head); 70 (convertible); 95 (fixed-head DB4 GTs).

BODY STYLES Fixed-head coupe or convertible.

CONSTRUCTION Pressed-steel and tubular inner chassis frame, with aluminum-alloy outer panels.

ENGINES Inline six 3670cc/3749cc.

POWER OUTPUT 240 bhp at 5500 rpm.

TRANSMISSION Four-speed manual (with optional overdrive).

SUSPENSION *Front:* independent by wishbones, coil springs, and telescopic shock absorbers; *Rear:* live axle located by trailing arms and Watt linkage with coil springs and lever-arm dampers.

BRAKES Four-wheel disc.

MAXIMUM SPEED 140+ mph (225+ km/h)

0–60 MPH (0–96 KM/H) 8 sec

0–100 MPH (0–161 KM/H) 20.1 sec

A.F.C. 14–22 mpg (3.6–7.8 km/l)

ASTON SMILE
The vertical bars in this car's radiator grille show it to be a so-called Series 4 DB4, built between September 1961 and October 1962.

NO PRETENSIONS
There is no doubt that the DB4 has got serious attitude. Its lines may be Italian, but it has none of the dainty delicacy of some contemporary Ferraris and Maseratis—the Aston's spirit is somehow true Brit.

TRUNK PANEL
Complex curves meant the trunk lid was one of the most difficult-to-produce panels in the entire car. Their hand-built nature means no two Astons are alike.

LIGHTS
Rear lights and front indicators were straight off the utilitarian Land Rover.

BOND MATERIAL
The DB4's stance is solid and butch, but not brutish—more British Boxer than lumbering Bulldog, aggressive yet refined. It is an ideal blueprint for a James Bond car.

CLASSIC STYLING
Clothed in an Italian body by Carrozzeria Touring of Milan, the DB4 possessed a graceful yet powerful elegance. Under the aluminum shell was Tadek Marek's twin-cam straight-six engine, which evolved from Aston's racing program.

BUMPERS
Bumper overriders were from the British Mk2 Ford Zephyr and Zodiac.

ENGINE
It looks very much like the contemporary Jaguar XK twin-cam straight-six, but Tadek Marek's design is both more powerful and vastly more complicated. Triple SU carburetors show this to be a Vantage engine with larger valves and an extra 20 bhp.

UPHOLSTERY
While rear seats in the fixed-head offer limited space, just look at the richness and quality of the Connolly leather. The ride wasn't quite as impressive, though—rear suspension was through basic lever-arm units.

SUSPENSION
Front suspension was double wishbones with coil springs and telescopic shocks.

ASTON MARTIN *V8*

A NEAR TWO-TON GOLIATH powered by an outrageous handmade 5.3-liter engine, the DBS V8 was meant to be Aston's money-earner for the 1970s. Based on the six-cylinder DBS of 1967, the V8 did not appear until April 1970. With a thundering 160 mph (257 km/h) top speed and incredible sub seven-second 0–60 time, Aston's new bulldog instantly earned a place on every millionaire's shopping list. The trouble was that it drove into a worldwide recession—in 1975 the Newport Pagnell factory produced just 19 cars. Aston's bank managers were worried men, but the company pulled through. The DBS became the Aston Martin V8 in 1972 and continued until 1989, giving birth to the legendary 400 bhp Vantage and gorgeous Volante Convertible. Excessive, expensive, impractical, and impossibly thirsty, the DBS V8 and AM V8 are wonderful relics from a time when environmentalism was just another word in the dictionary.

ASTON LINES
Smooth tapering cockpit line is an Aston hallmark echoed in the current DB7.

NEW CONSTRUCTION
DBS was one of the first Astons with a chassis and departed from the traditional Superleggera tubular superstructure of the DB4, 5, and 6. Like Ferraris and Maseratis, Aston prices were ballyhooed up to stratospheric levels in the Eighties.

REAR ASPECT
Prodigious rear overhang makes the rear aspect look cluttered.

REAR WINDOW
Thin rear window gave the driver limited rearward vision.

SPOILER
Discreet rear spoiler was part of the ...ntly sweeping fender line.

TWIN PIPES
Handmade bumpers covered huge twin exhausts —a gentle reminder of this Aston's epic V8 grunt.

B391 AJD

OWNERS WITH PEDIGREE
Cars with incredible presence, Astons were good enough for James Bond, King Hussein of Jordan, Peter Sellers, and even the Prince of Wales—who has owned a DB6 Volante from new.

POWER BULGE
Massive hood power bulge was to clear four carburetors.

ASTON MARTIN V8

ENGINE
The alloy V8 was first seen in Lola sports-racing cars. The massive air-filter box covers a quartet of twin-choke Weber carbs, which guzzle one gallon of fuel for every 13 miles (4.6 km/l), and much less if you enjoy yourself.

EIGHTIES' PRICE
In the Eighties, top quality DBSs changed hands for $75,000 plus.

POWER UNIT
V8's engine churned out over 300 bhp, but later models could boast 400 bhp.

FRONT END
Shapely "cliff-hanger" nose was always a DBS trademark.

BOND CAR
A 1984 AM V8 Volante featured in the James Bond film *The Living Daylights*, with Timothy Dalton. In 1964 a DB5 was the first Aston to star alongside James Bond in the film *Goldfinger*, this time with Sean Connery.

SPOILER
Chin spoiler and undertray helped reduce front-end lift at higher speeds.

B391 A

CLASSY CABIN

Over the years the DBS was skillfully updated, without losing its traditional ambience. Features included leather and wood surroundings, air-conditioning, electric windows, and radio cassette. Nearly all V8s were ordered with Chrysler TorqueFlite auto transmission.

BODYWORK
V8's aluminum body was hand smoothed and lovingly finished.

SUMPTUOUS FIXTURES
As with most Astons, the interior was decked out in the finest quality leather and wood.

SPECIFICATIONS

MODEL Aston Martin V8 (1972–89)

PRODUCTION 2,842 (including Volante and Vantage)

BODY STYLE Four-seater coupe.

CONSTRUCTION Aluminum body, steel platform chassis.

ENGINE Twin OHC alloy 5340cc V8.

POWER OUTPUT Never released but approx 345 bhp (Vantage 400 bhp).

TRANSMISSION Three-speed auto or five-speed manual.

SUSPENSION Independent front, De Dion rear.

BRAKES Four-wheel disc.

MAXIMUM SPEED 161 mph (259 km/h); 173 mph (278 km/h) (Vantage)

0–60 MPH (0–96 KM/H) 6.2 sec (Vantage 5.4 sec)

0–100 MPH (0–161 KM/H) 14.2 sec (Vantage 13 sec)

A.F.C. 13 mpg (4.6 km/l)

Audi *Quattro Sport*

One of the rarest and most iconic Audis ever built was the 155 mph (250 km/h) Quattro Sport. With a short wheelbase, all-alloy 300 bhp engine, and a body made of aluminum-reinforced fiberglass and Kevlar, it has all the charisma, and nearly all the performance, of a Ferrari GTO. The Quattro changed the way we think about four-wheel drive. Before 1980, four-wheel drive systems had foundered through high cost, weight, and lousy road behavior. Everybody thought that if you bolted a four-wheel drive system onto a performance coupe it would have ugly handling, transmission whine, and an insatiable appetite for fuel. Audi's engineers proved that the accepted wisdom was wrong, and by 1982, the Quattro was a World Rally Champion. Gone but not forgotten, the Quattro Sport is now a much admired collectors' item.

FUNCTIONAL INTERIOR
While the dashboard layout is nothing special, everything is typically Germanic—clear, neat, and easy to use. The only touch of luxury in the Quattro is half-leather trim.

RALLY SUCCESS
In competition trim, Audi's remarkable turbocharged engine was pushing out 400 bhp, and by 1987, the fearsome S1 Sport generated 509 bhp. To meet Group B homologation requirements, only 220 Sports were built, and only a few destined for sale to some very lucky private owners.

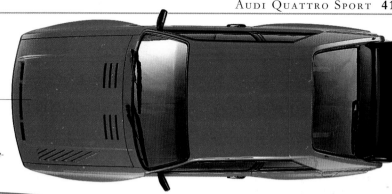

HOOD
*Long nose and
d bulge cover the
ntercooler for the
turbo unit.*

ROOF
*Roof sections were
made of aluminum-
onded fiberglass.*

HAND-CRAFTED BODY
*Bodyshells were welded by a
team of just 22 craftsmen.*

HOT PROPERTY

From any angle the Quattro Sport is
testosterone on wheels, with a butch
and aggressive four-square stance. The
cinder-block styling, though, meant that
the Quattro's aerodynamics were poor.

SPECIFICATIONS

MODEL Audi Quattro Sport (1983–87)
PRODUCTION 220 (all LHD)
BODY STYLE Two-seater, two-door coupe.
CONSTRUCTION Monocoque body from
Kevlar, aluminum, fiberglass, and steel.
ENGINE 2133cc five-cylinder turbocharged.
POWER OUTPUT 304 bhp at 6500 rpm.
TRANSMISSION Five-speed manual, four-
wheel drive.
SUSPENSION All-around independent.
BRAKES Four-wheel vented discs with
switchable ABS.
MAXIMUM SPEED 155 mph (250 km/h)
0–60 MPH (0–96 KM/H) 4.8 sec
0–100 MPH (0–161 KM/H) 13.9 sec
A.F.C. 17 mpg (6 km/l)

LIMITED EDITION
Of the 1,700 Audis produced each day in the mid-1980s, only three were Quattros, and of a year's output only a tiny amount were Sports.

REAR LIGHTS
Darkened rear lights were included across the whole Quattro line in 1984.

FOUR-SEATER?
While it looked like a four-seater, in practice only two could fit in.

RIDE QUALITY
Though the ride was harder than on normal Quattros, steering was quicker.

ARCHES
Box wheel arches are a Quattro hallmark, and essential to cover the fat 9J×15 wheels.

ENGINE

The five-cylinder 2133cc alloy engine is 50 lb (22.7 kg) lighter than the stock item, with twin overhead cams, four valves per cylinder, a giant turbocharger and Bosch LH-Jetronic injection. Center Torsen differential gives a 50/50 front-to-rear split. Rear differential lock disengages when the car passes 15 mph (24 km/h).

TURBOCHARGER

Turbo lag was a big problem on early Quattros; from 20–60 mph (32–96 km/h) in top it was slower than a 900cc VW Polo.

TECHNICAL TRAILBLAZER

Four-wheel drive cars are now part of most large carmakers' model lines and, along with airbags and antilock brakes (ABS), have played their part toward safer driving. We must thank the car that started it all, the Audi Quattro.

AUSTIN *Mini Cooper*

THE MINI COOPER WAS ONE of Britain's great motor sport legends, an inspired confection that became the definitive rally car of the Sixties. Because of its size, maneuverability, and front-wheel drive, the Cooper could dance around bigger, more unwieldy cars and scuttle off to victory. The hot Mini was a perfect blend of pin-sharp steering, terrific handling balance, and a feeling that you could get away with almost anything. Originally the brainchild of race car builder John Cooper, the Mini's designer, Alec Issigonis, thought it should be a "people's car" rather than a performance machine and did not like the idea of a souped-up Mini. Fortunately BMC (British Motor Corporation) did, and agreed to a trial run of just 1,000 cars. One of their better decisions.

SPOTLIGHT
Roof-mounted spotlight could be rotated from inside the car.

TIRES
Radial tires were on the Cooper S but not the standard Cooper.

RALLY REAR

24 PK wears the classic Mini rally uniform of straight-through exhaust, Minilite wheels, roll bar, twin fuel tanks, and lightweight stick-on license plates. BMC had a proactive Competitions Department.

COOPER S

The Cooper S, built between 1963–67, came in a choice of 970 or 1071cc engines and had wider wheels and different badging from the stock Cooper.

WINDSHIELD
Windshield was glass, but all other windows were made out of Plexiglas to save weight.

LICENSE PLATE
Competitions departments often swapped license plates, bodyshells, and chassis numbers, making it hard to identify genuine ex-race Coopers.

SPEEDY CORNERING
With a low center of gravity and a wheel at each extreme corner, the Mini had the perfect credentials for tramlike handling.

RACING PEDIGREE
In the 1964 Monte Carlo Rally, the Cooper produced a giant-killing performance, trouncing 4.7-liter Fairlanes to win. It never looked back, winning the '62 and '64 Tulip Rallies, the '63 Alpine Rally, the '65 and '67 Monte Carlo, and more than 25 other prestigious races.

RARE BLOCK

Though this is a 1071cc example, the 970cc version was the rarest of all Coopers, with only 964 made.

ENGINE

The 1071cc A-series engine would rev to 7,200 rpm, producing 72 bhp. Crankshaft, con-rods, valves, and rockers were all toughened, and the Cooper also had a bigger oil pump and beefed-up gearbox. Lockheed disc brakes and servo provided the stopping power.

GRILLE

Front grille was quick-release to allow access for emergency repairs to distributor, oil cooler, starter motor, and alternator.

RACE EXPERIENCE

This example, 24 PK, was driven by Sir Peter Moon and John Davenport in the 1964 Isle of Man Manx Trophy Rally. But, while leading the pack on the penultimate stage of the rally at Druidale, 24 PK was badly rolled and needed a complete reshell. Many race Coopers led a hard life, often rebuilt and reshelled several times.

PRICE TO PAY
The price difference between the Cooper and the S was £569 ($860) for the standard car and £695 ($1,050) for the S.

LIGHTS
For night rally stages, Coopers needed maximum illumination. Straps held on the headlight protectors.

SPECIFICATIONS

MODEL Austin Mini Cooper (1963–69)

PRODUCTION 145,000 (all models)

BODY STYLE Sedan.

CONSTRUCTION All steel two-door monocoque mounted on front and rear sub-frames.

ENGINES Four-cylinder 970cc/ 997cc/998cc/1071cc/1275cc.

POWER OUTPUT 65 bhp at 6500 rpm to 76 bhp at 5800 rpm.

TRANSMISSION Four-speed, no synchromesh on first.

SUSPENSION Independent front and rear suspension with rubber cones and wishbones (Hydrolastic from late 1964).

BRAKES Lockheed front discs with rear drums.

MAXIMUM SPEED 100 mph (161 km/h)

0–60 MPH (0–96 KM/H) 12.9 sec

0–100 MPH (0–161 KM/H) 20 sec

A.F.C. 30 mpg (10.6 km/l)

INTERIOR
The Cooper has typical rally-car features: wood-rim Moto-Lita wheel, fire extinguisher, Halda trip meter, tachometer, stopwatches, and maplight. The only features that would have been standard equipment are the center speedo, heater, and switches.

Austin-Healey *Sprite Mk1*

Some automotive academics believe all the best car designs have a recognizable face. If that is the case, few cars have a cuter one than this little fellow, with that ear-to-ear grinning grille and those wide-open, slightly astonished eyes. Of course, it is those trademark bulging peepers that prompted the nickname "Frogeye," by which everyone now recognizes this engaging little character. So much of the Frogeye's character was borne of necessity. The Donald Healey Motor Company and Austin had already teamed up with the Austin-Healey 100. In 1958, its little brother, the Sprite, was born, a spartan sports car designed down to a price and based on the engine and running gear of the Austin A35 sedan, with a bit of Morris Minor too. Yet the Frogeye really was a sports car and had a sweet raspberry exhaust note to prove it.

DECEPTIVE LOOKS

At just under 11 ft 5 in (3.5 m), the Frogeye is not quite as small as it looks. Its pert looks were only part of the car's cult appeal; for with its firm, even harsh, ride it had a traditional British sports car feel. A nimble performer, you could hustle it along a twisty road, cornering flat and clicking through the gears.

REAR VIEW
Plexiglas rear window offered only limited rear vision.

ENGINE

The Austin-Morris A-series engine was a little gem. It first appeared in the Austin A35 sedan and went on to power several generations of Mini *(see pages 44–47)*. In the Frogeye it was modified internally with extra-strong valve springs and equipped with twin SU carburetors to give 50 bhp gross (43 bhp net). By today's standards it's no road burner, but in the late Fifties it was a peppy little performer.

ENGINE ACCEESS
Rear-hinged alligator hood gives great engine access and makes the Frogeye a delight for tinkerers.

LOW DOWN
The Frogeye's low stance aided flat cornering. Ground clearance was better than it looked: just under 5 in (12.7 cm).

BUMPERS
Bumpers with overriders were a sensible and popular extra.

GVS 668

RACING LINKS

Sprites put up spirited performances at
Le Mans and Sebring in Florida, making club
racing affordable to ordinary enthusiasts.

THE FROG'S EYES

Donald Healey's original design incorporated
retracting headlights like the later Lotus Elan
(see pages 344–45), but extra cost ruled these ou
As it was, the protruding headlight pods create
a car with a character all of its own. The
complex one-piece hood in which the lamps
are set is made up of four main panels.

DUAL LIGHTS
Sidelights doubled
as flashing
indicators.

GVS 668

LATER INCARNATION

The design has a classic simplicity, free of needless chrome embellishment; there is no external door handle to interrupt the flowing flanks. In 1961 the Frogeye was reclothed in a more conventional skin, and these follow-on Sprites, also badged as MG Midgets, lasted until 1979.

ROUND RUMP
It is not so much a trunk, because it does not open; more a luggage locker with access behind the rear seats.

GEAR STICK
Stubby gear stick was nicely positioned for the driver.

COZY COCKPIT
The Frogeye fits like a glove. Side curtains rather than wind-down windows gave some extra elbow room and everything is within reach for the sporty driver—speedo on the right and tachometer on the left.

SPECIFICATIONS

MODEL Austin-Healey Sprite Mk1 (1958–61)

PRODUCTION 38,999

BODY STYLE Two-seater roadster.

CONSTRUCTION Unitary body/chassis.

ENGINE BMC A-Series 948cc, four-cylinder, overhead valve.

POWER OUTPUT 43 bhp at 5200 rpm.

TRANSMISSION Four-speed manual, synchromesh on top three ratios.

SUSPENSION *Front:* Independent, coil springs and wishbones; *Rear:* Quarter-elliptic leaf springs, rigid axle.

BRAKES Hydraulic, drums all around.

MAXIMUM SPEED 84 mph (135 km/h)

0–60 MPH (0–96 KM/H) 20.5 sec

A.F.C. 35–45 mpg (12.5–16 km/l)

AUSTIN-HEALEY *3000*

THE HEALEY HUNDRED WAS A sensation at the 1952 Earl's Court Motor Show in London. Austin's Leonard Lord had already contracted to supply the engines, but when he noticed the sports car's impact, he decided he wanted to build it too—it was transformed into the Austin-Healey 100. Donald Healey had spotted a gap in the American sports car market between the Jaguar XK120 *(see pages 296–99)* and the cheap and cheerful MG T series *(see pages 366–69)*. His hunch was right, for about 80 percent of all production went Stateside. Over the years this rugged bruiser became increasingly civilized. In 1956, it received a six-cylinder engine in place of the four, but in 1959 the 3000 was born. It became increasingly refined, with front disc brakes, then wind-up windows, and ever faster. Our featured car is the last of the line, a 3000 Mk3. Although perhaps verging on grand-tourer territory, it was still one of the fastest Big Healeys and has become a landmark British sports car.

WELL MATURED

The Austin-Healey put on weight over the years, became gradually more refined, and stayed true to its original sports car spirit. It developed into a surefooted thoroughbred.

WHEELS AND WHITEWALLS

Wire wheels with knock-off hubs were options on some models, standard on others; whitewalls usually signify an American car.

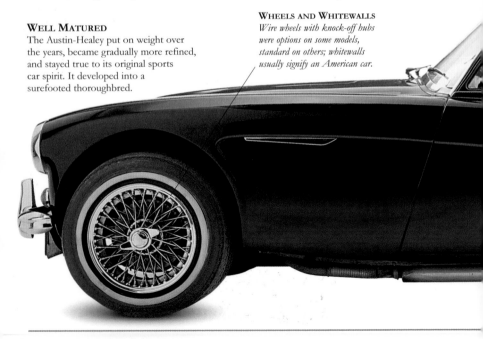

HOT PIT
Heat buildup from the engine and underfloor exhaust made for a warm ride.

COMFORTS
Updated weather equipment was an improvement on earlier efforts, which took two people 10 minutes to erect.

HOOD SCOOP
All six-cylinder Healeys, both the 100/6 and the 3000, featured a hood scoop; the longer engine pushed the radiator forward, with the scoop clearing the underhood protrusion to aid airflow.

WINDSHIELD

In 1962, the 3000 acquired a wrap-around windshield and wind-up windows, as the once raw sports car adopted trappings of sophistication.

ENGINE

Under the hood of the biggest of the so-called Big Healeys is the 2912cc straight-six, designated the 3000. This is the butchest of the big bangers, pumping out a hefty 150 bhp.

STYLING INFLUENCES

The two major influences on the Healey's changing faces were the needs of the American market and the impositions of Austin, both as parts supplier and as frugal keeper of purse strings. But from the start, the styling was always a major asset, and what you see here in the 3000 Mk3 is the eventual culmination of those combined styling forces.

REFINED REAR

The first prototype rear-end treatments featured faddish fins that were replaced by a classic round rump.

INCREASED LUXURY

Once spartan, the cockpit of the Austin-Healey became increasingly luxurious, with a polished veneer dash, glove compartment, fine leather, and rich carpet. One thing remained traditional—engine heat meant the cockpit was always a hot place to be.

HEALEY GRIN

From the traditional Healey diamond grille, the mouth of the Austin-Healey developed into a wide grin.

MORE POWER

The Americans bought more Healeys than anyone else and wanted more oomph. So in 1959 the 2639cc six-cylinder of the Healey 100/6 was bored out to 2912cc and rounded up to give the model name 3000.

SPECIFICATIONS

MODEL Austin-Healey 3000 (1959–68)

PRODUCTION 42,926 (all 3000 models)

BODY STYLES Two-seater roadster, 2+2 roadster, 2+2 convertible.

CONSTRUCTION Separate chassis/body.

ENGINE 2912cc overhead-valve, straight-six.

POWER OUTPUT 3000 Mk1: 124 bhp at 4600 rpm. 3000 Mk2: 132 bhp at 4750 rpm. 3000 Mk3: 150 bhp at 5250 rpm.

TRANSMISSION Four-speed manual with overdrive.

SUSPENSION *Front:* Independent coil springs and wishbones, antiroll bar; *Rear:* Semi-elliptic leaf springs. Lever-arm shock absorbers all around.

BRAKES Front discs; rear drum.

MAXIMUM SPEED 110–120 mph (177–193 km/h)

0–60 MPH (0–96 KM/H) 9.5–10.8 sec

A.F.C. 17–34 mpg (6–12 km/l)

BENTLEY *R-Type Continental*

IN ITS DAY THE BENTLEY CONTINENTAL, launched in 1952, was the fastest production four-seater in the world and acclaimed as "a modern magic carpet which annihilates distance." The R-Type Conti is still rightly considered one of the greatest cars of all time. Designed for the English country gentleman, it was understated, but had a lithe, sinewy beauty rarely seen in other cars of its era. Rolls-Royce's brief was to create a fast touring car for plutocrat customers, and to do that they had to reduce both size and weight. Aluminum construction helped the weight, while wind tunnel testing created that slippery shape. Those emergent fins at the back were not for decoration—they actually aided the car's directional stability. But such avant-garde development did not come cheap. In 1952, the R-Type Continental was the most expensive production car in the world and cost the same as a very large and agreeable house.

POSTWAR CLASSIC

In 1952, with wartime austerity a fading memory, this was one of the flashiest and most rakish cars money could buy. Today, this exemplar of breeding and privilege stands as a resplendent memorial to the affluence and optimism of Fifties Britain. Collectors seem to agree that the Continental is the finest postwar Bentley and one of the world's all-time great cars.

EXPORT ONLY
Such was the cost of the Continental that it was first introduced on an export-only basis.

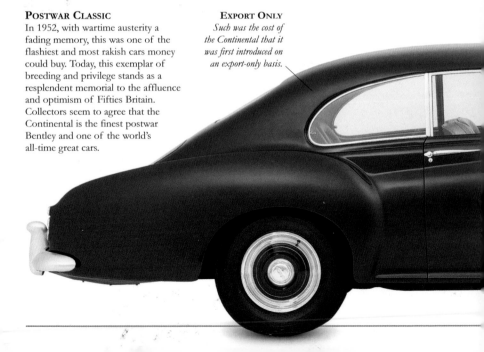

QUALITY RIDE
The Continental was a car that begged you to press its accelerator pedal to the floor and reassured you with its powerful brakes.

DESIGN SIMILARITIES
The Continental bears an uncanny resemblance to a Pininfarina R-Type prototype shown at the 1948 Paris Salon.

RADIATOR
Classic Gothic radiator shell was considered far more sporting than Rolls-Royce's Doric example.

UKL 109

LIGHTS
Front fog lights used to be known as "pass lights" for overtaking.

AERODYNAMIC TESTS

The Continental spent much time in the wind tunnel to establish air drag during forward motion. Sweeping rear quarters directed the wind over the rear wheels, which were covered in spats to assist airflow. During prototype testing, it was found that a normal set of six-ply tires lasted for only 20 miles (32 km).

REAR FENDERS

Gently tapering rear fenders funneled air away into a slipstream; the Continental's aerodynamics were way ahead of its time.

ALUMINUM CONSTRUCTION

Not only was the body made from lightweight aluminum—courtesy of H. J. Mulliner & Co. Ltd.—but also the side window and shield frames. The prototype had high quality alloy bumpers; production cars had steel ones.

CARBURETORS

Carburation was by two SU HD8 units.

WEIGHT

Body weight was kept to a minimum because no Fifties' tires could cope with speeds over 120 mph (193 km/h).

ENGINE

Continentals used a 4-liter straight-six engine of 4566cc—increased to 4887cc in May 1954 and known as the big bore engine. It allowed the car to reach 50 mph (80 km/h) in first gear.

SPECIFICATIONS

MODEL Bentley R-Type Continental (1952–55)

PRODUCTION 208

BODY STYLE Two-door, four-seater touring sedan.

CONSTRUCTION Steel chassis, alloy body.

ENGINES 4566 or 4887cc straight-sixes.

POWER OUTPUT Never declared, described as "sufficient."

TRANSMISSION Four-speed synchromesh manual or auto option.

SUSPENSION Independent front with wishbones and coil springs, rear live axle with leaf springs.

BRAKES Front disc, rear drums.

MAXIMUM SPEED 115 mph (185 km/h)

0–60 MPH (0–96 KM/H) 13.5 sec

0–100 MPH (0–161 KM/H) 36.2 sec

A.F.C. 19.4 mpg (6.9 km/l)

REAR WINDOW
Pillar box rear window was a throwback to prewar cars.

TRUNK SPACE
Trunk was considered large enough to carry luggage for touring.

REAR ASPECT
Rear flanks are like the tense haunches of a sprinter.

WHEELS
Prototypes had spats covering the rear wheels.

PLUSH DASH
The beautifully detailed dashboard mirrored the Continental's exterior elegance. The first R-Types had manual gearboxes with a right-hand floor-mounted stick, thus reflecting the car's sporting character. Later models were offered with automatic boxes.

BENTLEY *Flying Spur*

ARGUABLY THE MOST BEAUTIFUL postwar Bentley, the Flying Spur was the first four-door Continental. Initially, Rolls-Royce would not allow builder H. J. Mulliner to use the name Continental, insisting it should only apply to two-door cars. After months of pressure from Mulliner, R.R. relented and allowed the shapely car to be known as a proper Continental. More than worthy of the hallowed name, the Flying Spur was launched in 1957, using the standard S1 chassis. In 1959 it inherited R.R.'s 220 bhp, oversquare, light-alloy V8, and by July 1962 the body shell was given the double headlight treatment and upgraded into what some consider to be the best of the breed—the S3 Flying Spur. Subtle, understated, and elegant, Flying Spurs are rare, and in their day were among the most admired and refined machines in the world. Although sharing much with the contemporary Standard Steel Bentley, the Spur's list price was half as much more as the stock item.

INTERIOR
Interior includes carefully detailed switchgear, the finest leather and walnut, and West of England cloth.

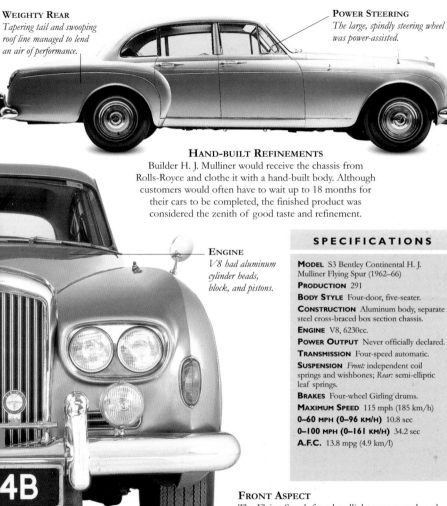

WEIGHTY REAR
Tapering tail and swooping roof line managed to lend an air of performance.

POWER STEERING
The large, spindly steering wheel was power-assisted.

HAND-BUILT REFINEMENTS

Builder H. J. Mulliner would receive the chassis from
Rolls-Royce and clothe it with a hand-built body. Although
customers would often have to wait up to 18 months for
their cars to be completed, the finished product was
considered the zenith of good taste and refinement.

ENGINE
V 8 had aluminum cylinder heads, block, and pistons.

SPECIFICATIONS

MODEL S3 Bentley Continental H. J.
Mulliner Flying Spur (1962–66)

PRODUCTION 291

BODY STYLE Four-door, five-seater.

CONSTRUCTION Aluminum body, separate
steel cross-braced box section chassis.

ENGINE V8, 6230cc.

POWER OUTPUT Never officially declared.

TRANSMISSION Four-speed automatic.

SUSPENSION *Front:* independent coil
springs and wishbones; *Rear:* semi-elliptic
leaf springs.

BRAKES Four-wheel Girling drums.

MAXIMUM SPEED 115 mph (185 km/h)

0–60 MPH (0–96 KM/H) 10.8 sec

0–100 MPH (0–161 KM/H) 34.2 sec

A.F.C. 13.8 mpg (4.9 km/l)

FRONT ASPECT

The Flying Spur's four-headlight nose was shared
with the standard steel Bentley S3, along with a
lowered radiator and hood line. The body was
constructed from hand-rolled aluminum.

BENTLEY *Continental Supersports*

THE 2003 CONTINENTAL GT with its magnificent W12 engine changed Bentley forever. Compact, rapid, reliable, and fashionable, the Conti (to use its street name) is one of the Crewe firm's most admired products and brought the Bentley brand to a younger customer. In 2009, the Supersports was launched as the fastest production Bentley ever, and the first to run on gas and biofuel (E85 ethanol). A special Quickshift tiptronic six-speed automatic gearbox reduced gear change times by 50 percent, and a Torsen T3 four-wheel-drive system made the Supersports surefooted enough to break the world speed record on ice at 205 mph (330 km/h). But despite the epic performance this is an amazingly refined supercar with superb steering and a truly magic carpet ride.

SIT LIGHTLY
Seat frames in the Supersports are carbon fiber to save weight.

THE PEOPLE'S POWER PLANT
The VW-designed twin-turbocharged six-liter W12 engine is one of the world's best. The cylinders are arranged in four banks of three to save space, but even in standard GT tune this engine still develops a mighty 552 bhp.

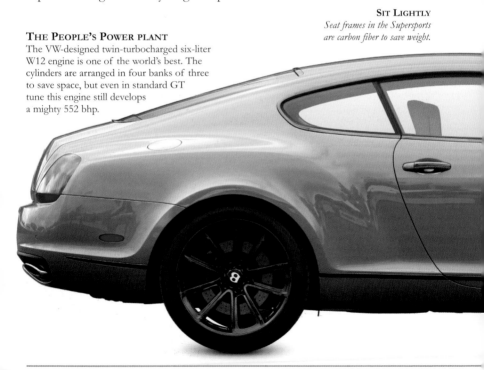

KEEPING COOL
Huge grille and vents cool engine and brakes.

SPECIFICATIONS

MODEL Bentley Continental Supersports (2009)

PRODUCTION N/A

BODY STYLE Four-seater, two-door coupe.

CONSTRUCTION Alloy panels, steel chassis.

ENGINE 5,998cc, W12 Twin Turbo.

POWER OUTPUT 621 bhp.

TRANSMISSION Six-speed tiptronic automatic.

SUSPENSION Independent all around.

BRAKES Four-wheel discs.

MAXIMUM SPEED 205 mph (330 km/h)

0–60 MPH (0–96 KM/H) 3.7 sec

0–100 MPH (0–161 KM/H) 8.9 sec

A.F.C. 15 mpg (6.4 km/l)

SUPERSPORTS CLONES
The superfast Bentley has become so iconic and desirable that owners of "ordinary" Conti GTs often put on the revised bumpers and black rims to make their cars look like Supersports. There's now a flourishing global industry "pimping" up all Continentals.

MONSTER BRAKES
Ceramic brakes are the most powerful ever fitted to a production car.

NOSE JOB
Front apron is unique to Supersports and is plastic to save weight.

BMW *507*

WHO WOULD HAVE THOUGHT that in the mid-Fifties BMW would have unveiled something as voluptuously beautiful as the 507? The company had a fine pre–World War II heritage that culminated in the crisp 328, but it did not resume car manufacturing until 1952, with the curvy, but slightly plump, six-cylinder 501 sedan. Then, at the Frankfurt show of late 1955 they hit us with the 507, designed by Count Albrecht Goertz. The 507 was a fantasy made real; not flashy, but dramatic and with poise and presence. BMW hoped the 507 would straighten out its precarious finances, winning sales in the lucrative American market. But the BMW's exotic looks and performance were more than matched by an orbital price. Production, which had been largely by hand, ended in March 1959 after just 252—some say 253—had been built. In fact, the 507 took BMW to the brink of financial oblivion; yet if that had been the last BMW it would have been a beautiful way to die.

TEUTONIC LINKS
Mounted on a tubular-steel chassis cut down from sedans, Albrecht Goertz's aluminum body is reminiscent of the contemporary— and slightly cheaper—Mercedes-Benz 300SL roadster; from the front it resembles the later AC Aces and Cobra *(see pages 12–19).*

BRAKES
Most 507s were built with all-around Alfin drum brakes. Some later cars had more effective front disc brakes.

DOOR HANDLES
Like the bumpers, the door handles were surprisingly discreet—if not particularly easy to use.

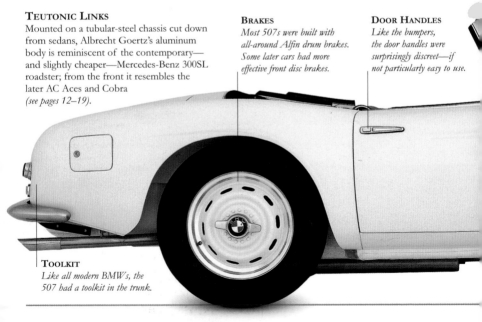

TOOLKIT
Like all modern BMWs, the 507 had a toolkit in the trunk.

SPECIFICATIONS

MODEL BMW 507 (1956–59)

PRODUCTION 252/3, most LHD

BODY STYLE Two-seater roadster.

CONSTRUCTION Box section and tubular steel chassis; aluminum body.

ENGINE All-aluminum 3168cc V8, two valves per cylinder.

POWER OUTPUT 150 bhp at 5000 rpm; some later cars 160 bhp at 5600 rpm.

TRANSMISSION Four-speed manual.

SUSPENSION *Front:* Unequal-length wishbones, torsion-bar springs and telescopic shock absorbers; *Rear:* Live axle, torsion-bar springs.

BRAKES Drums front and rear; front discs and rear drums on later cars.

MAXIMUM SPEED 125 mph (201 km/h); 135–140 mph (217–225 km/h) with optional 3.42:1 final drive.

0–60 MPH (0–96 KM/H) 9 sec

A.F.C. 18 mpg (6.4 km/)

DRIVING CONDITIONS
As a drive, the 507 tended toward marked understeer; so instant was throttle response that the tail easily spun out.

HOOD VENT
Ornate chrome-plated grilles in the front sides covered functional engine-bay air vents.

OPTIONAL POWER
Souped-up 160 bhp versions of the 507 were good for 140 mph (225 km/h).

WHEELS
Knock-off Rudge wheels like this were the most sought-after option.

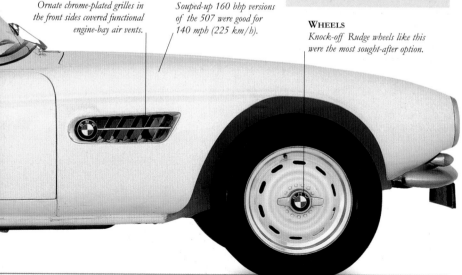

RAKISH BODY

The 507's body is an all-aluminum affair atop a simple tubular chassis. Brightwork is kept to the minimum, accentuating the clean lines. The brightwork included on the car is kept simple; the rear bumpers, for example, have no bulky overriders.

ENGINE

The 3.2-liter all-aluminum engine was light and powerful. Twin Zenith carbs are the same as those of the contemporary Porsches.

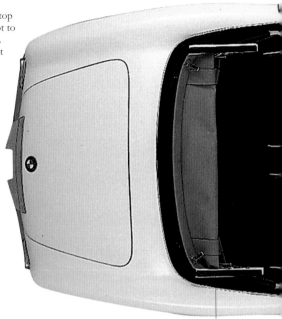

TOP

You rarely see a 507 with its top raised, but it is simple to erect and remarkably handsome.

PIPE MUSIC

The BMW had a brisk, wholesome bark and unmistakable creamy wuffle of a V8.

BEEMER BADGING

Eight BMW stylized propeller rounde including those on wheel trims and eared spinners, grace the 507, nine if you include the badge in the center of the steering wheel.

ENGINE PROBLEMS
*The 3.2-liter engine tended
to run too hot in traffic and
too cool on the open road.*

HORN-PULLS
*The interior was clearly inspired
by US styling of the period,
with gimmicky horn-pulls
behind the steering wheel.*

INTERIOR
The 507, unlike the contemporary 503, has
a floor-mounted stick to operate the four-
speed gearbox. Dash consists of a clock,
speedometer, and tachometer. Some cars
had internally adjustable door mirrors.

BMW *3.0CSL*

ONE LITTLE LETTER CAN MAKE SO much difference. In this case it is the L at the end of the name tag that makes the BMW 3.0CSL so special. The BMW CS pillarless coupes of the late Sixties and early Seventies were elegant and good-looking tourers. But add that L, and you have a legend. The letter actually stands for "Leichtmetall," and when tacked to the rump of the BMW it amounts to warpaint. The original CSL of 1974 had a 2985cc engine developing 180 bhp, no front bumper, and a mixture of aluminum and thin steel body panels. In August 1972, a cylinder-bore increase took the CSL's capacity to 3003cc with 200 bhp and allowed it into Group 2 for competition purposes. But it is the wild-winged, so-called "Batmobile" homologation special that really boils the blood of boy racers. An ultimate road car, great racer, rare, short-lived and high-priced, this charismatic, pared-down Beemer has got classic credentials.

GOOD LOOKER
Even mild rather than wild and winged, the CSL is certainly one of the best-looking cars of its generation. With its pillarless look, the cabin is light and airy, despite the black interior. But all that glass made it hot; air vents behind the BMW rear-pillar badge helped a little.

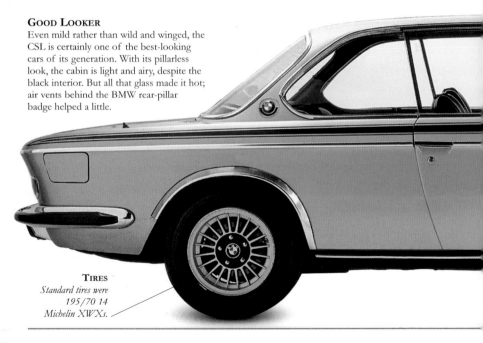

TIRES
Standard tires were 195/70 14 Michelin XWXs.

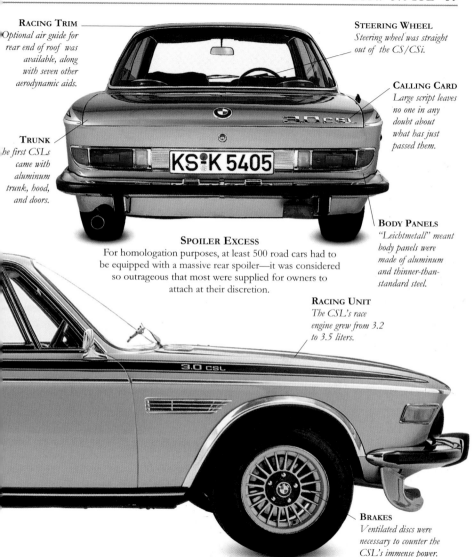

RACING TRIM
Optional air guide for rear end of roof was available, along with seven other aerodynamic aids.

STEERING WHEEL
Steering wheel was straight out of the CS/CSi.

CALLING CARD
Large script leaves no one in any doubt about what has just passed them.

TRUNK
The first CSLs came with aluminum trunk, hood, and doors.

SPOILER EXCESS
For homologation purposes, at least 500 road cars had to be equipped with a massive rear spoiler—it was considered so outrageous that most were supplied for owners to attach at their discretion.

BODY PANELS
"Leichtmetall" meant body panels were made of aluminum and thinner-than-standard steel.

RACING UNIT
The CSL's race engine grew from 3.2 to 3.5 liters.

BRAKES
Ventilated discs were necessary to counter the CSL's immense power.

ENGINE

In genuine racing trim, the Batmobile's 3.2-litre straight-six engine gave nearly 400 bhp and, for 1976, nearly 500 bhp with turbocharging. But road cars like this British-spec 3003cc 3.0CSL gave around 200 bhp on fuel injection.

SEVENTIES' BARGAIN

Just after the 1973 fuel crisis, you could pick up a CSL for very little money.

ENGINE UPGRADE

Early CSLs had a carburetor-fed 2985cc engine developing 180 bhp; after 1972, capacity increased to 3003cc, shown here, for homologation purposes.

BUMPER-TO-BUMPER

German-market CSLs had no front bumper and a fiberglass bumper; this car's metal items show it to be a British-spec model.

TRACK SUCCESS

The CSLs were the first BMWs developed under the company's new Motorsport department which was set up in 1972. The model produced immediate success for BMW, initially in Europe and then on tracks in the United States. The CSL won all but one of the European Touring Car Championships between 1973 and 1979.

INTERIOR

British-spec CSLs, like this car, retained Scheel lightweight bucket seats, but had carpets, electric windows (front and rear), power steering, and a sliver of wood.

LIMITED EDITION

500 fuel-injected versions of the CSL were offered in Britain.

SPECIFICATIONS

MODEL BMW 3.0CSL (1971–74)

PRODUCTION 1,208 (all versions)

BODY STYLE Four-seater coupe.

CONSTRUCTION Steel monocoque, steel and aluminum body.

ENGINES 2985cc, 3003cc, or 3153cc in-line six.

POWER OUTPUT 200 bhp at 5500 rpm (3003cc).

TRANSMISSION Four-speed manual.

SUSPENSION *Front:* MacPherson struts and antiroll bar; *Rear:* semitrailing swinging arms, coil springs, and antiroll bar.

BRAKES Servo-assisted ventilated discs front and rear.

MAXIMUM SPEED 135 mph (217 km/h)

0–60 MPH (0–96 KM/H) 7.3 sec (3003cc)

0–100 MPH (0–161 KM/H) 21 sec (3003cc)

A.F.C. 22–25 mpg (7.8–8.8 km/l)

DO-IT-YOURSELF

Road-going cars were only slightly lighter than the CS and CSi; they even had BMW's trademark toolkit, neatly hinged from the underside of the trunk lid.

BMW *M1*

THE M1—A SIMPLE NAME, a simple concept. M stood for Motorsport GmbH, BMW's separate competition division. And the number one? Well, this was going to be a first for this time BMW was not just going to develop capable racers from competent sedans and coupes. It was going to build a high-profile, beat-all racer, with road-going versions basking in the reflected glory of on-track success. The first prototype ran in 1977, with the M1 entering production in 1978. By the end of manufacture in 1980, a mere 457 racing and road-going M1s had been built, making it one of the rarest and most desirable of modern BMWs. Though its racing career was only briefly distinguished, it is as one of the all-time ultimate road cars that the M1 stands out, for it is not just a 160 mph (257 km/h) "autobahnstormer." It is one of the least demanding supercars to drive, a testament to its fine engineering, and is in many ways as remarkable as the gorgeous 328 of the 1930s.

INTERNATIONAL CONSTRUCTION
The M1 had widespread international influences. From a concept car created in 1972 by Frenchman Paul Bracq, the final body shape was created in Italy by Giorgio Giugiaro's ItalDesign in Turin. Lamborghini also contributed to the engineering. Yet somehow it all comes together in a unified shape, and, with the double kidney grille, the M1 is still unmistakably a BMW.

SUSPENSION
Suspension was a mix of springs, wishbones, and telescopic shocks.

LEFTIES
All BMW M1s were left-hand drive.

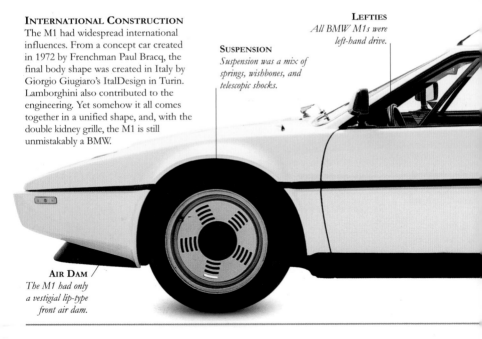

AIR DAM
The M1 had only a vestigial lip-type front air dam.

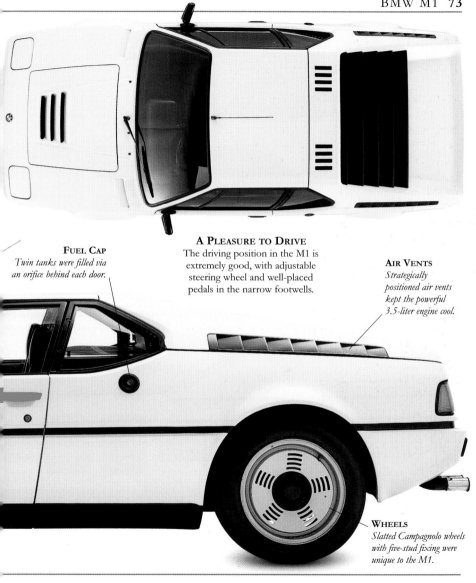

FUEL CAP
Twin tanks were filled via an orifice behind each door.

A PLEASURE TO DRIVE
The driving position in the M1 is extremely good, with adjustable steering wheel and well-placed pedals in the narrow footwells.

AIR VENTS
Strategically positioned air vents kept the powerful 3.5-liter engine cool.

WHEELS
Slatted Campagnolo wheels with five-stud fixing were unique to the M1.

CYLINDER HEAD
The cylinder head was a light-alloy casting, with two chain-driven overhead cams operating four valves per cylinder.

ENGINE

The M1's 3453cc straight-six engine uses essentially the same cast-iron cylinder block as BMW's 635CSi coupe, but with a forged-alloy crankshaft and slightly longer connecting rods.

MIRRORS
Big door mirrors—essential for maneuvering the M1—were electrically adjusted.

MZ·X 498

DARK INTERIOR

The all-black interior is somber, but fixtures are all to a high standard; unlike those of many supercars, the heating and ventilation systems actually work. However, rearward visibility through the slatted, heavily buttressed engine cover is severely restricted.

REAR LIGHTS
Large rear light clusters were the same as those of the 6-series coupe and 7-series sedan models.

MZ X 4984

HEADLIGHTS
Retractable headlights were backed up by grille-mounted driving lights.

SPECIFICATIONS

MODEL BMW M1 (1978–80)

PRODUCTION 457

BODY STYLE Two-seater mid-engined sports.

CONSTRUCTION Tubular steel space-frame with fiberglass body.

ENGINE Inline six, four valves per cylinder, dohc 3453cc.

POWER OUTPUT 277 bhp at 6500 rpm.

TRANSMISSION Combined ZF five-speed gearbox and limited slip differential.

SUSPENSION Coil springs, wishbones, and Bilstein gas-pressure telescopic shock absorbers front and rear.

BRAKES Servo-assisted ventilated discs all around.

MAXIMUM SPEED 162 mph (261 km/h)

0–60 MPH (0–96 KM/H) 5.4 sec

A.F.C. 24–30 mpg (8.5–10.6 km/l)

PURE M1 RACING

BMW teamed up with FOCA (Formula One Constructors' Association) to create the Procar series —M1-only races planned primarily as supporting events for Grand Prix meetings in 1979 and 1980.

BUGATTI *Veyron Grand Sport*

THE VEYRON IS QUITE SIMPLY the greatest car ever made. This isn't just the fastest production car in the world, it's a technological *tour de force* that defies physics, gravity, and common sense. With a 0–62 mph (0–100 km/h) time of less than 2.7 seconds, the acceleration of the Veyron's open-top version, the Grand Sport, has been described as "like falling out of an airplane," yet its road manners are the pinnacle of civility. The legendary 16-cylinder, quad-turbocharged engine develops 1,001 bhp, yet it can brake from 62 mph (100 km/h) to a standstill in only 103 ft (31.4 m). The Veyron is more than just a million-pound supercar, it's a global celebrity in its own right.

BUGATTI REINVENTED
When VW bought the Bugatti brand in 1998 nobody could have guessed their plans for such a stunning reinvention, or that they would create the world's most audacious supercar so quickly. In 1999, they surprised the world by showing the first concept, and by 2005 had created an automotive masterpiece that will never be repeated in our lifetime.

TARGA TOP
Grand Sport versions have a removable, lightweight, transparent polycarbonate roof.

WING BRAKE
Air brake rises in 0.4 seconds and has the stopping power of an ordinary hatchback.

SPECIFICATIONS

MODEL Bugatti Veyron 16.4 Grand Sport (2008)

PRODUCTION 450 (all variants)

BODY STYLE Two-door, two-seater open-top sports car.

CONSTRUCTION Carbon-fiber composite and alloy.

ENGINE 7,993cc W16.

POWER OUTPUT 1,001 bhp.

TRANSMISSION Seven-speed, sequential, dual-clutch automatic.

SUSPENSION Computer-controlled double wishbones front and rear.

BRAKES Carbon-fiber, silicone carbide discs plus rear airbrake.

MAXIMUM SPEED 253 mph (407 km/h)

0–62 MPH (0–100 KM/H) less than 2.7 sec

A.F.C. 9.5 mpg (4 km/l)

EPIC GEARBOX
Steering wheel has magnesium gearbox paddles for the seven-speed direct-shift, dual-clutch, computer-controlled automatic made by Ricardo in England. Shift speed is 150 milliseconds and the car's torque is an incredible 1,250 Nm at 2,200–5,500 rpm.

OPEN AIR
With roof removed, speeds of up to 217 mph (350 km/h) are possible.

GREAT BRAKES
Brakes are cross-drilled, radially vented silicon carbide discs.

COOL DOWN
Seven separate radiators keep engine, gearbox, and differential cool.

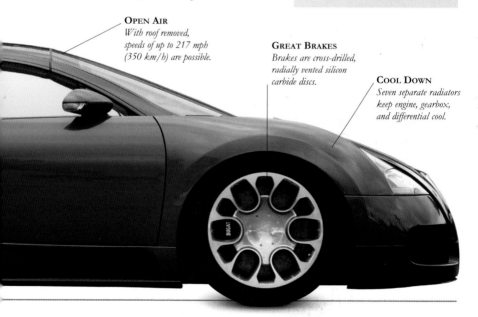

Buick *Roadmaster* (1949)

The '49 Roadmaster took the market's breath away. With a low silhouette, straight hood, and fastback styling, it was a poem in steel. The first Buick with a truly new postwar look, the '49 was designed by Ned Nickles using GM's new C-body. It also boasted two bold new styling motifs: Ventiports and an aggressive 25-tooth "Dollar Grin" grille. Harley Earl's aesthetic of aeronautical entertainment did the trick, and Buick notched up nearly 400,000 sales that year. Never mind that the windshield was still two-piece, that there was no power steering, and the engine was a straight-eight—it looked gorgeous and came with the new Dynaflow automatic transmission. The Roadmaster, like the '49 Cadillac, was a seminal car and the first flowering of the most flamboyant decade of car design ever seen.

Serious Cachet

For years GM's copywriters crowed that "when better cars are built, Buick will build them," and in a sense that hyperbole was true. In its day, the gloriously voluptuous Roadmaster was a serious set of wheels, only one step down from a Cadillac, and to own one meant you really had arrived.

Spotlight
Spotlight with mirror was a $25 option.

Ventiport Status
Cheaper Buicks had only three Ventiports; the lavish Roadmaster had four.

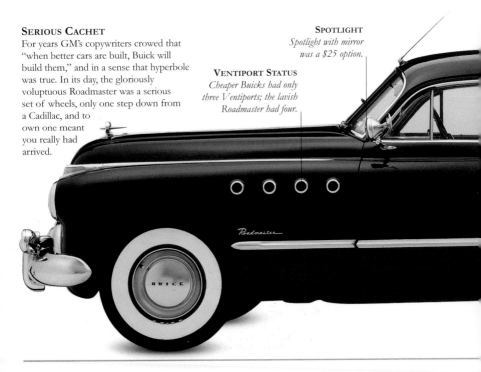

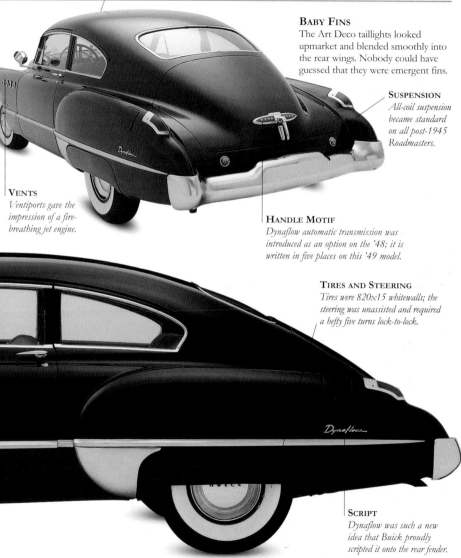

BABY FINS
The Art Deco taillights looked upmarket and blended smoothly into the rear wings. Nobody could have guessed that they were emergent fins.

SUSPENSION
All-coil suspension became standard on all post-1945 Roadmasters.

VENTS
Ventiports gave the impression of a fire-breathing jet engine.

HANDLE MOTIF
Dynaflow automatic transmission was introduced as an option on the '48; it is written in five places on this '49 model.

TIRES AND STEERING
Tires were 820x15 whitewalls; the steering was unassisted and required a hefty five turns lock-to-lock.

SCRIPT
Dynaflow was such a new idea that Buick proudly scripted it onto the rear fender.

ADVERTISING
The '49's class set the trend for later Roadmasters, with the copywriters eager to stress that the model was the "Buick of Buicks."

Sovereign right of a successful man

Roadmaster

SIGN OF THE TIMES
The Roadmaster may have shared its body with the Oldsmobile 98 and the Cadillac Series 62, but it gave Buick a distinction never seen before. Big, bold, and brash, the '49 was perfect for its time, and it began the trend for lower, sleeker styling. Optimistic, opulent, and glitzy, it carried strident styling cues that told people a block away that this was no ordinary car, this was a Buick—even better the very best Buick money could buy.

CLASSY REAR
Elegant flourish completed the swooping teardrop rear.

STYLING
The GM C-body had closed quarters and Sedanette styling.

DYNA FLOW

18 363
52 WYOMING

EARLY TRADEMARKS
Gun-sight hood ornament, bucktooth grille, and Ventiports were flashy styling metaphors that would become famous Buick trademarks. Although divided by a center pillar, the windshield glass was actually curved.

ENGINE
The Roadie had a Fireball straight-eight cast-iron 320cid engine.

GRILLE
The classic vertical grille bars were replaced for the 1955 model year.

DASHBOARD
The instrument panel was new for '49 and described as "pilot centered" because the speedo was positioned straight ahead of the driver through the steering wheel.

SPECIFICATIONS

MODEL 1949 Buick Roadmaster Series 70 Sedanette

PRODUCTION 18,415 (1949)

BODY STYLE Two-door fastback coupe.

CONSTRUCTION Steel body and chassis.

ENGINE 320cid straight-eight.

POWER OUTPUT 150 bhp.

TRANSMISSION Two-speed Dynaflow automatic.

SUSPENSION Front and rear coil springs.

BRAKES Front and rear drums.

MAXIMUM SPEED 100 mph (161 km/h)

0–60 MPH (0–96 KM/H) 17 sec

A.F.C. 20 mpg (7 km/l)

Buick *Roadmaster* (1957)

In 1957, America was gearing up for the Sixties. Little Richard screamed his way to the top with "Lucille" and Elvis had nine hits in a row. Jack Kerouac penned his immortal novel *On the Road*, inspiring carloads of Americans to seek the adman's "Promised Land" along Ike's new interstates. Fins and chrome were applied with a shovel and General Motors spent several hundred million dollars refashioning their Buick model line. The Roadmaster of 1957 was low and mighty, a massive 17 ft 11 in (5.46 m) long and 6 ft (1.83 m) wide. Power was up to 300 bhp, along with trendy dorsal fins, sweepspear body moldings, and a trio of chrome chevrons on the rear quarters. Four Ventiports, a Buick trademark harking back to the original 1949 Roadmaster, still graced the sweeping front fenders. But America did not take to Buick new look, particularly some of the Roadmaster's fashionable jet-age design motifs.

PLANE STYLING
Aircraft design exerted a big influence on automotive styling in the Fifties, and the '57 Roadmaster was no exception. With wraparound windshield, cockpitlike roof area, and turbine-style wheel covers, a nation of Walter Mittys could imagine themselves vapor-trailing through the stratosphere.

CABIN OR COCKPIT?
Rakish swooping roof line borrowed heavily from bubble cockpits of jet fighters.

HEIGHT
The '57 Roadmaster was lower and sleeker than previous models.

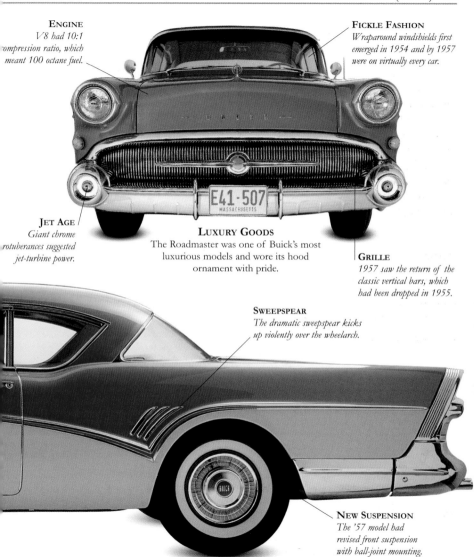

ENGINE
V8 had 10:1 compression ratio, which meant 100 octane fuel.

FICKLE FASHION
Wraparound windshields first emerged in 1954 and by 1957 were on virtually every car.

JET AGE
Giant chrome protuberances suggested jet-turbine power.

LUXURY GOODS
The Roadmaster was one of Buick's most luxurious models and wore its hood ornament with pride.

GRILLE
1957 saw the return of the classic vertical bars, which had been dropped in 1955.

SWEEPSPEAR
The dramatic sweepspear kicks up violently over the wheelarch.

NEW SUSPENSION
The '57 model had revised front suspension with ball-joint mounting.

E41·507
MASSACHUSETTS

TRUNK

The cavernous trunk could accommodate almost anything you could buy at the mall in the consumer-driven Fifties.

ENGINE

The hot Buick's 5.9-liter V8 pushed out 300 bhp; it was capable of 112 mph (180 km/h) and 0 to 60 mph (96 km/h) in 10 seconds. Dynaflow transmission had variable pitch blades which changed their angle like those of an airplane propeller.

STYLING EXCESS

Vast chrome rear bumper made for a prodigious overhang, with massive Dagmarlike overriders, razor-sharp taillights, and fluted underpanel—a stylistic nightmare. One interesting new feature was the fuel cap, now positioned in a slot above the rear license plate.

FIN DETAIL

The Roadmaster showed that, by 1957, tail-fin fashion was rising to ridiculous heights. Unfortunately, by '57 the Roadmaster looked very much like every other American car. Gone was that chaste individuality, and Buick began to lose its reputation as a maker of high quality cars—production fell by 24 percent this year.

LIMITED VISION
Small tinted rear windshield didn't offer much assistance to the driver in reversing situations.

SPECIFICATIONS

MODEL Buick Roadmaster (1957)

PRODUCTION 36,638 (1957)

BODY STYLE Two-door, five-seater hardtop coupe.

CONSTRUCTION X-braced chassis with steel body.

ENGINE V8, 364cid.

POWER OUTPUT 250 bhp at 4400 rpm.

TRANSMISSION Dynaflow two-speed automatic.

SUSPENSION Independent coil springs.

BRAKES Hydraulic servo drums all around.

MAXIMUM SPEED 112 mph (180 km/h)

0–60 MPH (0–96 KM/H) 10.5 sec

0–100 MPH (0–161 KM/H) 21.2 sec

A.F.C. 12 mpg (4.2 km/l)

POWER STEERING
Power-assisted steering and Dynaflow automatic transmission became standard on all Roadmasters from 1953.

GM BADGING
Badge at the center of the steering wheel indicates that Buicks were built at GM's factory in Flint, Michigan.

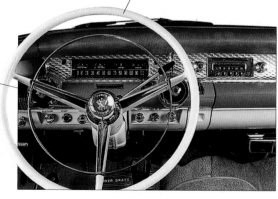

INTERIOR
oadmaster standard special equipment cluded a Red Liner speedometer, glove ompartment lamp, trip mileage indicator, nd a color-coordinated dash panel. From)55 Roadmasters could be ordered with a noice of 10 types of interior trim.

Buick *Limited Riviera* *(1958)*

WHEN YOUR FORTUNES ARE FLAGGING, you pour on the chrome. As blubbery barges go, the '58 Limited has to be one of the gaudiest. Spanning 19 ft (5.78 m) and tipping the scales at two tons, the Limited is empirical proof that 1958 was not Buick's happiest year. Despite all that twinkling kitsch and the reincarnated Limited badge, the bulbous Buick bombed. For a start, GM's Dynaflow automatic transmission was not up to Pontiac's Hydra-Matic standards, and the Limited's brakes were disinclined to work. Furthermore, in what was a recession year for the industry, the Limited had been priced into Cadillac territory—$33 more than the Series 62. Total production for the Limited in 1958 was a very limited 7,436 units. By the late Fifties, Detroit had lost its way, and the '58 Limited was on the road to nowhere.

TRIMMINGS
Interiors were trimmed in gray cloth and vinyl or Cordaveen. Seat cushions had Double-Depth foam rubber.

CHILD OF THE FIFTIES
Buick's answer to an aircraft carrier was a riot of ornamentation that went on for half a block. At rest, the Limited looked like it needed a fifth wheel to support that weighty rear overhang.

BODY STYLES
As well as this four-door Riviera, the 700 Series also included a two-door version, a stripped chassis model, and a convertible.

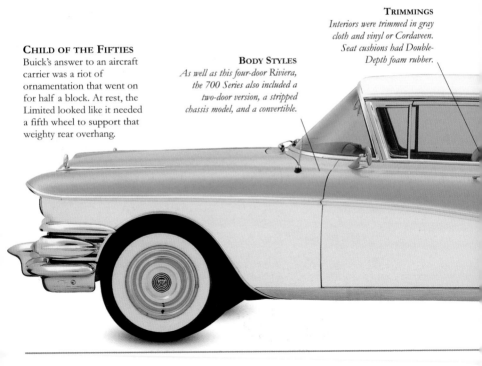

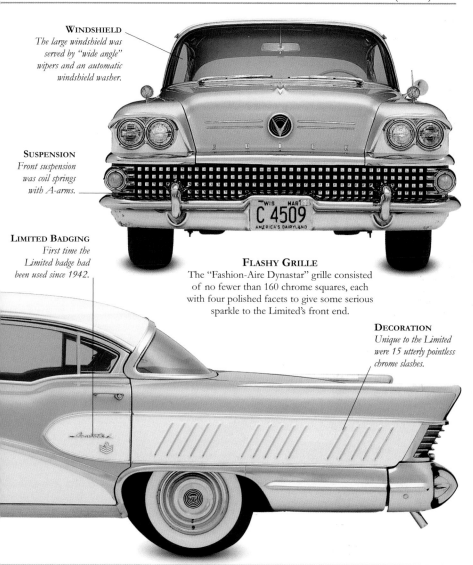

WINDSHIELD
The large windshield was served by "wide angle" wipers and an automatic windshield washer.

SUSPENSION
Front suspension was coil springs with A-arms.

LIMITED BADGING
First time the Limited badge had been used since 1942.

FLASHY GRILLE
The "Fashion-Aire Dynastar" grille consisted of no fewer than 160 chrome squares, each with four polished facets to give some serious sparkle to the Limited's front end.

DECORATION
Unique to the Limited were 15 utterly pointless chrome slashes.

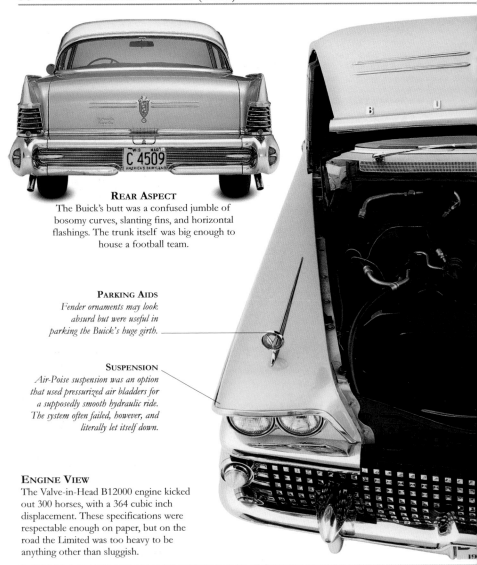

REAR ASPECT

The Buick's butt was a confused jumble of
bosomy curves, slanting fins, and horizontal
flashings. The trunk itself was big enough to
house a football team.

PARKING AIDS

*Fender ornaments may look
absurd but were useful in
parking the Buick's huge girth.*

SUSPENSION

*Air-Poise suspension was an option
that used pressurized air bladders for
a supposedly smooth hydraulic ride.
The system often failed, however, and
literally let itself down.*

ENGINE VIEW

The Valve-in-Head B12000 engine kicked
out 300 horses, with a 364 cubic inch
displacement. These specifications were
respectable enough on paper, but on the
road the Limited was too heavy to be
anything other than sluggish.

CHROME TRIM
The metal with a shiny coating could be found on everything from food mixers to radios in the Fifties.

ECONOMY
Producing 13 mpg (4.6 km/l), the Limited was thirsty.

SPECIFICATIONS

MODEL Buick Limited Riviera Series 700 (1958)

PRODUCTION 7,436 (1958, all Series 700 body styles)

BODY STYLES Two- and four-door, six-seater hardtops, two-door convertible.

CONSTRUCTION Steel monocoque.

ENGINE 364cid V8.

POWER OUTPUT 300 bhp.

TRANSMISSION Flight-Pitch Dynaflow automatic.

SUSPENSION *Front:* coil springs with A-arms; *Rear:* live axle with coil springs. Optional air suspension.

BRAKES Front and rear drums.

MAXIMUM SPEED 110 mph (177 km/h)

0–60 MPH (0–96 KM/H) 9.5 sec

A.F.C. 13 mpg (4.6 km/l)

HORN
Horn-pulls were pretty much standard on every US car in the Fifties.

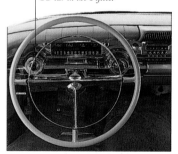

INTERIOR
Power steering and brakes were essential and came as standard. Other standard equipment included an electric clock, cigarette lighters, and electric windows.

BUICK *Riviera (1964)*

IN '58, SO THE STORY GOES, GM's design supremo Bill Mitchell was entranced by a Rolls-Royce he saw hissing past a London hotel. "What we want," said Mitchell, "is a cross between a Ferrari and a Rolls." By August 1960, he'd turned his vision into a full-size clay mock-up. One of the world's most handsome cars, the original '63 Riviera locked horns with Ford's T-Bird and was GM's attempt at a "Great New American Classic Car." And it worked. Separate and elegant, the Riv was a clever amalgam of razor edges and chaste curves, embellished by just the right amount of chrome. Beneath the exquisite lines was a cross-member frame, a 401cid V8, power brakes, and a two-speed Turbine Drive tranny. In the interests of exclusivity, Buick agreed that only 40,000 would be made each year. With ravishing looks, prodigious performance, and the classiest image in town, the Riv ranks as one of Detroit's finest confections.

CLASS APPEAL
The Riv was America's answer to the Bentley Continental, and pandered to Ivy League America's obsession with aristocratic European thoroughbreds like Aston Martin, Maserati, and Jaguar.

FINE-LINE DESIGN
Superbly understated, razor-edged styling made for a clean, crisp-looking machine.

DIMENSIONS
Relatively compact, the Riviera was considerably shorter and lighter than other big Buicks.

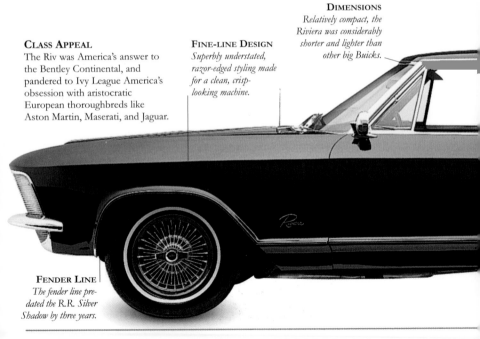

FENDER LINE
The fender line pre-dated the R.R. Silver Shadow by three years.

SPECIFICATIONS

MODEL Buick Riviera (1964)

PRODUCTION 37,958 (1964)

BODY STYLE Two-door hardtop coupe.

CONSTRUCTION Steel body and chassis.

ENGINE 425cid V8

POWER OUTPUT 340–360 bhp.

TRANSMISSION Two- or three-speed automatic.

SUSPENSION Front and rear coil springs.

BRAKES Front and rear drums.

MAXIMUM SPEED 120–125 mph (193–201 km/h)

0–60 MPH (0–96 KM/H) 8 sec

A.F.C. 12–16 mpg (4.2–5.7 km/l)

CONWAY TWITTY
The crooner of such tunes as "It's Only Make Believe"
owned the '64 Riv on these pages, and he personalized
it with his own license plate.

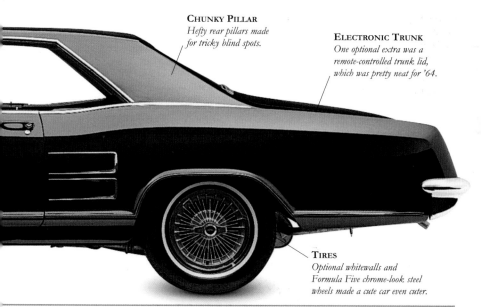

CHUNKY PILLAR
*Hefty rear pillars made
for tricky blind spots.*

ELECTRONIC TRUNK
*One optional extra was a
remote-controlled trunk lid,
which was pretty neat for '64.*

TIRES
*Optional whitewalls and
Formula Five chrome-look steel
wheels made a cute car even cuter.*

CLASSIC RIV FRONT
'63 and '64 Rivs have classic exposed double headlights. For reasons best known to itself, Buick gave '65 cars headlights that were hidden behind electrically-operated, clam-shell doors.

ENGINE
'64s had a 425cid Wildcat V8 that could be tickled up to 360 horses, courtesy of dual four-barrels. *Car Life* magazine tested a '64 Riv with the Wildcat unit and stomped to 60 mph (96 km/h) in a scintillating 7.7 seconds.

ROVER TRANSF
Buick sold the tool for the old 401 to Rover, who used it great success on its Range Rover.

ENGINE OPTION
'65 saw a Gran Sport option with 360 bhp mill, limited slip diff, and "Giro-Poise" roll control.

INTERIOR
The sumptuous Riv was a full four-seater, with the rear seat divided to look like buckets. The dominant V-shaped center console mushroomed from between the front seats to blend into the dashboard. The car's interior has a European ambience that was quite uncharacteristic for the period.

GRILLE
The grille was inspired by the Ferrari 250GT.

T-BIRD BEATER
High-rolling price of $4,333 was actually $153 cheaper than Ford's T-Bird.

W-SHAPE
he purposeful W-section front could have come straight out of an Italian styling house. The classy Riviera soon became the American Jaguar.

BUICK *Riviera* (1971)

THE '63 RIVIERA HAD BEEN one of Buick's best sellers, but by the late Sixties it was lagging far behind Ford's now-luxurious Thunderbird. However, the Riviera easily outsold its stablemate, the radical front-wheel drive Toronado; but for '71 Buick upped the stakes by unveiling a new Riviera that was a little bit special. The new model had become almost a caricature of itself, now bigger and brasher than it ever was before. Handsome and dramatic, the "boat-tail," as it was nicknamed, had its stylistic roots in the split rear window Sting Ray of '63. It was as elegant as Jackie Onassis and as hard-hitting as Muhammad Ali. Its base price was $5,251, undercutting the arch-rival T-Bird by a wide margin. Designer Bill Mitchell nominated it as his favourite car of all time, and, while sales of Rivieras hardly went crazy, at last Buick had a flagship model that was the envy of the industry. It was the coupe in which to make a truly stunning entrance.

ENGINE
The Riviera came with GM's biggest mill, the mighty 455. The hotter Gran Sport option made the massive V8 even smoother and quieter and offered big-buck buyers a shtonking 330 bhp. One reviewer said of the GS-engined car, "there's nothing better made on these shores."

GRILLE
The lines of the boat-tail were not only beautiful at the rear but were carried right through to the thrusting, pointed grille.

ARCHES
Wheel arches were made open and went against the trend for skirted fenders.

CHUNKY REAR
The muscular rear flanks flow into the boat-tail rear. Only a Detroit stylist would graft a huge chrome point to the back of a car.

FINE LINES
Daring lines such as these had never before been seen on a production car.

SPECIFICATIONS

MODEL Buick Riviera (1971)

PRODUCTION 33,810 (1971)

BODY STYLE Two-door coupe.

CONSTRUCTION Steel body and box-section chassis.

ENGINE 455cid V8.

POWER OUTPUT 315–330 bhp.

TRANSMISSION Three-speed Turbo Hydra-Matic automatic.

SUSPENSION *Front:* independent coil springs; *Rear:* self-leveling pneumatic bellows over shocks.

BRAKES Front discs, rear drums.

MAXIMUM SPEED 125 mph (201 km/h)

0–60 MPH (0–96 KM/H) 8.4 sec

A.F.C. 12–15 mpg (4.2–5.3 km/l)

CABIN
The Seventies cabin was plush but plasticky.

INTERIOR
After 1972, the rear seat could be split 60/40 —pretty neat for a coupe. The options list was infinite, and you could swell the car's sticker price by a small fortune. Tilt steering wheel came as standard.

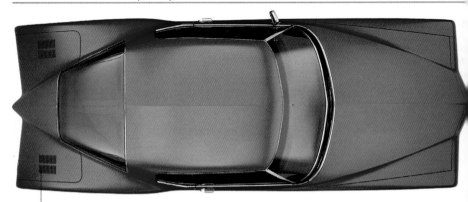

AIR VENTS
Vents were part of the air-conditioning system and unique to '71 Rivieras.

OVERHEAD BEAUTY
The Riviera's styling may have been excessive, but it still made a capacious five-seater, despite the fastback roof line and massive rear window. The 122 in (3.1 m) wheelbase made the '71 boat-tail longer than previous Rivieras.

PILLARLESS STYLE
With the side windows down, the Riv was pillarless, further gracing those swooping lines.

SUPREME STOPPING POWER
The Riviera drew praise for its braking, helped by a Max Trac antiskid option. The Riv could stop from 60 mph (96 km/h) in 135 ft (41 m), a whole 40 ft (12 m) shorter than its rivals.

TINTED SHIELD
Soft-Ray tinted glass helped keep things cool.

BRAKES
Discs on the front helped create a quality braking system.

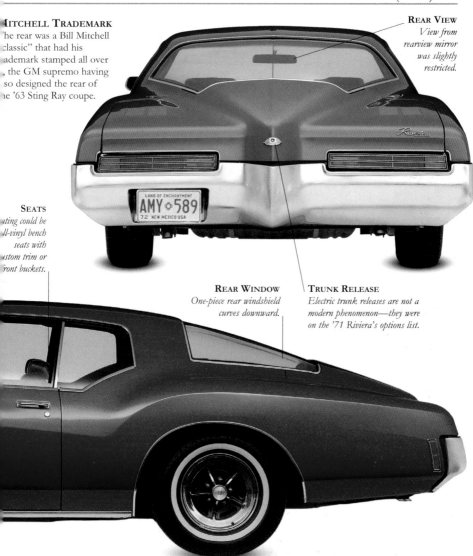

MITCHELL TRADEMARK
The rear was a Bill Mitchell "classic" that had his trademark stamped all over it, the GM supremo having also designed the rear of the '63 Sting Ray coupe.

REAR VIEW
View from rearview mirror was slightly restricted.

SEATS
Seating could be all-vinyl bench seats with custom trim or front buckets.

REAR WINDOW
One-piece rear windshield curves downward.

TRUNK RELEASE
Electric trunk releases are not a modern phenomenon—they were on the '71 Riviera's options list.

LAND OF ENCHANTMENT
AMY ◦ 589
72 NEW MEXICO USA

CADILLAC *Series 62*

WE OWE A LOT TO THE '49 Cadillac. It brought us tail fins and a high-compression V8. Harley Earl came up with those trendsetting rear rudders, and John F. Gordon the performance motor. Between them they created the basic grammar of the postwar American car. In 1949 the one millionth Caddy rolled off the production line, and the stunning Series 62 was born. Handsome and quick, it was a complete revelation. Even the haughty British and Italians nodded sagely in admiration and, at a whisker under $3,000, it knocked the competition dead in their tracks. As Cadillac ads boasted: "The new Cadillac is not only the world's most beautiful and distinguished motor car, but its performance is a challenge to the imagination." The American Dream and the finest era in American cars began with the '49 Cadillac.

INTERIOR
The cabin was heavily chromed and oozed quality. Colors were gray-blue or brown with wool carpets to match, and leather or cloth seats. Steering was Saginaw, with standard four-speed auto transmission.

UNDER THE HOOD
While styling was similar to that of the '48 model, the new OHV V8 in the '49 was an innovation.

CADDY INSPIRATION

1948 was the year of the fin and the year of the crème des Cadillac. Cadillac designers Bill Mitchell, Harley Earl, Frank Hershey, and Art Ross had been smitten by a secret P-38 Lockheed Lightning fighter plane. Cadillac also had Ed Cole's OHV V8, some 10 years in the making. With a brief to reduce weight and increase compression, the end result was an engine with more torque and better mileage than any other at the time.

WINDSHIELD
Curved windscreen was a novelty for a 1949 car.

CADDY BADGING
The "V" emblem below the crest denoted V8 power; the basic badge design remained unaltered until 1952.

SPECIFICATIONS

MODEL Cadillac Series 62 (1949)

PRODUCTION 92,554 (all body styles)

BODY STYLE Two-door, five-seater fastback.

CONSTRUCTION Steel body and chassis.

ENGINE 331cid V8.

POWER OUTPUT 162 bhp.

TRANSMISSION Four-speed Hydra-Matic automatic.

SUSPENSION *Front:* coil springs; *Rear:* leaf springs.

BRAKES Front and rear drums.

MAXIMUM SPEED 100 mph (161 km/h)

0–60 MPH (0–96 KM/H) 13.4 sec

A.F.C. 17 mpg (6 km/l)

SECRET CAP
Fuel cap was hidden under taillight, a Cadillac trait since 1941.

TAIL VIEW
The plane-inspired rear fins became a Caddy trademark and would reach a titanic height on '59 models.

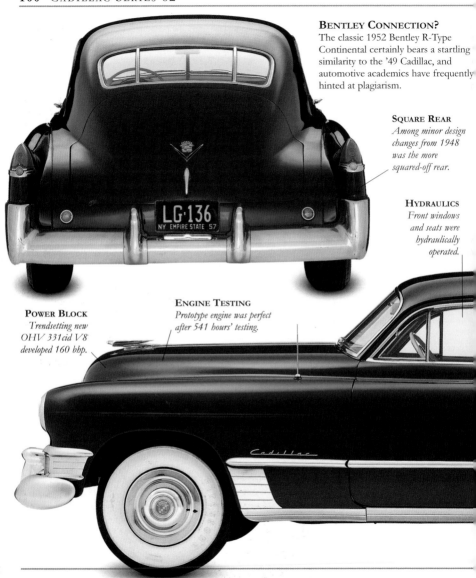

BENTLEY CONNECTION?
The classic 1952 Bentley R-Type Continental certainly bears a startling similarity to the '49 Cadillac, and automotive academics have frequently hinted at plagiarism.

SQUARE REAR
Among minor design changes from 1948 was the more squared-off rear.

HYDRAULICS
Front windows and seats were hydraulically operated.

POWER BLOCK
Trendsetting new OHV 331cid V8 developed 160 bhp.

ENGINE TESTING
Prototype engine was perfect after 541 hours' testing.

ELIEVE THE HYPE
adillac advertisements trumpeted that the
9 was "the world's most beautiful car,"
d the simple yet elegant styling
ught the public's
agination.

FINE LINES
*Glorious tapering
roof line.*

GRILLE
*Grille was
avier on the '49
than on the '48.*

TIRES
*Tires ran at only 24 psi,
making unassisted steering
heavy for the driver.*

DECORATION
*Chrome slashes were
inspired by aircraft
air intakes.*

CLASSIC STYLING
Hugely influential body design was
penned by Harley Earl and Julio Andrade
at GM's styling studios. Many of the '49
features soon found themselves on
other GM products such as
Oldsmobile and Buick.

CADILLAC *Eldorado Convertible* (1953)

FOR 1950s AMERICA, CARS DID NOT come much more glamorous than the 1953 Eldor
"A car apart—even from other Cadillacs," assured the advertising copy. The first Cad
to bear the Eldo badge, it was seen as the ultimate and most desirable American luxu
car, good enough even for Marilyn Monroe and Dwight Eisenhower. Conceived as a
limited edition, the '53 brought avant-garde styling cues from Harley Earl's Motoram
Exhibitions. Earl was Cadillac's inspired chief designer, while Motoramas were yearly
futuristic car shows where his whims of steel took on form. At a hefty $7,750, nearly
twice as much as the regular Cadillac Convertible and five times as much as an ordina
Chevrolet, the '53 was special. In 1954, Cadillac cut the price by 50 percent and soon
Eldorados were leaving showrooms like heat-seeking missiles. Today collectors regard
the '53 as the one that started it all—the first and most fabulous of the Eldorados.

POWER TOPPERS

At the time the '53 was America's most
powerful car, with a cast-iron V8, four-
barrel carburetor, and wedge cylinder head.
With the standard convertible weighing
300 lb (136 kg) less, the Eldorado was
actually the slowest of the Cadillacs.

AIR-CON WEIGHT

*Air-conditioning boosted the car's
weight to 4,800 lb (2,177 kg),
but top speed was still a brisk
116 mph (187 km/h).*

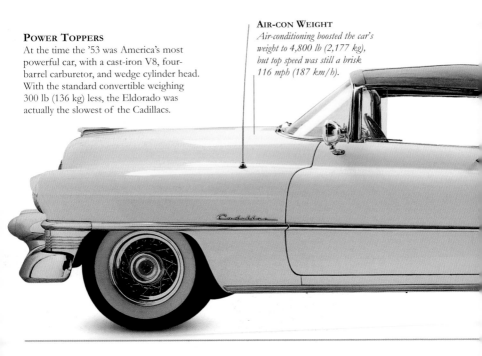

SPECIFICATIONS

MODEL Cadillac Eldorado Convertible (1953)

PRODUCTION 532 (1953)

BODY STYLE Five-seater convertible.

CONSTRUCTION Steel bodywork.

ENGINE 5424cc V8.

POWER OUTPUT 210 bhp at 4150 rpm.

TRANSMISSION Three-speed Hydra-Matic Dual-Range automatic.

SUSPENSION *Front:* independent MacPherson strut; *Rear:* live axle with leaf springs.

BRAKES Front and rear drums.

MAXIMUM SPEED 116 mph (187 km/h)

0–60 MPH (0–96 KM/H) 12.8 sec

0–100 MPH (0–161 KM/H) 20 sec

A.F.C. 14–20 mpg (5–7 km/l)

FUTURISTIC STYLING
The twin exhausts emerge from the rear bumper—
the beginnings of "jet-age" styling themes which would
culminate in the outrageous 42-in (107-cm) fins on the
1959 Cadillac Convertible *(see pages 106–09).*

MATERIAL
*Top was made
of Orlon acrylic.*

SLICK DESIGN
*The top disappeared neatly
below a steel tonneau panel,
giving the Eldorado a much
cleaner uninterrupted line
than other convertibles.*

SPARE WHEEL
*The trunk-mounted spare
wheel was an after-market
continental touring kit.*

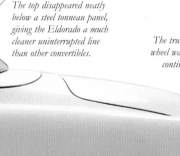

TIRES
*Slick whitewall tires and chrome wire wheels
were standard on the Eldorado Convertible.*

TOP OF THE LINE
As Cadillac's finest flagship, the Eldorado had image by the bucketful. The 331 cubic inch V8 engine was the most powerful yet, and the body line was ultrasleek.

WINDSHIELD
The standard Cadillac wraparound windshield was first seen on the '53.

TWO-WAY MIRROR
The heavily chromed, hand-operated swiveling spotlight doubled up as a door mirror.

CHROME STYLING
Dagmars were so-called after a lushly upholstered starlet of the day.

ANTENNA
Antenna picked up reception for self-tuning radio.

DASHBOARD
Standard equipment on the Eldo convertible was Hydra-Matic transmission, hydraulic window lifts, leather and cloth upholstery, tinted glass, vanity and side mirrors, plus a self-tuning radio.

BODY COLOR
Colors available were Alpine White, Aztec Red, Azure Blue, and Artisan Ochre.

CADILLAC *Convertible*

NO CAR BETTER SUMS UP AMERICA at its peak than the 1959 Cadillac—a rocket-styled starship for orbiting the galaxy of new freeways in the richest and most powerful country on earth. With 42 in (107 cm) fins, the '59 Caddy marks the zenith of American car design. Two tons in weight, 20 ft (6.1 m) long, and 6 ft (1.83 m) wide, it oozed money, self-confidence, and unchallenged power. Under a hood almost the size of Texas nestled an engine almost as big as California. But while it might have looked like it was jet-powered, the '59 handled like the *Exxon Valdez*. So what. The '59 Caddy will always be remembered as a glorious monument to the final years of shameless American optimism. And for a brief, hysterical moment the '59 was the preeminent American car, the ultimate in crazed consumerism. Not a car, but an exemplar of its time that says more about Fifties America than a trunk of history books. The '59 *was* the American Dream.

HALLOWED STATUS
With tail fins that rose a full 3½ ft (1.07 m) off the ground, the '59 is an artifact, a talisman of its times. Not a car, but a styling icon, wonderfully representative of the end of an era —the last years of American world supremacy and an obsession with space travel and men from Mars.

WINDSHIELD
Steep, wraparound windshield could have come straight out of a fighter plane.

QUARTERLIGHTS
Chrome door quarterlights could be swiveled from inside the car.

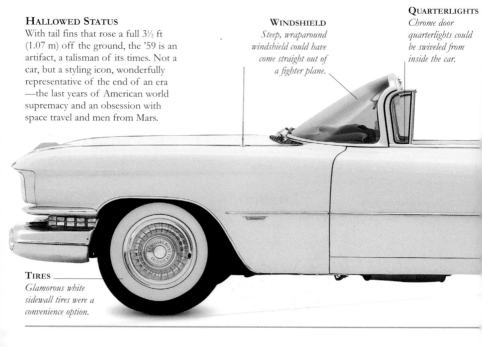

TIRES
Glamorous white sidewall tires were a convenience option.

TOP
*With top furled, the
Cadillac had a
dartlike profile.*

LIGHTS
*Egg-shaped ruby
taillights were
pure jet age.*

EXCESS REAR
Commentators at the time actually thought the '59
too garish. So did Cadillac, which took 6 in (15.5 cm)
off the fins in the following model year.

DOORS
*Massive slab-sided
doors gave easy
entrance and exit.*

TRUNK
*Trunk was cavernous
and could hold five
wheels and tires.*

PENNSYLVANIA
XSU·385

EXTRAVAGANT LENGTH
*The '59's length meant that its turning
circle was a massive 24 ft (7.3 m).*

SPACIOUS
Interior was vast, a true six-seater with acres of room.

HOOD STATUS

With a hood the size of an aircraft carrier, the '59 Caddy was perfect for a society where a car's importance was defined by the length of its nose. The price to pay for such excess was that the front end was notorious for vibration. To help with the comfort factor, electrically operated seats, windows, and trunk could all be ordered.

INTERIOR CHOICES

In addition to power brakes and steering, auto transmission, central locking, and tinted glass, you could also specify automatic headlight dimming.

SPECIFICATIONS

MODEL Cadillac Eldorado Convertible (1959)

PRODUCTION 11,130 (1959)

BODY STYLE Two-door, six-seater convertible.

CONSTRUCTION X-frame chassis, steel body.

ENGINE 6.3-liter (390cid) V8.

POWER OUTPUT 325/345 bhp at 4800 rpm.

TRANSMISSION GM Hydra-Matic three-speed automatic.

SUSPENSION All-around coil springs with optional Freon-12 gas suspension.

BRAKES Four-wheel hydraulic power-assisted drums.

MAXIMUM SPEED 112 mph (180 km/h)

0–60 MPH (0–96 KM/H) 10.3 sec

0–100 MPH (0–161 KM/H) 23.1 sec

A.F.C. 8 mpg (2.8 km/l)

ENGINE

The monster 6.3-liter V8 engine had a cast-iron block, five main bearings, and hydraulic valve lifters, pushing out a not inconsiderable 325 bhp at 4800 rpm.

HIDDEN LIGHTS
Extravagant mounds of chrome might look like turbines but concealed reversing lights.

TAIL VIEW
The '59's outrageous fins, which are the highest of any car in the world, are accentuated by its very low profile— 3 in (8 cm) lower than the '58 model's already modest elevation.

CADILLAC *Eldorado* (1976)

BY 1976, CADILLACS HAD BECOME so swollen that they plowed through corners, averaged 13 mpg (4.6 km/l), and were as quick off the line as an M24 tank. Despite a massive 500cid V8, output of the '76 Eldo was a lowly 190 brake horsepower, with a top speed of just 109 mph (175 km/h). Something had to change, and Cadillac's response had been the '75 Seville. But the '76 Eldo marked the end of an era for another reason—it was the last American convertible. Cadillac was the final automobile manufacturer to delete the ragtop from their model lineup and, when they made the announcement that the convertible was to be phased out at the end of '76, the market fought to buy up the last 200. People even tried to cut in line by claiming they were distantly related to Cadillac's founder. One 72-year-old man in Nebraska bought six. A grand American institution had quietly passed away.

FIXTURES
Interiors could be specified in Merlin Plaid, lush velour, Mansion Knit, or 11 types of Sierra Grain leather.

TRADITIONAL SETUP
Big and slab-sided, the '76 Eldo used a front-wheel drive arrangement that had first been used on the '67 Eldorado and is still used today. The '76 Convertible had big vital statistics, measuring 225 in (5.7 m) long, 80 in (2 m) wide, and costing $10,354.

FUNKY MIRROR
The heavy chrome adjustable door mirror was electrically operated and incorporated a thermometer that displayed the outside temperature.

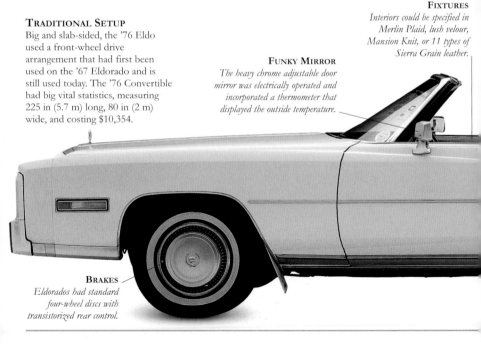

BRAKES
Eldorados had standard four-wheel discs with transistorized rear control.

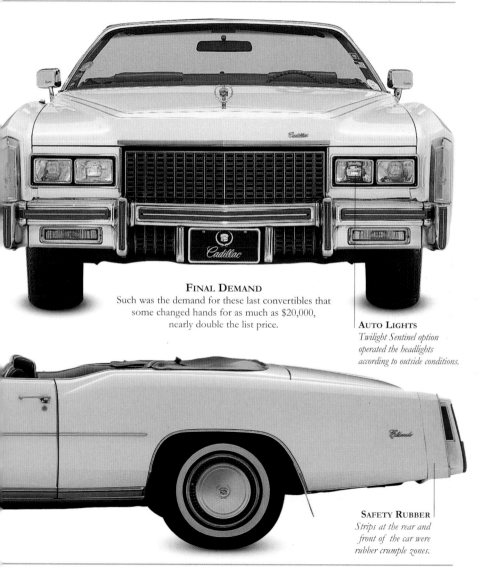

FINAL DEMAND
Such was the demand for these last convertibles that
some changed hands for as much as $20,000,
nearly double the list price.

AUTO LIGHTS
*Twilight Sentinel option
operated the headlights
according to outside conditions.*

SAFETY RUBBER
*Strips at the rear and
front of the car were
rubber crumple zones.*

ECONOMY CLASS
Raised compression ratios an
a recalibrated carburetor gave
the Eldo better fuel economy
than might be expected from
such a mammoth block.
Hydro-Boost power
brakes were needed
to stop the 5,153 l
(2,337 kg) colossus

SUSPENSION
*Independent coil
springs were
complemented
by automatic
level control.*

WOOD
*Interior wood was called
"distressed pecan grain."*

INTERIOR
Technically advanced
options were always
Cadillac's forte. The Eldo
was available with an
airbag, Dual Comfort
front seats with fold-
down armrests, and a
six-way power seat.

COLOR CHOICE
*Eldos could be
ordered in 21
body colors.*

SPECIFICATIONS

MODEL Cadillac Eldorado Convertible
(1976)

PRODUCTION 14,000 (1976)

BODY STYLE Two-door, six-seater
convertible.

CONSTRUCTION Steel body and chassis.

ENGINE 500cid V8.

POWER OUTPUT 190 bhp.

TRANSMISSION Three-speed Hydra-Matic
Turbo automatic.

SUSPENSION Front and rear independent
coil springs with automatic level control.

BRAKES Four-wheel discs.

MAXIMUM SPEED 109 mph (175 km/h)

0–60 MPH (0–96 KM/H) 15.1 sec

A.F.C. 13 mpg (4.6 km/l)

NGINE

ready strangled by
hission pipery, the need to
aximize every gallon meant that the
g 500bhp V8 was embarrassingly lethargic
hen it came to speed. Even lower ratio
ar axles were used to boost mileage.

SPACE
*Even with the top up, the
Eldo was gargantuan inside.*

NVERTOR
*ll Eldorados
d a catalytic
convertor as
standard.*

ADILLAC NAME
e Cadillac shield harkens
ck to 1650 and the original
ench Cadillac family.
ench model names were
ed in 1966 with the Calais
d DeVille lines.

REFLECTORS
*Slightly superfluous in that
not many drivers would
miss this giant on the road.*

CHEVROLET *Corvette* (1954)

A CARICATURE OF A EUROPEAN roadster, the first Corvette of 1953 was more show than go. With typical arrogance, Harley Earl was more interested in the way it looked saw a huge market for a new type of auto opium. With everybody's dreams looking exactly the same, the plastic 'Vette brought a badly needed shot of designed-in diversity. Early models may have been cramped and slow, but they looked like they'd been lifted straight off a Motorama turntable, which they had. Building them was a nightmare though, and for a while GM lost money on each one. Still, nobody minded because Chevrolet now had a new image—as the company that came up with the first American sports car.

EXHIBITION SUCCESS
The 'Vette's shape was based on the 1952 EX-122 show car, and this was one of the few Motorama dream cars to go into production virtually unchanged. The original plan to produce the 'Vette in steel was shelved after widespread acclaim for the fiberglass body from visitors to Motorama.

PERFORMANCE
Performance was not in the Jaguar XK120 league, with a modest 107 mph (172 km/h) top speed.

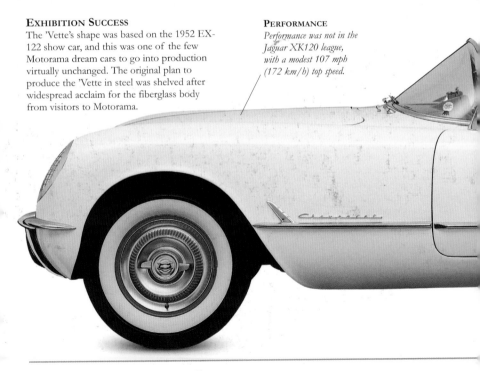

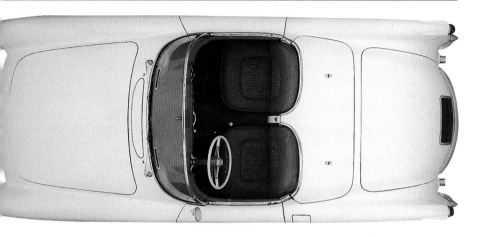

OVERVIEW

The cleverly packaged fiberglass body was rather tricky to make, with no less than 46 different sections. The soft top folded out of sight below a neat lift-up panel.

INTERNAL HANDLES
Like the British sports cars it aped, the '54 'Vette's door handles lived on the inside.

SUSPENSION
Outboard-mounted rear leaf springs helped cornering stability.

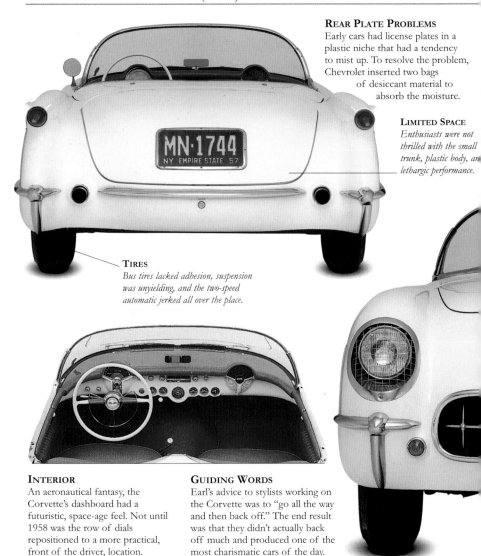

REAR PLATE PROBLEMS

Early cars had license plates in a plastic niche that had a tendency to mist up. To resolve the problem, Chevrolet inserted two bags of desiccant material to absorb the moisture.

LIMITED SPACE

Enthusiasts were not thrilled with the small trunk, plastic body, and lethargic performance.

TIRES

Bus tires lacked adhesion, suspension was unyielding, and the two-speed automatic jerked all over the place.

INTERIOR

An aeronautical fantasy, the Corvette's dashboard had a futuristic, space-age feel. Not until 1958 was the row of dials repositioned to a more practical, front of the driver, location.

GUIDING WORDS

Earl's advice to stylists working on the Corvette was to "go all the way and then back off." The end result was that they didn't actually back off much and produced one of the most charismatic cars of the day.

ENGINE
The souped-up Blue Flame Six block may have had triple carburetors, higher compression, and a high-lift cam, but it was still old and wheezy. 'Vettes had to wait until 1955 for the V8 they deserved.

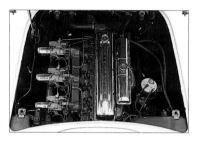

SPECIFICATIONS

MODEL Chevrolet Corvette (1954)

PRODUCTION 3,640 (1954)

BODY STYLE Two-door, two-seater sports.

CONSTRUCTION Fiberglass body, steel chassis.

ENGINE 235.5cid straight six.

POWER OUTPUT 150 bhp.

TRANSMISSION Two-speed Powerglide automatic.

SUSPENSION *Front:* coil springs; *Rear:* leaf springs with live axle.

BRAKES Front and rear drums.

MAXIMUM SPEED 107 mph (172 km/h)

0–60 MPH (0–96 KM/H) 8–12 sec

A.F.C. 20 mpg (7 km/l)

BODY COLOR
Oddly enough, 80 percent of all '54 Corvettes were painted white.

GUARDS
Stone guards on lights were culled from European racing cars, but criticized for being too feminine.

ITALIAN SMILE
Earl admitted that the shark-tooth grille was robbed from contemporary Ferraris.

BUMPERS
Impact protection may have been vestigial, but the fiberglass body took knocks well.

CHEVROLET *Bel Air (1957)*

CHEVROLET CALLED THEIR '57 LINE "sweet, smooth, and sassy," and the Bel Air was exactly what America wanted—a junior Cadillac. Finny, trim, and handsome, and with Ed Cole's Super Turbo-Fire V8, it boasted one of the first production engines to pump out one horsepower per cubic inch, and was the first mass-market "fuelie" sedan with Ramjet injection. Chevy copywriters screamed "the Hot One's even hotter," and Bel Airs became kings of the street. Production that year broke the 1½ million barrier and gave Ford the fright of its life. The trouble was that the "Hot One" was forced to cool it when the Automobile Manufacturers' Association urged carmakers to put an end to their performance hysteria. Today, the Bel Air is one of the most widely coveted US collector's cars and the perfect embodiment of young mid-Fifties America. In the words of the Billie Jo Spears song, "Wish we still had her today; the good love we're living, we owe it to that '57 Chevrolet."

BODY STYLE
Other body styles available included a two-door hardtop.

POPULAR AND STYLISH
At $2,511, the Bel Air Convertible was the epitome of budget-priced good taste, finding 47,562 eager buyers. Low, sleek, and flashy, it could almost out-glam the contemporary Caddy ragtop.

BUICK STYLE
The Bel Air's Ventiports only lasted a couple of years.

ENGINE
Only 1,503 fuel-injected Bel Airs were sold.

Ornamentation

he rather clumsy bombsight hood ornament ould be fairly described as the '57 Bel Air's only minor stylistic blemish. he public liked it, though.

French Decoration

Chevrolet's fleur-de-lis, a reminder of their French roots.

Safety Measures

Seat belts and shoulder straps were available on the lengthy options list.

Perfectly Formed

Immediately after it was introduced, it was rightly hailed as a design classic. Elegant, sophisticated, and perfectly proportioned, the '57 Bel Air is one of the finest postwar American autos of all.

Longer Model

The '57 Bel Air was 2½ in (6.3 cm) longer than the '56 model.

A TRUE CLASSIC

The '57 Bel Air sums up America's most prosperous decade better than any other car of the time. Along with hula-hoops, drive-in movies, and rock 'n' roll, it has become a Fifties icon. It was loved then because it was stylish, solid, sporty, and affordable, and it's loved now for more or less the same reasons; plus it simply drips with nostalgia.

INTERIOR

The distinctive two-tone interiors were a delight. Buyers could opt for a custom color interior, power convertible top, tinted glass, vanity mirror, ventilated seat pads, power windows, and even a tissue dispenser.

POWER OPTION

The Bel Air Convertible could be equipped with an optional power-operated top.

SPEEDOMETER

Speedo read to 120, and larger-engined models nearly broke through the dial.

BEHIND THE WHEEL

The small-block Turbo-Fire V8 packed 185 bhp in base two-barrel trim and 270 bhp with the optional Rochester four barrel. Ramjet injection added a hefty $500 to the sticker price.

AIR STYLE
Chevrolet, like every other US car manufacturer at the time, was eager to cash in on the jet age, but in reality this '55 Bel Air four-door sedan looks positively dumpy next to the fighter plane.

HIDDEN CAP
In common with Lincoln and Cadillac, Chevrolet incorporated the fuel caps into the chrome molding at the rear edge of the left tail fin.

RESTRAINED FINNAGE
Subtle rear fins are almost demure compared with other contemporary efforts.

SPECIFICATIONS

MODEL Chevrolet Bel Air Convertible (1957)

PRODUCTION 47,562 (1957)

BODY STYLE Two-door convertible.

CONSTRUCTION Steel body and box-section chassis.

ENGINES 265cid, 283cid V8s.

POWER OUTPUT 162–283 bhp (283cid V8 fuel injected).

TRANSMISSION Three-speed manual with optional overdrive, optional two-speed Powerglide automatic, and Turboglide.

SUSPENSION *Front:* independent coil springs; *Rear:* leaf springs with live axle.

BRAKES Front and rear drums.

MAXIMUM SPEED 90–120 mph (145–193 km/h)

0–60 MPH (0–96 KM/H) 8–12 sec

A.F.C. 14 mpg (5 km/l)

CHEVROLET *Bel Air Nomad* (1957)

IF YOU THOUGHT BMW AND MERCEDES were first with the sporting uptown carry-all, think again. Chevrolet kicked off the genre as far back as 1955. The Bel Air Nomad was a development of Harley Earl's dream wagon based on the Chevrolet Corvette; and although it looked like other '55 Bel Airs, the V8 Nomad was the most expensive Chevy ever. But despite the fact that *Motor Trend* described the '57 Nomad as "one of the year's most beautiful cars," with only two doors its appeal was limited, its large glass area made the cabin too hot, and the tailgate let in water. No surprise then that it was one of Chevy's least popular models. Sales never broke the magic 10,000 barrier and, by 1958, the world's first sportwagon, and now a milestone car, had been dropped.

ROOF FIRST
The Nomad was the first car to use nonstructural corrugations on the roof.

INTERIOR
Two-tone trim could be complemented by power seat, tinted glass, and seat belts.

STYLE REVIVAL
The Nomad was essentially a revival of the original Town and Country theme and a reaction against the utilitarian functionalism of the boxy wooden wagons that had become ubiquitous in suburban America.

ENGINE
Base unit was a 235cid six; grunty 265cid V8 was available.

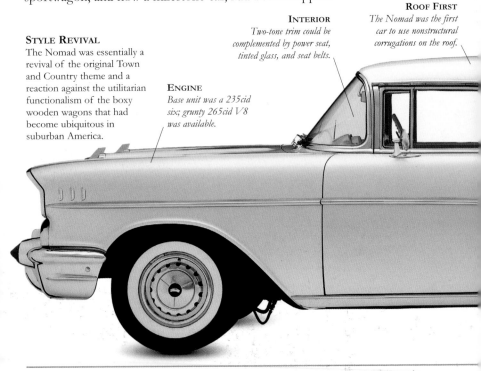

SPECIFICATIONS

MODEL Chevrolet Bel Air Nomad (1957)

PRODUCTION 6,103 (1957)

BODY STYLE Two-door station wagon.

CONSTRUCTION Steel body and chassis.

ENGINES 235cid six, 265cid V8.

POWER OUTPUT 123–283 bhp.

TRANSMISSION Three-speed manual with overdrive, two-speed Powerglide automatic, and optional Turboglide.

SUSPENSION *Front:* coil springs; *Rear:* leaf springs.

BRAKES Front and rear drums.

MAXIMUM SPEED 90–120 mph (145–193 km/h)

0–60 MPH (0–96 KM/H) 8–11 sec

A.F.C. 15–19 mpg (5.3–6.7 km/l)

IMMEDIATE HIT
Unveiled in January 1954, the Motorama Nomad—created by Chevy stylist Carl Renner—was such a hit that a production version made it into the '55 brochures.

DECORATED TAIL
The classic Harley Earl embellished tailgate was taken straight from the Motorama Corvette and was widely praised.

'VETTE LINES
Motorama 'Vette roof line was adapted for production Nomads in just two days.

CHEVROLET *3100 Stepside*

CHEVY WAS ON A HIGH in the mid-Fifties. With the 'Vette, the Bel Air, and their new V8, it was America's undisputed top car manufacturer. A boundless optimism percolated through all divisions, even touching such prosaic offerings as trucks. And the definitive Chevy carry-all has to be the '57 pickup. It had not only that four-stroke overhead-valve V8 mill, but also various options and a smart new restyle. No wonder it was nicknamed "a Cadillac in drag." Among the most enduring of all American design statements, the '57 had clean, well-proportioned lines, a minimum of chrome, and integrated fenders. Chevrolet turned the pickup from a beast of burden into a personalized workhorse complete with all the accessories of gracious living usually seen in a boulevard cruiser.

ENGINE
The small-block V8 produced 150 bhp and could cruise at 70 mph (113 km/h). From '55, all Chevys used open-drive instead of an enclosed torque-tube driveline.

WRAPAROUND SHIELD
De Luxe models had a larger, wraparound windshield, and two-tone seats, door trims, and steering wheel.

INTERIOR
The Stepside was as stylized inside as out, with chrome switches, swing-out ashtrays, and a V-shaped speedo.

TIMBER BED
Wooden bed floors helped to protect
the load area and added a quality feel
to Chevy's Stepside.

SPECIFICATIONS

MODEL Chevrolet 3100 Stepside (1957)

PRODUCTION Not available.

BODY STYLE Two-seater, short-bed pickup.

CONSTRUCTION Steel body and chassis.

ENGINES 235cid six, 265cid V8.

POWER OUTPUT 130–145 bhp.

TRANSMISSION Three-speed manual with optional overdrive, optional three-speed automatic.

SUSPENSION *Front:* coil springs; *Rear:* leaf springs.

BRAKES Front and rear drums.

MAXIMUM SPEED 80 mph (129 km/h)

0–60 MPH (0–96 KM/H) 17.3 sec

A.F.C. 17 mpg (6 km/l)

MULTIPLE CHOICES
Chevy's '57 pickups can be identified
by the new trapezoid grille and a
flatter hood than '56 models. Buyers
had a choice of short or long bed,
De Luxe or standard trim, and 11
exterior colors. Engines were the
235cid Thriftmaster six or the
265cid Trademaster V8.

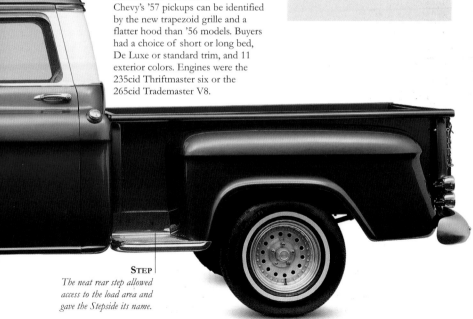

STEP
*The neat rear step allowed
access to the load area and
gave the Stepside its name.*

CHEVROLET *Impala*

IN THE SIXTIES, unbridled consumerism began to wane. America turned away from the politics of prosperity and, in deference, Chevrolet toned down its finny Impala. The '59's gothic cantilevered batwings went, replaced by a much blunter rear deck. WASP America was developing a social conscience and Fifties excess just wasn't cool anymore. However, the '60 Impala was no shrinking violet. Tired of gorging on gratuitous ornamentation, US drivers were offered a new theology—performance. Freeways were one long concrete loop, premium gas was cheap, and safety and environmentalism were a nightmare still to come. For $333, the Sports Coupe could boast a 348cid, 335 bhp Special Super Turbo-Thrust V8. The '59 Impala was riotous and the '60 stylistically muddled, but within a year the unruliness would disappear altogether. These crossover Chevrolets are landmark cars—they ushered in a new decade that would change America and Americans forever.

RESTRAINED STYLING
The front of the Impala was meant to be quiet and calm and a million miles from the deranged dentistry of mid-Fifties grille treatments. The jet-fighter cockpit and quarter-panel missile ornaments were eerie portents of the coming decade of military intervention.

LUXURY EXTRAS
Chevy's trump card was an option list normally found on luxury cars, like air-conditioning, power steering and windows, and six-way power seat.

NATION'S FAVORITE
The Impala was America's best-selling model in 1960.

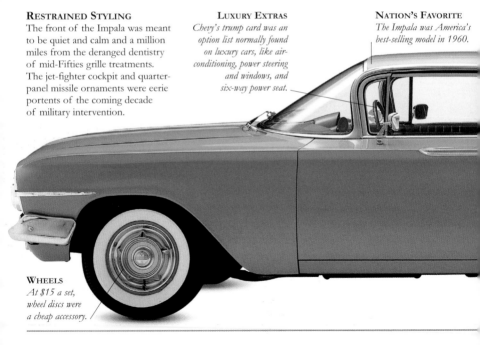

WHEELS
At $15 a set, wheel discs were a cheap accessory.

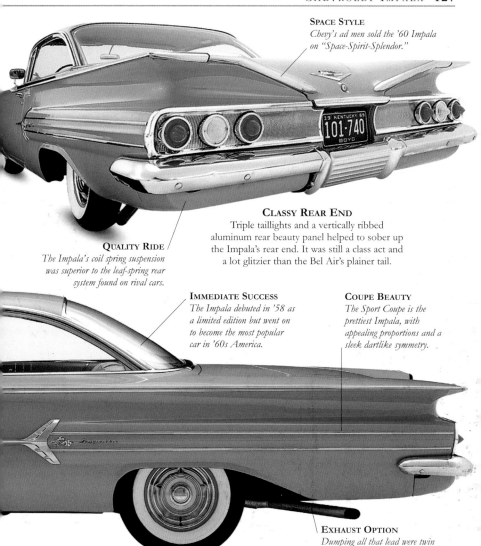

SPACE STYLE
Chevy's ad men sold the '60 Impala on "Space-Spirit-Splendor."

CLASSY REAR END
Triple taillights and a vertically ribbed aluminum rear beauty panel helped to sober up the Impala's rear end. It was still a class act and a lot glitzier than the Bel Air's plainer tail.

QUALITY RIDE
The Impala's coil spring suspension was superior to the leaf-spring rear system found on rival cars.

IMMEDIATE SUCCESS
The Impala debuted in '58 as a limited edition but went on to become the most popular car in '60s America.

COUPE BEAUTY
The Sport Coupe is the prettiest Impala, with appealing proportions and a sleek dartlike symmetry.

EXHAUST OPTION
Dumping all that lead were twin exhausts, a bargain $19 option.

STEERING WHEEL
The sporty steering wheel was inspired by the Corvette.

INTERIOR
Inside, the Impala was loaded with performance metaphor: central speedo, four gauges, and a mock sports steering wheel with crossed flags. This car incorporates power windows and dual Polaroid sun visors.

TRIPLE LIGHTS
The triple taillights had disappeared in '59 but returned for the '60 model; they went on to become a classic Impala styling cue.

LENGTHY FRAME
Impalas were big, riding on a 119-in (302-cm) wheelbase.

TIRES
Slick whitewalls were yours for just $36.

TAME FINS
The '60 Impala sported much tamer Spread Wing fins that copied a seagu in flight. They were an answer to charges that the '59's uproarious rear end was downright dangerous.

MODEL RANGE
Body styles were four-door sports sedan, pillarless sport coupe, stock four-door sedan, and convertible.

SPECIFICATIONS

MODEL Chevrolet Impala Sports Coupe (1960)

PRODUCTION Not available.

BODY STYLE Two-door coupe.

CONSTRUCTION Steel body, separate chassis.

ENGINES 235cid straight six, 283cid, 348cid V8s.

POWER OUTPUT 135–335 bhp (348cid turbo V8).

TRANSMISSION Three-speed manual, optional four-speed manual, two-speed Powerglide automatic, Turboglide automatic.

SUSPENSION *Front:* upper and lower A-arms, coil springs; *Rear:* coil springs with live axle.

BRAKES Four-wheel disc.

MAXIMUM SPEED 90–135 mph (145–217 km/h)

0–60 MPH (0–96 KM/H) 9–18 sec

A.F.C. 12–16 mpg (4.2–5.7 km/l)

EXTRA BOOST
Impalas could be warmed up considerably with some very special engines.

RACING MODELS

The Impala impressed on circuits all over the world. In 1961, some models were deemed hot enough to run with European track stars like the Jaguar Mark II, as driven by Graham Hill.

ENGINE

Two V8 engine options offered consumers seven heady levels of power, from 170 to 335 horses. Cheapskates could still specify the ancient Blue Flame Six, which wheezed out a miserly 135 bhp. Seen here is the 185 bhp, 283cid V8. Impalas could be invigorated with optional Positraction, heavy-duty springs, and power brakes.

CHEVROLET *Corvette Sting Ray (1966)*

THE CHEVROLET CORVETTE IS AMERICA'S native sports car. The "plastic fantastic," born in 1953, is still fantastic more than half a decade later. Along the way, in 1992, it notched up a million sales, and it is still hanging in there. Admittedly it has mutated over the years, but it has stayed true to its roots in one very important aspect. Other American sports car contenders, like the Ford Thunderbird *(see pages 274–77),* soon abandoned any sporting pretensions, adding weight and middle-aged girth, but not the Corvette. All Corvette fans have their favorite eras: for some it is the purity of the very first generation from 1953; others favor the glamorous 1956–62 models; but for many, the Corvette came of age in 1963 with the birth of the Sting Ray.

HIDDEN LIGHTS
Twin, pop-up headlights were hidden behind electrically operated covers; more than a gimmick, they aided aerodynamic efficiency.

BADGING
Corvettes from 1963 to 1967 were known as Sting Rays; the restyled 1968 model *(see pages 142–45)* was renamed as Stingray, one word. The checkered flag on the front of the hood denotes sporting lineage, while the red flag bears the GM logo and a fleur-de-lis.

CHASSIS
New chassis frame was introduced in 1963.

INTERIOR

The Batmobile-style interior, with twin-hooped dash, is carried over from earlier Corvettes but updated in the Sting Ray. The deep-dished, wood-effect wheel comes close to the chest, and power steering was an option.

SEATING

Seats were low and flat, rather than figure hugging.

BRAKES

In 1965 the Sting Ray got four-wheeled disc brakes in place of all-around drums.

SPECIFICATIONS

MODEL Chevrolet Corvette Sting Ray (1963–69)

PRODUCTION 118,964

BODY STYLES Two-door sports convertible or fastback coupe.

CONSTRUCTION Fiberglass body; X-braced pressed-steel box-section chassis.

ENGINES OHV V8, 5359cc (327cid), 6495cc (396cid), 7008cc (427cid).

POWER OUTPUT 250–375 bhp (5359cc), 390–560 bhp (7008cc).

TRANSMISSION Three-speed manual, opt'l. four-speed manual or Powerglide auto.

SUSPENSION Independent all around. *Front:* Unequal-length wishbones with coil springs; *Rear:* Transverse leaf.

BRAKES Drums to 1965, then discs.

MAXIMUM SPEED 152 mph (245 km/h, 7008cc).

0–60 MPH (0–96 KM/H) 5.4 sec (7008cc).

0–100 MPH (0–161 KM/H) 13.1 sec (7008cc).

A.F.C. 9–16 mpg (3–5.7 km/l).

A MITCHELL CLASSIC

The Sting Ray was a bold design breakthrough, giving concrete expression to many of the ideas of new GM styling chief, Bill Mitchell. He reputedly regarded the 1963 Sting Ray as his finest piece of work. More than half of all production was in convertible roadsters, for which a hardtop was an option.

OVERHEAD VIEW

You can tell this is a "small block" engine—the hood power bulge was widened to accommodate the "big block" unit. Three-speed manual transmission was standard, with two-speed automatic and three types of manual four-speed shift optional.

ENGINE OPTIONS

Sting Rays came in three engine sizes—naturally all V8s—with a wide range of power options from 250 bhp to more than twice that. This featured car is a 1966 Sting Ray with "small block" 5359cc V8 and Holley four-barrel carb.

LIMITED TRUNK
Fuel tank and spare tire took up most of the trunk space.

HARDTOP OPTION
Until 1963, all Corvettes were open roadsters; but with the arrival of the Sting Ray, a fixed-head coupe was now also available. The distinctive two-piece back window used on the 1963 model makes it the most sought-after fixed-head Sting Ray.

SIDE EXHAUST
Aluminum strip concealed side-mounted exhaust option.

CHEVROLET *Corvair Monza*

BY 1960, SALES OF DINOSAURS were down, small-car imports were up, and Detroit finally listened to a market screaming for economy compacts. Then along came Chevrolet's adventurous answer to the Volkswagen Beetle, the pretty, rear-engined Corvair, which sold for half the price of a Ford Thunderbird. But problems soon arose. GM's draconian cost-cutting meant that a crucial $15 suspension stabilizing bar was omitted, and early Corvairs handled like pigs. The suspension was redesigned in '65, but it was too late. Bad news also came in the form of Ralph Nader's book *Unsafe at Any Speed*, which lambasted the Corvair. The new Ford Mustang, which had become the hot compact, didn't help either. By 1969, it was all over for the Corvair. GM's stab at downsizing had been a disaster.

IMPRESSING THE PRESS
After very few styling changes for the first five years, the new body design for '65 had a heavy Italian influence with smooth-flowing, rounded lines that impressed the automotive press. *Car and Driver* magazine called it "the best of established foreign and domestic coachwork."

SIDE MIRROR
Shatter-resistant side mirror came as standard.

RAGTOP NUMBERS
Only 26,000 convertibles were sold in '65.

MAINLY AUTOMATIC
Despite the public's interest in economy, 53 percent of all Corvairs had automatic transmission.

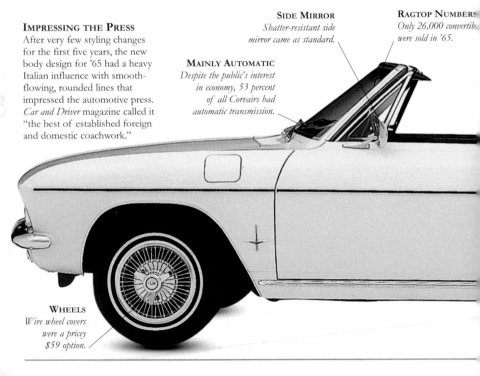

WHEELS
Wire wheel covers were a pricey $59 option.

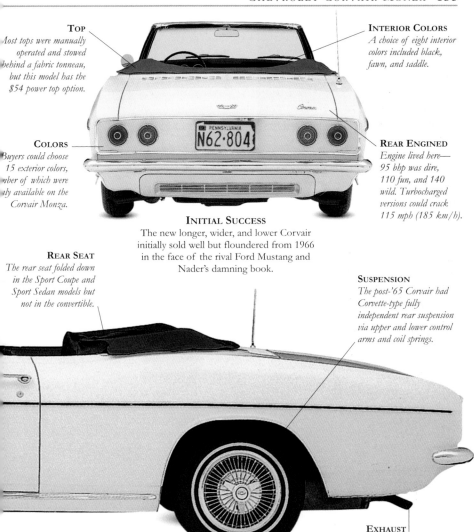

TOP
*Most tops were manually
operated and stowed
behind a fabric tonneau,
but this model has the
$54 power top option.*

INTERIOR COLORS
*A choice of eight interior
colors included black,
fawn, and saddle.*

COLORS
*Buyers could choose
15 exterior colors,
number of which were
only available on the
Corvair Monza.*

REAR ENGINED
*Engine lived here—
95 bhp was dire,
110 fun, and 140
wild. Turbocharged
versions could crack
115 mph (185 km/h).*

INITIAL SUCCESS
The new longer, wider, and lower Corvair
initially sold well but floundered from 1966
in the face of the rival Ford Mustang and
Nader's damning book.

REAR SEAT
*The rear seat folded down
in the Sport Coupe and
Sport Sedan models but
not in the convertible.*

SUSPENSION
*The post-'65 Corvair had
Corvette-type fully
independent rear suspension
via upper and lower control
arms and coil springs.*

EXHAUST
*Long-life exhaust system
consisted of aluminized silencer.*

PENNSYLVANIA
N62·804

STORAGE SPACE
Rear-engined format meant that storage space under the hood was massive.

INTERIOR
The all-vinyl interior was very European, with bucket seats and telescopic steering column. The restrained steering wheel and deep-set instruments could have come straight out of a BMW. The dials were recessed to reduce glare and deep-twist carpeting added an air of luxury to the cockpit. Options on offer included a windshield-mounted automatic compass and a hand-rubbed walnut steering wheel.

BLOCK FEATURES
All Corvairs had an automatic choke and aluminum cylinder heads.

TIRES
White sidewalls could be ordered for an extra $29.

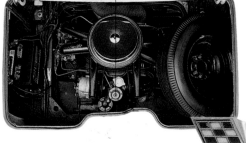

ENGINE
Corvair buyers had a choice of alloy, air-cooled, horizontal sixes. The base unit was a 164cid block with four Rochester carbs developing 140 bhp. The hot turbocharged motors were able to push out a more respectable 180 bhp.

POWER READING
The 140 badge represented the Corvair's power output.

END OF THE LINE

By the end of '68, sales of the handsome Monza Coupe were down to just 6,800 units, and GM decided to pull the plug in May '69. Those who had bought a '69 Corvair were given a certificate worth $150 off any other '69–'70 Chevrolet.

SPECIFICATIONS

MODEL Chevrolet Corvair Monza (1966)

PRODUCTION 60,447 (1966, Monza only)

BODY STYLES Two- and four-door, four-seater coupe and convertible.

CONSTRUCTION Steel unitary body.

ENGINES 164cid flat sixes.

POWER OUTPUT 95–140 bhp.

TRANSMISSION Three-speed manual, optional four-speed manual, and two-speed Powerglide automatic.

SUSPENSION Front and rear coil springs.

BRAKES Front and rear drums.

MAXIMUM SPEED 105–120 mph (169–193 km/h)

0–60 MPH (0–96 KM/H) 11–15.2 sec

A.F.C. 20 mpg (7 km/l)

PRODUCTION

1965 model year production peaked at 205,000 units. Ford's Mustang did half a million in the same year.

FIRST MONZAS

The early Corvair Monzas, with deluxe trim and automatic transmission, were a big hit. In 1961, over 143,000 were sold, which amounted to over half the grand Corvair total.

WINDOWS

Side windows were made of specially curved glass.

ANTENNA

Power-operated rear antenna was an option.

CHEVROLET *Camaro RS Convertible*

RUMORS THAT GENERAL MOTORS had at last come up with something to steal sales from Ford's hugely successful Mustang *(see pages 278–85)* swept through the American auto industry in the spring of 1966. Code-named Panther, the Camaro was announced to newspaper reporters on June 29, 1966, touching down in showrooms on September 21. The Pony Car building-block philosophy was simple: sell a basic machine and allow the customer to add their own extras. The trouble was that the Camaro had an options list as arcane and complicated as a lawyer's library. From Strato-Ease headrests to Comfort-Tilt steering wheel, the Camaro buyer really was spoiled for choice. But it worked. Buyers ordered the Rally Sport equipment package for their stock Camaros, and suddenly they were kings of the street. Go-faster, twin-lined body striping, hidden headlights, and matte black taillight bezels were all calculated to enhance the illusion of performance pedigree. Especially if he or she could not afford the real thing—the hot Camaro SS.

CLEAN STYLING
The market accepted the Camaro as a solid response to the Ford Mustang. Its styling was cleaner, more European, and less boxy, and it drove better than the Ford. Despite all this, Camaro sales were still considerably less than the Mustang.

PRODUCTION SOURCES
First-generation Camaros were mainly built in Norwood, Ohio, but some also came out of the Van Nuys plant in California.

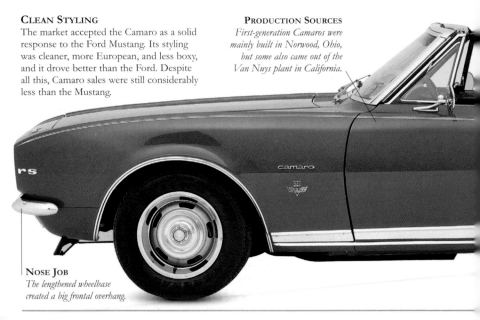

NOSE JOB
The lengthened wheelbase created a big frontal overhang.

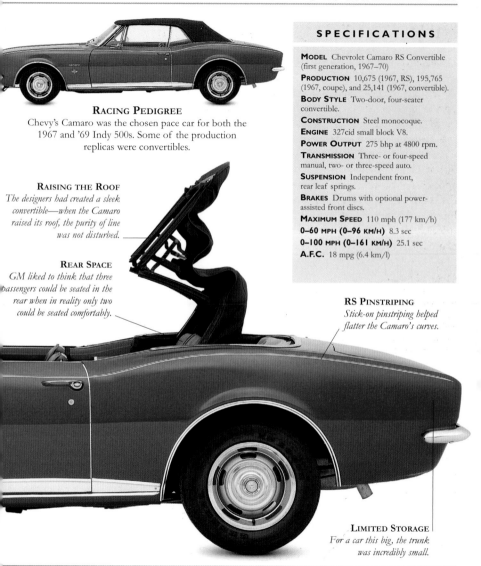

RACING PEDIGREE

Chevy's Camaro was the chosen pace car for both the 1967 and '69 Indy 500s. Some of the production replicas were convertibles.

RAISING THE ROOF

The designers had created a sleek convertible—when the Camaro raised its roof, the purity of line was not disturbed.

REAR SPACE

GM liked to think that three passengers could be seated in the rear when in reality only two could be seated comfortably.

SPECIFICATIONS

MODEL Chevrolet Camaro RS Convertible (first generation, 1967–70)

PRODUCTION 10,675 (1967, RS), 195,765 (1967, coupe), and 25,141 (1967, convertible).

BODY STYLE Two-door, four-seater convertible.

CONSTRUCTION Steel monocoque.

ENGINE 327cid small block V8.

POWER OUTPUT 275 bhp at 4800 rpm.

TRANSMISSION Three- or four-speed manual, two- or three-speed auto.

SUSPENSION Independent front, rear leaf springs.

BRAKES Drums with optional power-assisted front discs.

MAXIMUM SPEED 110 mph (177 km/h)

0–60 MPH (0–96 KM/H) 8.3 sec

0–100 MPH (0–161 KM/H) 25.1 sec

A.F.C. 18 mpg (6.4 km/l)

RS PINSTRIPING

Stick-on pinstriping helped flatter the Camaro's curves.

LIMITED STORAGE

For a car this big, the trunk was incredibly small.

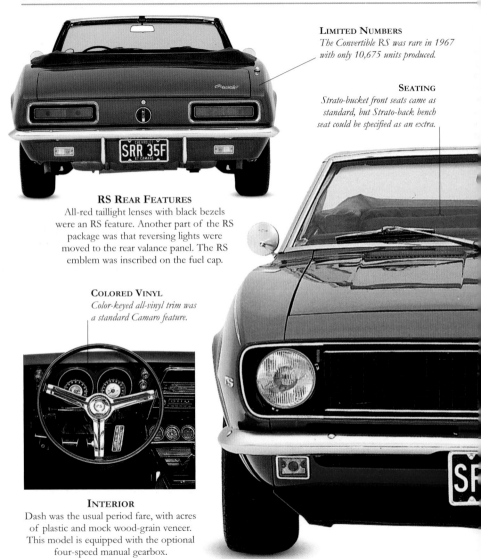

LIMITED NUMBERS
The Convertible RS was rare in 1967 with only 10,675 units produced.

SEATING
Strato-bucket front seats came as standard, but Strato-back bench seat could be specified as an extra.

RS REAR FEATURES
All-red taillight lenses with black bezels were an RS feature. Another part of the RS package was that reversing lights were moved to the rear valance panel. The RS emblem was inscribed on the fuel cap.

COLORED VINYL
Color-keyed all-vinyl trim was a standard Camaro feature.

INTERIOR
Dash was the usual period fare, with acres of plastic and mock wood-grain veneer. This model is equipped with the optional four-speed manual gearbox.

RACING OPTION

Trans Am Racing spawned the Z28 Camaro, a thinly-veiled street racer, designed to take on the Shelby Mustang. Top speed was 124 mph (200 km/h) and 0-60 came up in 6.7 seconds. Only available as a coupe, it was designed for those who put speed before comfort so could not be ordered with automatic transmission or air-conditioning.

ENGINE

The basic V8 power plant for Camaros was the trusty small block cast-iron 327cid lump, which, with a bit of fine-tuning, evolved into the 350cid unit of the desirable SS models. Compression ratio was 8.8:1, and it produced 210 bhp.

MIRROR CHANGE

By 1968 the circular side mirrors had been replaced by rectangular ones.

POWER RATING

American horsepower was all about cubic inches (cid), not cubic centimeters (cc) as in Europe, and the RS proudly badged its 327 cubic inch capacity.

CHEVROLET *Corvette Stingray (1969)*

THE AUTOMOTIVE PRESS REALLY lashed into the '69 Shark, calling it a piece of junk, a low point in Corvette history, and the beginning of a new trend toward the image-and-gadget car. Instead of testing the 'Vette, *Car and Driver* magazine simply recited a litany of glitches and pronounced it "too dire to drive," sending ripples of rage through GM. To be frank, the '69 was not the best 'Vette ever. Styling was boisterous, trunk space vestigial, the seats had you sliding all over the place, and the general build was shoddy. Two great engines saved the day, the 327cid and three incarnations of the big-block 427. With the hottest L88 version hitting 60 mph (96 km/h) in five-and-a-half seconds and peaking at 160 mph (257 km/h), these were cars that were race-ready from the showroom floor. Despite the vitriol, the public liked their image, gadgets, and grunt, buying 38,762 of them, a production record unbroken for the next six years—empirical proof that, occasionally, car journalists do talk hot air.

AGGRESSIVE POSTURE
The Stingray filled its wheelarches very convincingly with an aggressive, menacing presence. Any similarity to the European sports cars that inspired the original Corvettes had by now withered away, to be replaced by a new, threatening personality. In the annals of automotive history, there is no car with more evil looks than this 1968–72 generation Corvette.

STINGRAY BADGE
Chevy stopped calling their 'Vette the Sting Ray in 1968 but thought better of it in '69, reinstating the name as one word.

VENTILATION
Trim liners for side fender slots only appeared in the '69 model year.

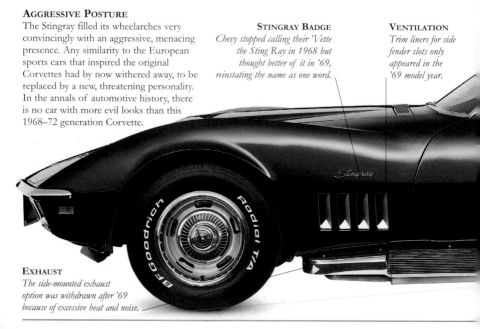

EXHAUST
The side-mounted exhaust option was withdrawn after '69 because of excessive heat and noise.

WINDOW
*Rear window
demister was
an option.*

RACK
*Rear rack helped since
there wasn't much
room in the trunk.*

WHEELS
*Wheel-rim width
increased to 8 in
(20 cm) in 1969,
wide enough to
climb walls.*

RAD 'VETTE
*A four-wheel-drive,
mid-engined
prototype 'Vette
was developed but
canceled in 1969.*

NEW DIRECTIONS

The '69 Stingray was styled by GM's Dave Hols and owed
little to the original Sting Ray. But this was the dawn of
the '70s, and while it might not have had the purest shape,
it reeked muscle from every vent.

ANTENNA
*AM/FM radio option
was offered for the first
time in 1968.*

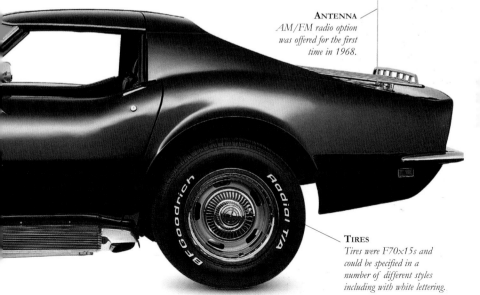

TIRES
*Tires were F70x15s and
could be specified in a
number of different styles
including with white lettering.*

SHARK-BASED DESIGN

GM chief Bill Mitchell was an admirer of sharks—"they are exciting to look at"—and wanted to design a car with similar lines. In 1960 a prototype Mako Shark was made, and the end result was the 1963 Sting Ray. A further prototype in 1966, the Mako Shark I produced the 1968–72 generation of Stingra but the 'Vette collided with the energy crisis and would never be the same again.

ENGINE

If the stock 427 was not enough, there was always the 500 bhp ZL1, a 170 mph (274 km/h) racing option package. To discourage boy racers, no heater was installed in the ZL1; only two were ever sold to retail customers.

WINDSHIELD

Soft Ray tinted glass was an optional extra.

NOTABLE YEAR

1969 saw the 250,000th 'Vette come off the production line; it was a gold convertible.

BIG DADDY

With the 427 unit, the 'Vette was the biggest, heaviest, fastest, thirstiest, cheapest, and most powerful sports car on the market.

ENGINE OPTION

The first all-aluminum Corvette block was offered in 1969.

ROOF PANEL

Half of the '69 production were coupes with twin lift-off roof panels and a removable window—making this Stingray almost a convertible.

WIPER COVER

'68 and '69 'Vettes had a vacuum-operated lid which covered the windshield wipers when not in use. It was, though, a styling gimmick which malfunctioned with depressing regularity.

INTERIOR

A major drawback of the '69 was its sharply raked seats, which prevented the traditional Corvette arm-out-of-the-window pose. While the telescopic tilt column and leather trim were extras, the glove compartment had been introduced as standard in 1968.

SPECIFICATIONS

MODEL Chevrolet Corvette Stingray (1969)

PRODUCTION 38,762 (1969)

BODY STYLES Two-seater sports and convertible.

CONSTRUCTION Fiberglass, separate chassis.

ENGINES 327cid, 427cid V8s.

POWER OUTPUT 300–500 bhp.

TRANSMISSION Three-speed manual, optional four-speed manual, three-speed Turbo Hydra-Matic automatic.

SUSPENSION *Front:* upper and lower A-arms, coil springs; *Rear:* independent with transverse strut and leaf springs.

BRAKES Front and rear discs.

MAXIMUM SPEED 117–170 mph (188–274 km/h)

0–60 MPH (0–96 KM/H) 5.7–7.7 sec

A.F.C. 10 mpg (3.5 km/l)

HEADLIGHTS

The '69 retained hidden headlights, but now worked off a vacuum.

CHEVROLET *Monte Carlo*

NOW THE WORLD'S LARGEST PRODUCER of motor vehicles, Chevrolet kicked off the Seventies with their Ford Thunderbird chaser, the 1970 Monte Carlo. Hailed as "action and elegance in a sporty personal luxury package," it was only available as a coupe and came with power front discs, Elm-Burl dash-panel inlays, and a choice of engines that ranged from the standard 350cid V8 to the Herculean SS 454. At $3,123 in base form, it was cheap compared to the $5,000 needed to buy a Thunderbird. But the T-Bird had become as urbane as Dean Martin, and the Monte couldn't match the Ford's élan. Even so, despite a six-week strike that lost Chevrolet 100,000 sales, over 145,000 Monte Carlos found buyers which, compared to a mere 40,000 T-Birds, made Chevy's new personal luxury confection a monster hit.

SHARED CHASSIS
The Monte Carlo used the same platform as the redesigned 1969 Pontiac Grand Prix. Stylistically, the long hood and short trunk promised performance and power. The single headlights were mounted in square-shaped housings, and the grid-textured grille was simple and unadorned.

INTERIOR
The Monte Carlo's cabin was Chevrolet's most luxurious for the year, but was criticized for having limited front and rear legroom.

HIDDEN ANTENNA
The radio antenna was hidden in the windshield.

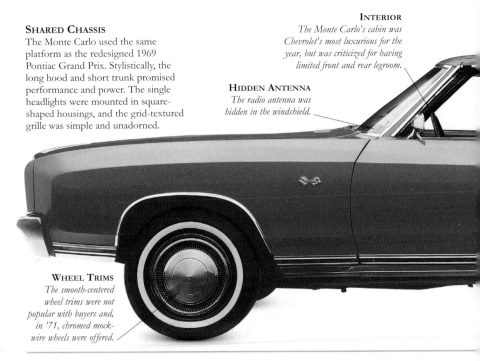

WHEEL TRIMS
The smooth-centered wheel trims were not popular with buyers and, in '71, chromed mock-wire wheels were offered.

SPEEDY UNIT
The massive 454 block made it a favorite with short-circuit stock car racers.

HEADLIGHTS
In '72, vertical parking lights were placed inboard of the headlights.

ENGINE
The potent SS 454 option was a modest $147 and could catapult the Monte Carlo to 60 mph (96 km/h) in less than eight seconds.

PILLAR
Prodigious rear pillar made city parking literally hit-or-miss.

SPECIFICATIONS

MODEL Chevrolet Monte Carlo (1970)

PRODUCTION 145,975 (1970)

BODY STYLE Two-door, five-seater coupe.

CONSTRUCTION Steel body and chassis.

ENGINES 350cid, 400cid, 454cid V8s.

POWER OUTPUT 250–360 bhp.

TRANSMISSION Three-speed manual, optional two-speed Powerglide automatic, Turbo Hydra-Matic three-speed automatic.

SUSPENSION *Front:* coil springs; *Rear:* leaf springs.

BRAKES Front and rear drums.

MAXIMUM SPEED 115–132 mph (185–211 km/h)

0–60 MPH (0–96 KM/H) 8–14 sec

A.F.C. 15–20 mpg (5.3–7 km/l)

VINYL ROOF
Black vinyl top was a $120 option. Buyers could also choose blue, dark gold, green, or white.

REAR STABILITY
Another option available, and used on this car, was rear antisway bars.

CHEVROLET *Nova SS*

THE NOVA NAME FIRST APPEARED in 1962 as the top-line model of Chevrolet's new Falcon-buster compact, the Chevy II. Evolving into a line in its own right, by '71 the Nova's Super Sport (SS) package was one of the smallest muscle cars ever fielded by Detroit. In an era when performance was on the wane, the diminutive banshee found plenty of friends among the budget drag-racing set. That strong 350cid V8 just happened to be a small-block Chevy, perfect for all those fine-tuned manifolds, carbs headers, and distributors courtesy of a massive tuning industry. Some pundits even went so far as hailing the Nova SS as the Seventies equivalent of the '57 Chevy. Frisk tough, and impudent, Chevy's giant killer could easily double the legal speed limit, an the SS was a Nova to die for. Quick and rare, only 7,016 '71 Novas sported the magic SS badge. Performance iron died a death in '72, making these last-of-the-line '71s perfect candidates for the "Chevy Muscle Hall of Fame."

DIFFERENT STYLING

Handsome, neat, and chaste, the Nova was a new breed of passenger car for the Seventies. Advertised as the "Not Too Small Car," it looked a lot like a scaled-down version of the Chevelle and debuted in this form in 1968 to rave reviews.

SAFETY REFLECTORS
Side markerlights were forced on the Nova after federal safety legislation was passed.

AIR CON
*Air conditioning was
an extra-cost option.*

LIGHTS
*Amber plastic
light lenses were
new for '71.*

INTERIOR
*Nova features included front
armrests, antitheft steering-
wheel-column lock, and
ignition key alarm system.*

ENGINE
The two- or four-barrel 350cid V8
ran on regular fuel and pushed out
270 ponies. At one point, Chevrolet
planned to squeeze the massive
454cid V8 from the Chevelle into
the Nova SS, but regrettably
dropped the idea.

STYLING
*The Nova's shell would last for
11 years and was shared with
Buick, Oldsmobile, and Pontiac.*

BLOCK
*In '71, the option of a four-
cylinder block was withdrawn on
the Nova; less than one percent of
'70 Nova buyers chose a four.*

ALLOYS
*The handsome
Sportmag five-
spoke alloys were
an $85 option.*

SPECIFICATIONS

MODEL Chevrolet Nova SS (1971)

PRODUCTION 7,016 (1971)

BODY STYLE Two-door, five-seater coupe.

CONSTRUCTION Steel unitary body.

ENGINE 350cid V8.

POWER OUTPUT 245 bhp.

TRANSMISSION Three-speed manual,
optional four-speed manual, and
three-speed automatic.

SUSPENSION *Front:* coil springs;
Rear: leaf springs.

BRAKES Front discs and rear drums.

MAXIMUM SPEED 120 mph (193 km/h)

0–60 MPH (0–96 KM/H) 6.2 sec

A.F.C. 20 mpg (7 km/l)

CHEVROLET *Camaro SS396*

AFTER A SUCCESSFUL DEBUT IN '67, the Camaro hit the deck in '72. Sluggish sales and a 174-day strike at the Lordstown, Ohio, plant meant Camaros were in short supply, and only 68,656 were produced that year. Worse still, 1,100 half-finished cars sitting on the assembly lines couldn't meet the impending '73 bumper impact laws, so GM was forced to junk all of them. There were some dark mutterings in GM boardrooms. Should the Camaro be canned? 1972 also saw the Super Sport (SS) package bow out. *Road & Track* magazine mourned its passing, hailing the SS396 as "the best car built in America in 1971." But the early Seventies were a bad trip for the automobile, and the Camaro would rise again; five years later it had risen from the ashes and was selling over a quarter of a million units. This is one American icon that refuses to die.

DURABLE DESIGN
The Camaro design survived an incredible 11 years without any serious alteration. It lured eyes and dollars away from the traditional European performance machines and became one of the most recognized American GTs of the Seventies. In addition to the SS package, Camaros could also be specified in Rally Sport (RS) and Z-28 performance guise.

SS NUMBERS
Only 6,562 Camaros had the SS equipment package in 1972 out of total Chevrolet sales for the year of 2,151,076.

STYLING
The Camaro was designed using computer technology; the smooth, horizontal surfaces blended together in an aerodynamically functional shape.

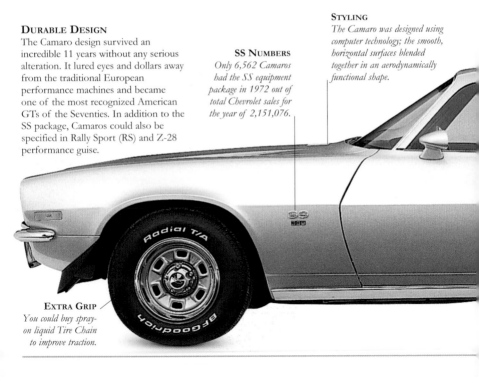

EXTRA GRIP
You could buy spray-on liquid Tire Chain to improve traction.

NASCAR Racer

Chevy spent big bucks to become performance
heavyweights, and the Camaro, along with the Chevelle,
was a successful racing model in the early '70s.

SPECIFICATIONS

Model Chevrolet Camaro SS396 (1972)

Production 6,562 (SS, 1972)

Body Style Two-door coupe.

Construction Steel body and chassis.

Engines 350cid, 396cid, 402cid V8s (SS).

Power Output 240–330 bhp.

Transmission Three-speed manual,
optional four-speed manual, and automatic.

Suspension *Front:* coil springs;
Rear: leaf springs.

Brakes Front power discs and rear drums.

Maximum Speed 125 mph (201 km/h)

0–60 mph (0–96 km/h) 7.5 sec

A.F.C. 15 mpg (5.3 km/l)

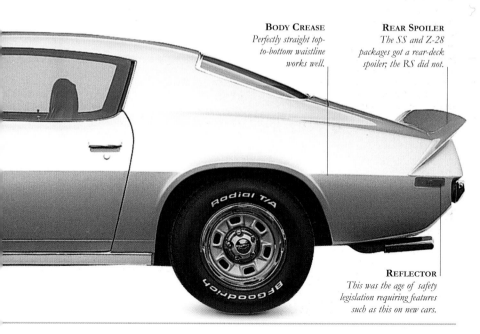

BODY CREASE
*Perfectly straight top-
to-bottom waistline
works well.*

REAR SPOILER
*The SS and Z-28
packages got a rear-deck
spoiler; the RS did not.*

REFLECTOR
*This was the age of safety
legislation requiring features
such as this on new cars.*

INTERIOR

Interiors were generally quite basic. Revisions for '72 were limited and mostly confined to the door panels, which now included map and coin holders under the door handles. The high-back seats are a clue that this is a post-'70 model.

COMFORT OPTIONS

Special instrumentation, center console, and Comfort-Tilt wheel were convenience options.

UNIQUE SS

Unlike other performance packs, the SS option gave the car a whole new look. The bolt-on front end was different, and included sidelights up alongside the headlights and recessed grille. SS spec usually included mini quarter-bumpers rather than the full-width item seen here.

CONCEALED WIPERS

SS and RS packages included hidden windshield wipers.

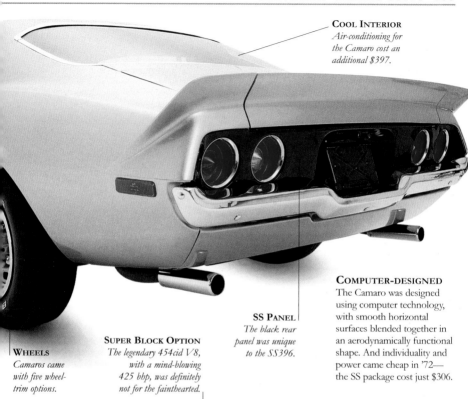

COOL INTERIOR
*Air-conditioning for
the Camaro cost an
additional $397.*

COMPUTER-DESIGNED
The Camaro was designed
using computer technology,
with smooth horizontal
surfaces blended together in
an aerodynamically functional
shape. And individuality and
power came cheap in '72—
the SS package cost just $306.

SS PANEL
*The black rear
panel was unique
to the SS396.*

WHEELS
*Camaros came
with five wheel-
trim options.*

SUPER BLOCK OPTION
*The legendary 454cid V8,
with a mind-blowing
425 bhp, was definitely
not for the fainthearted.*

ENGINE
Camaros came with a range
of engines to suit all
pocketbooks and for all
types of drivers. The entry-
level V8 was just $96 more
than the plodding straight
six. The block featured here
is the lively 396cid V8.
Under 5,000 owners chose a
six compared to nearly
64,000 who opted for
one of the V8 options.

ENGINE IDEA
*A 400cid engine
was planned
for mid-year
introduction but
it never made
the Camaro.*

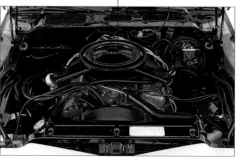

CHRYSLER *Imperial*

IN 1950 CHRYSLER WAS CELEBRATING its silver jubilee, an anniversary year with a sting in its tail. The Office of Price Stabilization had frozen car prices, there was a four-month strike, and serious coal and steel shortages were affecting the industry. The '50 Imperial was a Chrysler New Yorker with a special roof and interior trim from the Derham Body Company. The jewels in Chrysler's crown, the Imperials were meant to lock horns with the best of Cadillac, Packard, and Lincoln. With Ausco-Lambert disc brakes, Prestomatic transmission, and a MoPar compass, they used the finest technology Chrysler could muster. The trouble was only 10,650 Imperials drove out of the door in 1950, the hemi-head V8 wouldn't arrive until the next year, buyers were calling it a Chrysler rather than an Imperial, and that frumpy styling looked exactly like what it was—yesterday's dinner warmed up again.

BEASTS OF THE ROAD
Bulky, rounded Chryslers were some of the biggest cars on the road in 1950. The Imperials had Cadillac-style grilles, and the Crown Imperial was a long limousine built to rival the Cadillac 75.

WINDSHIELD
The windshield was still old-fashioned two-piece flat glass, which made the Imperial look rather antiquated.

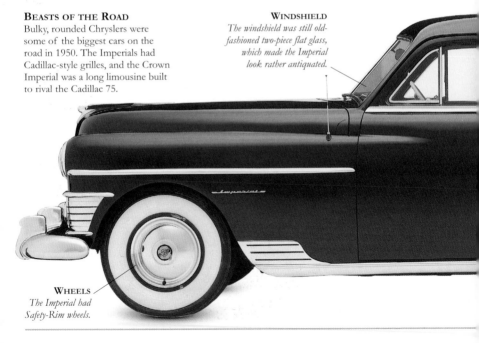

WHEELS
The Imperial had Safety-Rim wheels.

INTERIOR

Chrysler's interiors were as restrained and conservative
as the people who drove them. Turn-key ignition
replaced push-button in 1950, which was also
the first year of electric windows.

SPECIFICATIONS

MODEL Chrysler Imperial (1950)

PRODUCTION 10,650 (1950)

BODY STYLE Four-door sedan.

CONSTRUCTION Steel body and chassis.

ENGINE 323cid straight-eight.

POWER OUTPUT 135 bhp.

TRANSMISSION Prestomatic semiautomatic.

SUSPENSION *Front:* coil springs; *Rear:* live axle.

BRAKES Front and rear drums, optional front discs.

MAXIMUM SPEED 100 mph (161 km/h)

0–60 MPH (0–96 KM/H) 13 sec

A.F.C. 16 mpg (5.7 km/l)

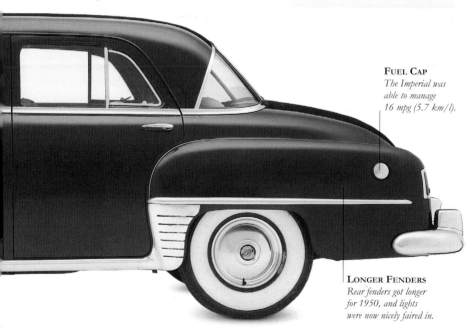

FUEL CAP
*The Imperial was
able to manage
16 mpg (5.7 km/l).*

LONGER FENDERS
*Rear fenders got longer
for 1950, and lights
were now nicely faired in.*

BIGGER BLOCK
*180 bhp hemi-head
V8 wouldn't arrive
till next year.*

WASHERS
*Windshield washers were
available as an option.*

ENGINE
The inline L-head eight developed 135
bhp and had a cast-iron block with
five main bearings. The carburetor was
a Carter single barrel, and Prestomatic
automatic transmission with fluid drive
came as standard.

SUSPENSION
*Imperials incorporated
Safety-Level ride.*

SEMI-AUTOMATIC TRANSMISSION
The semi-automatic gearbox allowed
the driver to use a clutch to pull away,
with the automatic taking over as
the car accelerated. Imperials had
a waterproof ignition system.

LENGTH
*Wheelbase measured 131½ in
(334 cm), which was 14 in (36 cm)
shorter than the Crown Imperial.*

REAR WINDOW
New "Clearbac" rear window used three pieces of glass that were divided by chrome strips.

LATE ARRIVAL
The celebrated designer Virgil Exner joined Chrysler in 1949 but arrived too late to improve the looks of the moribund Imperial. Despite Chrysler's problems, 1950 was a bumper year for American car production with the industry wheeling out a staggering 6,663,461 units.

TOP CAR
Imperials were seen as the cream of the Chrysler crop. Advertising for the Crown Imperial purred that it was "the aristocrat of cars."

IMPERIAL PRICING
The Imperial four-door sedan cost $3,055 before optional extras were added. The most expensive model in Chrysler's 1950 line was the eight-passenger Crown Imperial sedan, which cost $5,334. In keeping with its establishment image, an Imperial station wagon was never offered. One claim to fame was that MGM Studios used an Imperial-based mobile camera car in many of their film productions.

WEIGHT
The Imperial weighed just under 1,000 lb (454 kg) less than the Crown Imperial.

CHRYSLER *New Yorker*

WHY CAN'T THEY MAKE CARS that look this good anymore? The '57 New Yorker was the first and finest example of Chrysler's "Forward Look" policy. With the average American production worker earning $82.32 a week, the $4,259 four-door hardtop was both sensationally good-looking and sensationally expensive. The car's glorious lines seriously alarmed Chrysler's competitors, especially since the styling was awarded two gold medals, the suspension was by newfangled torsion bar, and muscle was courtesy of one of the most respected engines in the world—the hemi-head Fire Power. Despite this, "the most glamorous cars of a generation" cost Chrysler a whopping $300 million, and sales were disappointing. One problem was a propensity for rust, along with shabby fit and finish; another was low productivity—only a measly 10,948 four-door hardtop models were produced. Even so, the New Yorker was certainly one of the most beautiful cars Chrysler ever made.

ONE MAN'S SHOW
Chrysler stunned the world with their dartlike shapes of 1957. The unified design was created by the mind of one man—Virgil Exner—rather than by a committee, and it shows. Those prodigious rear fenders sweep up gracefully, harmonizing well with the gently tapering roof line.

AUTO FIRST
TorqueFlite automatic transmission was first seen this year.

MIRROR
Side mirror was an optional extra.

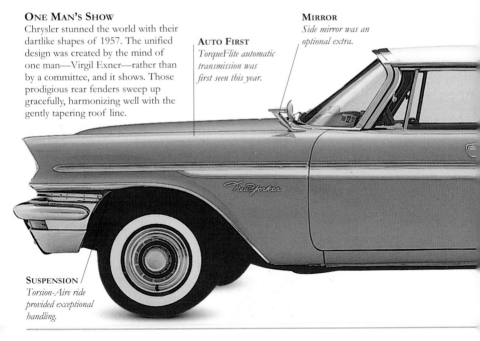

SUSPENSION
Torsion-Aire ride provided exceptional handling.

SIMPLE AND EFFECTIVE

Rather than looking overstyled, the rear end and deck are
actually quite restrained. The licence plate sits neatly in its
niche, the tail pipes are completely concealed, the bumper is
understated, and even the rear lights are not too heavy-handed.

SPECIFICATIONS

MODEL Chrysler New Yorker (1957)

PRODUCTION 34,620 (all body styles, 1957)

BODY STYLE Four-door, six-seater hardtop.

CONSTRUCTION Monocoque.

ENGINE 392cid V8.

POWER OUTPUT 325 bhp.

TRANSMISSION Three-speed TorqueFlite
automatic.

SUSPENSION *Front:* A-arms and
longitudinal torsion bar; *Rear:* semi-elliptic
leaf springs.

BRAKES Front and rear drums.

MAXIMUM SPEED 115 mph
(185 km/h)

0–60 MPH (0–96 KM/H) 12.3 sec

A.F.C. 13 mpg (4.6 km/l)

WINNING SHAPE
*The New Yorker's shape was so universally
acclaimed that it was awarded two Grand
Prix D'Honneur and two gold medals by
the Industrial Designers Institute.*

STLYISH ORNAMENTATION
*The New Yorker had few styling
excesses. Even the gratuitous slashes on
the rear wing did not look over the top.*

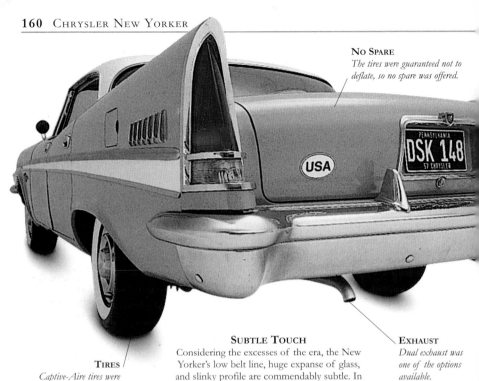

NO SPARE
The tires were guaranteed not to deflate, so no spare was offered.

USA

PENNSYLVANIA
DSK 148
57 CHRYSLER

TIRES
Captive-Aire tires were available, with promises that they wouldn't let themselves down.

SUBTLE TOUCH
Considering the excesses of the era, the New Yorker's low belt line, huge expanse of glass, and slinky profile are commendably subtle. In fact, if it wasn't for those outrageous fins, Chrysler's dreamboat might have ended up in the Museum of Modern Art.

EXHAUST
Dual exhaust was one of the options available.

INTERIOR
New Yorkers had everything. Equipment included power windows, a six-way power seat, Hi-Way Hi-Fi phonograph, Electro-Touch radio, rear seat speaker, Instant Air heater, handbrake warning system, Air-Temp air-conditioning, and tinted glass—an altogether impressive array of features for a 1957 automobile. There are still many modern luxury cars that don't have the same comprehensive specification of the Fifties' New Yorker.

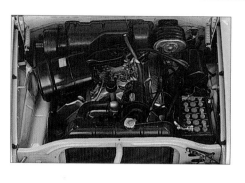

ENGINE

The top-of-the-line model had a top-of-the-line motor. The hemi-head was the largest production unit available in 1957. Bore and stroke were increased and displacement raised by nearly 10 percent. It was efficient, ran on low-octane gas, and could be highly tuned.

OTHER MODELS

The three other model lines for Chrysler in '57 were the Windsor, Saratoga, and 300C.

WAGON VERSION

One of the other models in the 1957 New Yorker lineup was a Town and Country Wagon, which was driven by the same impressive Fire Power V8 found in the sedan and hardtops.

CHRYSLER *300F* (1960)

"RED HOT AND RAMBUNCTIOUS" is how Chrysler sold the 300F. It may be one of the strangest slogans of any American automaker, but the 300F really was red hot and a serious flying machine that could better 140 mph (225 km/h). The rambunctious refer to the ram-air induction on the bad-boy 413cid wedge-head V8. Ram tuning had long been a way of raising torque and horsepower for drag racing, and it gave the 300F a wicked performance persona. One of Virgil Exner's happier designs, the 300F of '60 had unibody construction, a French Pont-A-Mousson four-speed gearbox, and front seats that swiveled toward you when you opened the doors. It also boasted an electro-luminescent instrument panel and Chrysler's best styling effort since 1957. But at $5,411, it was no surprise that only 964 coupes found buyers. Nevertheless, it bolstered Chrysler's image, and taught them plenty of tuning tricks for the muscle-car wars that were revving up just around the corner.

DOOR ACTION
Opening the door initiated the self-activating swiveling seats.

POWER AND GLORY
The 300F was one of America's most powerful cars, and a souped-up version recorded a one-way run of an amazing 189 mph (304 km/h) on the Bonneville salt flats. But despite the prodigious performance, it was deliberately understated compared with many contemporary Detroit offerings.

NONINLINE CARBS
The alternative carburetor positioning gave a steady buildup of power along the torque curve.

TIRES
Nylon whitewalls came as standard.

NICKNAME
The phrase "beautiful brutes" was coined to describe the 300 Series.

?NE FINS
?u could argue that the
?0F's fins started at the front
? the car and traveled along
?e side, building up to lethal,
?ggerlike points above the
?quisitely sculptured taillights.

PILLARLESS STYLE
With the window rolled down the 300F had a pillarless look.

LIMITED TIME
Within two years fins would disappear completely on the Chrysler letter series 300.

EXTRA GRIP
This particular model has Sure-Grip differential, a $52 option.

SPECIFICATIONS

MODEL Chrysler 300F (1960)

PRODUCTION 1,212 (1960, both body styles)

BODY STYLES Two-door coupe and convertible.

CONSTRUCTION Steel unitary body.

ENGINE 413cid V8.

POWER OUTPUT 375–400 bhp.

TRANSMISSION Three-speed push-button automatic, optional four-speed manual.

SUSPENSION *Front:* torsion bars; *Rear:* leaf springs.

BRAKES Front and rear drums.

MAXIMUM SPEED 140 mph (225 km/h)

0–60 MPH (0–96 KM/H) 7.1 sec

A.F.C. 12 mpg (4.2 km/l)

DASHBOARD

The "Astra-Dome" instrumentation was illuminated at night by electro-luminescent light, giving a soft, eerie glow that shone through the translucent markings on the gauges. It was technically very daring and boasted six different laminations of plastic, vitreous, and phosphor.

TACHOMETER
Center-mounted tachometer came as standard.

TINTED WINDOW
Solex tinted glass was a $43 optional extra.

DANGER FINS
The 300F's razor-sharp rear fins were criticized by Ralph Nader in his book Unsafe at Any Speed *as "potentially lethal."*

THE ONLY BLEMISH

The much-criticized fake spare-tire embellishment on the trunk was variously described as a toilet seat or trash can lid. This questionable rear deck treatment was officially known as "Flight-Sweep" and was also available on other Chryslers. Possibly the 300F's only stylistic peccadillo, it was dropped in '61.

QUIRKY SEAT SYSTEM
elf-activated swiveling seats
ere new for 1960 and pivoted
utward automatically when
ther door was opened.
s ironic that the burly
)0F's typical owner
as likely to be a
abby 40-year-old.

MIRROR
*Side mirror
was remote-
controlled.*

ANTENNA
*ower antenna was
a $43 option; this
car also has the
Golden Tone
radio ($124).*

SERIOUS STORAGE
The two-door shape meant that the rear deck was the size
of Indiana, and the cavernous trunk was large enough to
hold four wheels and tires.

CHRYSLER *300L* (1965)

BACK IN '55, CHRYSLER DEBUTED their mighty 300 "Letter Car." The most powerful automobile of the year, the 300C kicked off a new genre of gentleman's hot rod that was to last for more than a decade. Chrysler cleverly marked annual model changes with letters, running from the 300B in 1956 all the way through—the letter I excepted—to this 300L in 1965. And '65 was the swan-song year for the Letter Series speciality car. The 300L sat on high-performance rubber and suspension and was powered by a high-output 413cid 360 bhp mill breathing through a four-barrel Carter carb. By the mid-Sixties, though, the game had changed and Chrysler was pumping its money into muscle-car iron like the Charger and GTX, an area of the market where business was brisk. The 300L was the last survivor of an era when the Madison Avenue advertising men were still trying to persuade us that an automobile as long as a freight train could also be a sports car.

NEW DESIGN CHIEF
Styling of the 300L was by Elwood Engle, who had replaced Virgil Exner as Chrysler's chief of design. Although the company's advertising claimed that this was "The Most Beautiful Chrysler Ever Built," the "Crisp, Clean, Custom" look of '63–'64 had ballooned.

ROOMY INSIDE
Belt lines were lower and roof lines higher this year, which increased the glass area and made the interior feel even more cavernous.

SUSPENSION
Torsion-bar front suspension gave poise and accuracy.

TOUGH JOB

Competition was particularly stiff in '65, and the 300L had to fight hard against the Oldsmobile Starfire, the agonizingly pretty Buick Riviera, and the market leader, Ford's flashy Thunderbird. Only 2,405 300L hardtops were produced, and a measly 440 two-door convertibles rolled out of the factory.

SPECIFICATIONS

MODEL Chrysler 300L (1965)

PRODUCTION 2,845 (1965)

BODY STYLES Two-door hardtop and convertible.

CONSTRUCTION Steel unitary body.

ENGINE 413cid V8.

POWER OUTPUT 360 bhp.

TRANSMISSION Three-speed automatic, optional four-speed manual.

SUSPENSION *Front:* torsion bar; *Rear:* leaf springs.

BRAKES Front and rear drums.

MAXIMUM SPEED 110 mph (177 km/h)

0–60 MPH (0–96 KM/H) 8.8 sec

A.F.C. 12–14 mpg (4.2–5 km/l)

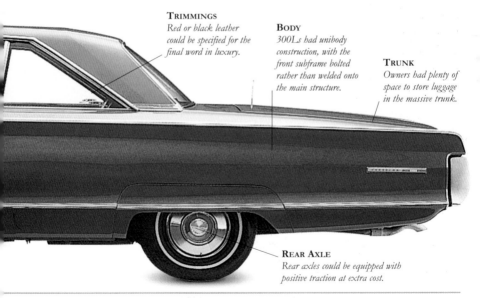

TRIMMINGS
Red or black leather could be specified for the final word in luxury.

BODY
300Ls had unibody construction, with the front subframe bolted rather than welded onto the main structure.

TRUNK
Owners had plenty of space to store luggage in the massive trunk.

REAR AXLE
Rear axles could be equipped with positive traction at extra cost.

CHRYSLER 300

COSTLY CAR
Coupes weighed in at a solid $4,090 with convertibles stickering at $4,545.

GRADUAL DEMISE
1961 saw the 300G, which was the last model to sport Exner's fins. The following year was arguably the start of the decline of the series, and by the time the famous 300 nameplate had reached its final year, the spark had gone. The 300L was not as quick as its forebears and is the least special of Chrysler's limited editions.

ALASKA 66
98506
1867 NORTH TO THE FUTURE 1967

HEADLIGHTS
These live behind a horizontally etched glass panel.

NEW BODY

*In '65 the Chrysler line changed
dramatically with a new corporate
C-body shared with upmarket
Dodges and the Plymouth Fury.*

COMFORT EXTRAS

*Options included tilting steering
wheel, Golden Tone radio,
cruise control, remote trunk
release, high-speed warning
system, and air-conditioning.*

INTERIOR

Front bucket seats plus a center console
were standard on the L, as was the new-for-
'65 column instead of push-button automatic
transmission. The rear seat was molded to
look like buckets but could actually
accommodate three people.

ENGINE

The non-Hemi V8 was tough and reliable, and
gave the 300L very respectable performance
figures. The L was quick, agile, and one of the
smoothest-riding Letter Series cars made, with
45 bhp more than the standard 300's unit.

CITROËN *Traction Avant*

LOVED BY POLITICIANS, POETS, and painters alike, the Traction Avant marked a watershed for both Citroën and the world's auto industry. A design prodigy, it was the first mass-produced car to incorporate a monocoque bodyshell with front-wheel drive and torsion bar springing, and it began Citroën's love affair with the unconventional. Conceived in just 18 months, the Traction Avant cost the French company dearly. By 1934, they had emptied the company coffers, laid off 8,000 workers, and on the insistence of the French government, were taken over by Michelin, who gave the Traction Avant the backing it deserved. It ran for over 23 years, with over three quarters of a million sedans, fixed-head coupes, and convertibles sold. Citroën's audacious sedan was the most significant and successful production car of its time, eclipsed only by the passage of 20 years and another *voiture revolutionnaire*, the Citroën DS.

WORLD BEATER
With aerodynamic styling, unitary steel body, and sweeping wings without running boards, the Traction Avant was a technical and aesthetic *tour de force.*

FRONT WHEEL
Front-wheel drive made for tenacious roadholding.

BEAUTY NOT BRAWN
Though the Avant had a 1911cc engine, it only pushed out 46 bhp.

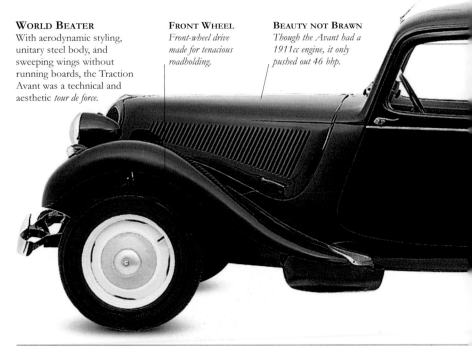

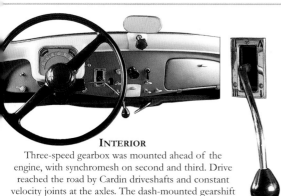

INTERIOR

Three-speed gearbox was mounted ahead of the engine, with synchromesh on second and third. Drive reached the road by Cardin driveshafts and constant velocity joints at the axles. The dash-mounted gearshift *(right)* lived on in the DS of 1955 *(see pages 178–81).*

REVISED TRUNK

In 1952, Citroën dispensed with the earlier "bob-tail" rear end and gave the Traction a "big trunk."

WHEEL

Michelin produced these Pilote wheels and tires for the Traction.

HOOD
Side-opening hood was a prewar feature.

ENGINE
The Traction's Maurice Sainturat–designed engine was new. "Floating Power" came from a short-stroke four-cylinder unit, with a three-bearing crankshaft and push-rod overhead valves—equating to seven French horsepower.

EASY ACCESS
Engine, gearbox, radiator, and front suspension were mounted on a detachable cradle for easy maintenance.

STYLISH DESIGN
The Art Deco door handle is typical of Citroën's obsession with form and function. Beautiful yet practical, it epitomizes André Lefevre's astonishing design. The chevron-shaped gears were also pioneered for smoothness and silence.

TRICKY DRIVER
The Traction looks and feels huge and was a real handful in tight spaces.

REAR WINDOW
*Small rear window
meant minimal
rearward visibility.*

SUSPENSION ATTRACTION
In 1954, as the car was approaching the end of its
life, the six-cylinder Traction Avant was known as
"Queen of the Road" because of its hydro-
pneumatic suspension—a mixture
of liquid and gas.

HOME COMFORTS
*Citroën advertising tried to woo
buyers with the line "on the
road... the comfort of home."*

FRONT SUSPENSION
*All-independent suspension with
torsion-bar springing, upper wishbones,
radius arms, friction shock absorbers,
and worm-and-roller steering (later
rack-and-pinion) gave crisp handling.*

UNIVERSAL APPROVAL
The world lavished unstinting praise
on the Traction Avant, extolling its
roadholding, hydraulic brakes, ride
comfort, and cornering abilities. Despite
the praise, it was this great grand *routier*
that devoured André Citroën's wealth
and pushed him to his deathbed.

REMOVABLE HOOD
*Any serious engine repairs
meant that the hood had to be
removed completely.*

CITROËN *2CV*

RARELY HAS A CAR BEEN SO ridiculed as the Citroën 2CV. At its launch at the 1948 Paris Salon, journalists lashed into this defenseless runabout with vicious zeal, and everyone who was near Paris at the time claimed to be the originator of the quip, "Do you get a can opener with it?" They all missed the point, for this minimal car was not meant to be measured against other cars; its true rival was the horse and cart, which Citroën boss Pierre Boulanger hoped to replace with his *toute petite voiture*—or very small car. As the *Deux Chevaux* it became much more than that and putt-putted into the history books, selling more than five million by the time of its eventual demise in 1990. As devotees of the 2CV say, "You either love them, or you don't understand them."

CAREFUL PLANNING

In 1935, Pierre Boulanger conceived a car to woo farmers away from the horse and cart. It would weigh no more than 661 lb (300 kg) and carry four people at 37 mph (60 km/h), while consuming no more than 56 mpg. The car that appears "undesigned" was in fact carefully conceived.

SIMPLE CHASSIS

Although designers flirted with notions of a chassisless car, cost dictated a more conventional sheet-steel platform chassis.

VISUAL ASSISTANCE
*Instructions on how to start
and stop the 2CV were
displayed behind the sun visor.*

INTERIOR
A speedo and ammeter
were the only concessions
to modernity. The original
fuel gauge was just a
calibrated stick.

SPECIFICATIONS

MODEL Citroën 2CV (1949–90)

PRODUCTION 5,114,966 (includes vans)

BODY STYLES Four-door convertible sedan, two-door van.

CONSTRUCTION Separate steel platform chassis, steel body.

ENGINES Air-cooled, horizontally opposed twin of 375cc, 425cc, 435cc, 602cc.

POWER OUTPUT 9, 12, 18, and 29 bhp, respectively.

TRANSMISSION Four-speed manual, front-wheel drive.

SUSPENSION Independent, interconnected coil-sprung.

BRAKES Drums all around.

MAXIMUM SPEED 375cc: 43 mph (69 km/h); 425cc: 49 mph (79 km/h); 435cc: 53 mph (85 km/h); 602cc: 72 mph (116 km/h).

0–60 MPH (0–96 KM/H) 30 sec (602cc)

A.F.C. 45–55 mpg (16–19.5 km/l)

BOLT ON
*All the body panels
simply unbolted, and even
the body shell was only
held in place by 16 bolts.*

SUSPENSION
*The sophisticated
independent
suspension system
gave a soft ride.*

STRAIGHTFORWARD DESIGN

The sober design purpose of the rolltop roof was to allow transportation of tall, bulky objects. It also happened that Citroën boss Pierre Boulanger was a six-footer who liked to wear a hat in a car. The minimal, but handy, lightweight, hammock-style seats lifted out to accommodate more goods or to provide picnic seating.

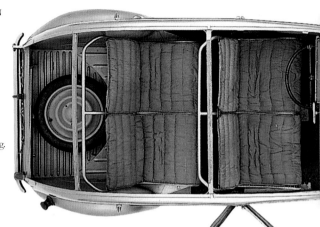

TRUNK
Roll-up canvas trunk lid of the original saved both weight and cost; a metal lid took over in 1957 on French cars.

DOORS
You were lucky to get them; prototypes featured waxed-cloth door coverings.

FUNCTIONAL DESIGN

The indicators are a good example of the functional design ethos. Why put a pair of indicators on the front and another pair on the back, when you could save the cost of two bulbs by giving your car cute "ears" that could be seen front and rear.

ENGINE

The original 375cc air-cooled twin, as seen here, eventually grew to all of 602cc, but all versions are genuinely happy to rev full out all day. In fact, most spend all their time being driven at maximum speed and seem to thrive on full revs. Engines are hard-working and long-lasting.

AIR VENT
Fresh air was obtained by opening the vent on the scuttle; a mesh strained out the insects and leaves.

NIQUE RIDE
othing drives like a Citroën 2CV—
e handling looks lurid as it leans
er wildly. The ride, though, is
ceptional, and the tenacious
p of those skinny
es is astonishing.
that and front-
eel drive too.

HEADLIGHT
*Prewar production
prototypes had only
one headlight.*

BODY COLORS
*Gray until late 1959,
hen the choice doubled
to include Glacier
Blue, with green and
ellow added in 1960.*

CITROËN *DS 21 Decapotable*

IN 1955, WHEN CITROËN FIRST drove prototypes of their mold-breaking DS through Paris, they were pursued by crowds shouting "La DS, la DS, voilà la DS!" Few other cars before or since were so technically and stylistically daring, and at its launch the DS created as many column inches as the death of Stalin. Cushioned on a bed of hydraulic fluid, with a semiautomatic gearbox, self-leveling suspension, and detachable body panels, it rendered half the world's cars out of date at a stroke. Parisian carmaker Henri Chapron produced 1,365 convertible DSs using the chassis from the Safari Estate model. Initially, Citroën refused to cooperate with Chapron but eventually sold the Decapotable models through their dealer network. At the time the stylish four-seater convertible was considered by many to be one of the most charismatic open-top cars on the market, and today genuine Chapron cars command seriously hefty premiums over the price of "ordinary" tin-top DS saloons

AERODYNAMIC PROFILE
The slippery, streamlined body cleaved the air with extreme aerodynamic efficiency. Body panels were detachable for easy repair and maintenance. Rear fenders could be removed for wheel changing in minutes, using just the car's wheelbrace.

RENOWNED OWNERS
Past owners of the DS include General de Gaulle, Brigitte Bardot, and the poet C. Day-Lewis.

THINNER REAR
On all DSs the rear track was narrower than the front.

INTERIOR
The inside was as innovative as the outside, with clever use of curved glass and copious layers of foam rubber, even on the floors.

SPECIFICATIONS

MODEL Citroën DS 21 Decapotable (1960–71)

PRODUCTION 1,365

BODY STYLE Five-seater convertible.

CONSTRUCTION All-steel body with detachable panels, steel platform chassis with welded box section side members.

ENGINE Four-cylinder 2175cc.

POWER OUTPUT 109 bhp at 5550 rpm.

TRANSMISSION Four-speed clutchless semiautomatic.

SUSPENSION Independent all around with hydro-pneumatic struts.

BRAKES *Front:* disc; *Rear:* drums.

MAXIMUM SPEED 116 mph (187 km/h)

0–60 MPH (0–96 KM/H) 11.2 sec

0–100 MPH (0–161 KM/H) 40.4 sec

A.F.C. 24 mpg (8.5 km/l)

DASHBOARD
Bertone's asymmetrical dashboard makes the interior look as futuristic as the rest of the car. The single-spoke steering wheel was a Citroën hallmark. The dash-mounted gear lever operated the clutchless semiautomatic box.

PROTECTION
Thin rubber overrider-type bumpers offered some protection.

NOSE JOB
The DS was known as the "Shark" because of its prodigious nose.

QUALITY CHOICE

Smooth Bertone-designed lines have made the Citroën DS a cult design icon and the cerebral choice for doctors, architects, artists, and musicians. Customers could specify almost any stylistic or mechanical extra.

BADGING

Citroën's double chevrons are modeled on helical gears.

LIGHT ALTERATION

A major change came in 1967 when the headlights and optional spot lights were faired in behind glass covers.

ENGINE

The DS 21's rather sluggish 2175cc engine developed 109 bhp and was never highly praised, having its origins in the prewar Traction Avant *(see pages 170–73).* Stopping power was provided by innovative inboard disc brakes with split circuits.

SPARE WHEEL

Spare wheel under the hood allowed for extra trunk space.

SUSPENSION
Fully independent suspension gave a magic-carpet ride.

STYLING
Citroën's advertising made much of the car's futuristic looks.

DS FAME
In 1962, the image of the DS received a boost when terrorists attacked President General De Gaulle. Despite being sprayed with bullets and having two flat tires, the presidential DS was able to swerve and speed away to safety.

NEAT TOUCHES
One of the Decapotable's trademarks was angled chrome-plated indicators perched on the rear fenders. Another was the novel suspension, which could be raised to clear rough terrain or navigate flooded roads.

A TRUE CLASSIC
Low, rakish, and space-age in appearance, the DS was so perfectly styled that it hardly altered shape in 20 years. The French philosopher Roland Barthes was captivated by the DS's design and compared its technical preeminence to the Gothic flourish of medieval cathedrals.

2 7 2 4 Y 33

CITROËN *SM*

THE CITROËN SM MAKES about as much sense as the Concorde, but since when have great cars had anything to do with common sense? It is certainly a flight of fancy, an extravagant, technical *tour de force* that, as a 16-ft (4.9-m) long streamliner, offered little more than 2+2 seating. The SM bristled with innovations—many of them established Citroën hallmarks—like swiveling headlights and self-leveling hydro-pneumatic suspension. It was a complex car—too complex in fact, with self-centering power steering and brakes that were both powered by (and virtually inoperable without) a high-compression engine-driven pump. And of course there was that capricious Maserati V6 motor. Yet once again Citroën had created an enduringly futuristic car where other "tomorrow cars of today" were soon exposed as voguish fads.

SLEEK AND SPEEDY

The SM's striking low-drag body was designed by ex-General Motors stylist Henri de Segur Lauve. The sleek nose and deep undertray, together with the noticeably tapered rear end, endow it with a slippery profile that gives a high level of aerodynamic efficiency. It is impressively stable at high speed.

COMPOUND CURVES

The tinted rear window, with compound curves and heating elements, must have cost a fortune to produce.

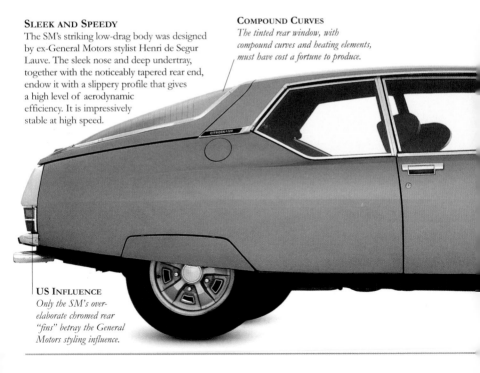

US INFLUENCE

Only the SM's over-elaborate chromed rear "fins" betray the General Motors styling influence.

SPECIFICATIONS

MODEL Citroën SM, SM EFI, and SM Auto (1970–75)

PRODUCTION 12,920 (all types, all LHD)

BODY STYLE Two-door, 2+2 coupe.

CONSTRUCTION All-steel unitary, with steel body and aluminum hood.

ENGINES All-aluminum 90-degree V6 of 2670cc (2974cc for SM Auto).

POWER OUTPUT SM: 170 bhp at 5500 rpm; 2974cc: 180 bhp at 5750 rpm.

TRANSMISSION Citroën five-speed manual or Borg-Warner three-speed automatic; front-wheel-drive.

SUSPENSION Hydro-pneumatic springing; independent transverse arms front, independent trailing arms rear.

BRAKES Discs all around.

MAXIMUM SPEED 137 mph (220 km/h) (SM EFI)

0–60 MPH (0–96 KM/H) 8.3 sec (SM EFI)

0–100 MPH (0–161 KM/H) 26–30 sec

A.F.C. 15–17 mpg (5.3–6.1 km/l)

DASHBOARD
The oval speedo and tachometer are visible through the single-spoke steering wheel, and the perennially confusing cluster of warning lights *(right)* are to the right.

WARNING LIGHTS
It took practice to decide in a hurry what each of the tiny warning lights actually meant.

ENGINE
Capacity was initially kept below 2.8 liters to escape France's punitive vehicle taxation system.

WHEELS
Lightweight wheels reinforced with carbon fiber were optionally available.

SURPRISING HANDLING

Despite its size and weight, the SM can actually be thrown around like a sports car. It rolls like a trawler in a heavy sea, and, like all front-wheel drivers, it understeers strongly but resolutely refuses to let go.

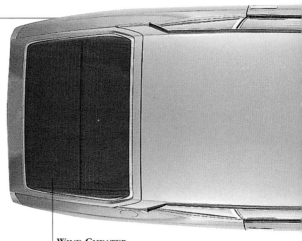

NOVEL LIGHTS
The SM had an array of six headlights, with the inner light on each side swiveling as the steering was turned.

WIND CHEATER
The tapering body is apparent in this overhead view.

PURELY FUNCTIONAL
The bulge in the tailgate above the rear license plate was for purely functional, aerodynamic reasons. It also suited the deeper license plates used on models in the US.

SUPPORTING ROLE
Like that of most front-wheel drive cars, the SM's rear suspension does little more than hold the body off the ground.

ENGINE

SM stands for Serié Maserati, and the exquisite Maserati all-aluminum V6 engine weighed just 309 lb (140 kg), was only 12 in (31 cm) long, but produced at least 170 bhp.

REAR CRAMP

Citroën's publicity material tried to hide the fact, but rear-seat legroom and headroom were barely sufficient for two large children.

RONTWARD VISIBILITY

im windshield pillars should have eant excellent visibility but, in ractice, the left-hand rive SM was sometimes fficult to place n the road.

BRAKES

nboard front disc brakes incorporated e handbrake mechanism.

CONTINENTAL *Mark II*

THAT THE FIFTIES AUTO INDUSTRY couldn't make a beautiful car is robustly disproved by the '56 Continental. As pretty as anything from Italy, the Mark II was intended to be a work of art and a symbol of affluence. William Ford was fanatical about his personal project, fighting for a chrome rather than plastic hood ornament costing $150, or the price of an entire Ford grille. But it was that tenacious attention to detail that killed the car. Even with the Mark II's huge $10,000 price tag, the Continental Division still hemorrhaged money. Poor sales, internal company struggles, and the fact that it was only a two-door meant that by '58 the Continental was no more. Ironically, one of the most beautiful cars Ford ever made was sacrificed to save one of the ugliest in the upcoming E-Car project—the Edsel.

PERSONAL LUXURY

The most expensive automobile in America, the $9,695 Continental really was the car for the stars. Elvis tried one as a change from his usual Cadillacs, and Jayne Mansfield owned a pearl-colored '57 with mink trim. The Continental was three years in the planning and was sold and marketed through a special Continental Division.

BODY HEIGHT
"Cow belly" frame was specifically designed to allow high seating with a low roof line.

LEATHER INTERIOR
The high-quality all-leather trim was specially imported from Bridge of Weir in Scotland.

RAGTOPS
Two special convertibles were built before the Continental was axed.

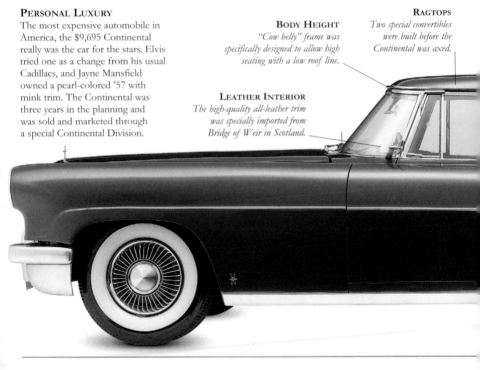

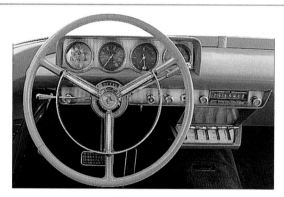

INTERIOR

The classically simple cabin could have come straight out of a British car. The interior boasted richly grained leathers and lavish fabrics. Self-tuning radio, four-way power seat, dual heater, and map lights were among an impressive array of standard features.

SPECIFICATIONS

MODEL Continental Mark II (1956)

PRODUCTION 2,550 (1956)

BODY STYLE Two-door, four-seater sedan.

CONSTRUCTION Steel body and chassis.

ENGINE 368cid V8.

POWER OUTPUT 300 bhp.

TRANSMISSION Turbo-Drive three-speed automatic.

SUSPENSION *Front:* independent coil springs; *Rear:* leaf springs.

BRAKES Front and rear drums.

MAXIMUM SPEED 115 mph (185 km/h)

0–60 MPH (0–96 KM/H) 12.1 sec

A.F.C. 16 mpg (5.7 km/l)

CABIN TEMPERATURE
Air-conditioning was the Continental's only extra-cost option.

PRICE OF CLAY
A pricey little number, even the Continental's prototype clay mock-up cost $1 million.

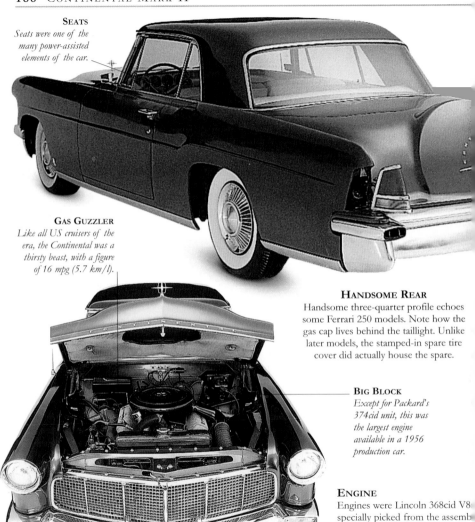

SEATS
Seats were one of the many power-assisted elements of the car.

GAS GUZZLER
Like all US cruisers of the era, the Continental was a thirsty beast, with a figure of 16 mpg (5.7 km/l).

HANDSOME REAR
Handsome three-quarter profile echoes some Ferrari 250 models. Note how the gas cap lives behind the taillight. Unlike later models, the stamped-in spare tire cover did actually house the spare.

BIG BLOCK
Except for Packard's 374cid unit, this was the largest engine available in a 1956 production car.

ENGINE
Engines were Lincoln 368cid V8 specially picked from the assemb line, stripped down, and hand-balanced for extra smoothness and refinement.

TINTED GLASS

This was one of the no-cost extras offered. Others included two-tone paint and an engraved nameplate.

SCRIPT

Continental tag revived the famous 1930s Lincolns of Edsel Ford.

SIMPLE FRONT ASPECT

With a sleek, clean front and simple die-cast grille, the only concession to contemporary Detroit ornamentation was how the direction indicators were faired into the front bumper.

OLLS KILLER

the rear of the car, trim fins, elegant mpers, and neat inset taillights meant at the Continental was admired on both es of the Atlantic. But though its target arket was Rolls-Royce territory, it turned t that the market wasn't large enough sustain volume production.

CLASSY BODY

High-quality bodies were specially finished by the Mitchell-Bentley Corporation of Ionia, Michigan.

FRENCH DEBUT

The Continental debuted on October 6, 1955 at the Paris Auto Show to rave reviews.

DAIMLER *SP250 Dart*

AN ECCENTRIC HYBRID, the SP250 was the car that sunk Daimler. By the late Fifties, the traditionalist Coventry-based company was in dire financial straits. Hoping to woo the car-crazy Americans, Daimler launched the Dart, with its odd pastiche of British and American styling themes, at the 1959 New York Show. Daimler had been making buses out of fiberglass, and the Dart emerged with a quirky, rust-free glass-reinforced-plastic body. The girder chassis was an unashamed copy of the Triumph TR2 *(see pages 444–47)*, and to keep the basic price down, necessities like heater, windshield wipers, and bumpers were made optional extras. Hardly a great car, the SP250 was a commercial failure, and projected sales of 7,500 units in the first three years dissolved into just 2,644, with only 1,200 going Stateside. Jaguar took over Daimler in 1960, and by 1964, Sir William Lyons had axed the sportiest car Daimler had ever made.

THE DART CONCEPT
The Dart was a Fifties concept born too late to compete with the New Wave of monocoque sports cars headed by the stunning E-Type. It stands as a memorial to both the haphazard Sixties British car industry and its self-destructive love affair with all things American.

HOOD
Fibreglass hood had a nasty habit of springing open at high speed.

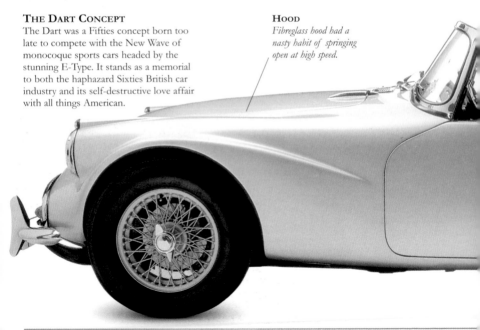

INTERIOR

The cockpit was pure British, with center gauges mounted on an aluminum plate, leather seats and dash, an occasional rear seat, fly-off handbrake, wind-up windows, and thick-pile carpets. Borg-Warner automatic transmission was an option but tended to slow the car down considerably.

REAR SEAT

Vestigial rear seat could just about accommodate one child.

SPECIFICATIONS

MODEL Daimler SP250 Dart (1959–64)

PRODUCTION 2,644 (1,415 LHD, 1,229 RHD)

BODY STYLE Two-door, two-seater sports convertible.

CONSTRUCTION Fiberglass body, steel girder chassis.

ENGINE Iron-block 2548cc V8.

POWER OUTPUT 140 bhp at 5800 rpm.

TRANSMISSION Four-speed manual or three-speed Borg-Warner Model 8.

SUSPENSION Independent front with wishbones and coil springs. Rear live axle with leaf springs.

BRAKES Four-wheel Girling discs.

MAXIMUM SPEED 125 mph (201 km/h)

0–60 MPH (0–96 KM/H) 8.5 sec

0–100 MPH (0–161 KM/H) 19.1 sec

A.F.C. 25 mpg (8.8 km/l)

ENGINE

The turbine-smooth, Edward Turner–designed V8 was the Dart's *tour de force*. If you were brave enough, it could reach 125 mph (201 km/h). With alloy heads and hemispherical combustion chambers, it was a gem of a unit that survived until 1969 in the Daimler 250 sedan.

IMPOSING SIGHT

The guppy-style front could never be called handsome, but when Sixties drivers caught it in their rearview mirrors, they knew to move over. The drastic plastic Dart was serious quick. Contemporary tests praised the Dart's performance and sweet-running V8.

FENDERS

Fluted fenders looked good and gave the body extra rigidity.

4068 WK

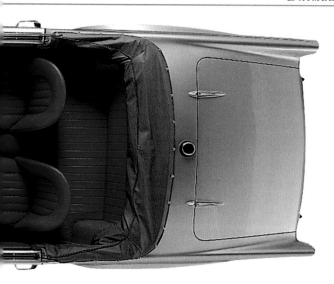

DART DEVELOPMENT

Dart development had three
phases: 1959–61 A-spec cars
came with no creature
comforts; April 1961 and
later B-specs had standard
bumpers, windshield wipers,
and chassis modifications;
while the last and most
refined C-specs, produced
from April 1963 to September
1964, boasted a heater and
cigar lighter as standard.

NEAT TOP
*Top furled away
neatly behind rear
seat, covered with
a fabric bag.*

EED STRAIN
high speed, the Dart was hard
rk; the chassis flexed, doors
ened on corners, and steering
s heavy. Road
ers admired its
ed but thought
chassis,
dling, and body
sh were poor.

UTE STYLING
*Chrome-on-brass
r light finishers
e monogrammed
h a dainty "D."*

4068 WK

DATSUN *Fairlady 1600*

THE SIMILARITY BETWEEN THE Datsun Fairlady and the MGB *(see pages 372–73)* is quite astonishing. The Datsun actually appeared first, at the 1961 Tokyo Motor Show, followed a year later by the MGB. Hardly a great car in its early 1500cc guise, the Fairlady improved dramatically over the years, a foretaste of the Japanese car industry's culture of constant improvement. The later two-liter, twin-carb, five-speed variants of 1967 could reach 125 mph (200 km/h) and even raised eyebrows at American sports car club races. Aimed at the American market, where it was known as the Datsun 1500, the Fairlady sold only 40,000 in nine years. But it showed Datsun how to make the legendary 240Z *(see pages 196–99)*, which became one of the world's best-selling sports cars.

BODY PANELS
The front fenders were bolted on for easy repair.

ENGINE
The 1595cc 90 bhp unit was the mainstay of the Fairlady line until 1970.

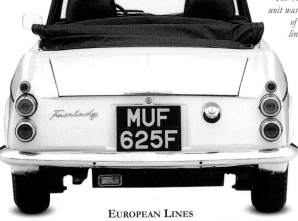

EUROPEAN LINES
Higher and narrower than the MGB, the Fairlady had an unmistakable and deliberate European look. However, of the 7,000 1500cc models sold, half went to the United States.

STYLING

Interestingly, no attempt was made to make the interior harmonize with the Fairlady's traditional exterior lines. The cockpit was typical of the period, with acres of black plastic.

SPECIFICATIONS

MODEL Datsun Fairlady 1600 (1965–70)

PRODUCTION Approx 40,000

BODY STYLE Two-seater sports convertible.

CONSTRUCTION Steel body mounted on box-section chassis.

ENGINE 1595cc four-cylinder.

POWER OUTPUT 90 bhp at 6000 rpm.

TRANSMISSION Four-speed all-synchro.

SUSPENSION *Front:* independent; *Rear:* leaf springs.

BRAKES Front wheel discs, rear drums.

MAXIMUM SPEED 105 mph (169 km/h)

0–60 MPH (0–96 KM/H) 13.3 sec

0–100 MPH (0–161 KM/H) 25 sec

A.F.C. 25 mpg (8.8 km/l)

PERIOD CHARM

Low and rakish with classically perfect proportions, the Fairlady has a certain period charm and is one of the best-looking Datsuns produced before 1965. Side views show the car at its best, while the messy rear and cluttered nose do not work as well.

DATSUN *240Z*

THROUGHOUT THE 1960s, Japanese carmakers were teetering on the brink of a sports car breakthrough. Toyota's 2000 GT *(see pages 442–43)* was a beauty, but with only 337 made, it was an exclusive curio. Honda was giving it a try too, with the dainty S600 and S800. As for Datsun, the MGB-lookalike Fairladies were relatively popular in Japan and the United States, but virtually unknown elsewhere. The revolution came with the Datsun 240Z, which at a stroke established Japan on the world sports car stage at a time when there was a gaping hole in that sector, particularly in the US. It was even launched in the States in October 1969, a month before its official Japanese release, and on a rising tide of Japanese exports to the US it scored a massive hit. It had the looks, performance, handling, and equipment levels. A great value sporting package that outsold all rivals.

TOP STYLIST
The lines of the 240Z were based on earlier styling exercises by Albrecht Goertz, master stylist of the BMW 507 *(see pages 64–67).*

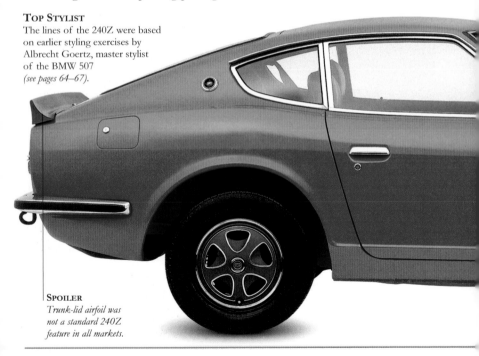

SPOILER
Trunk-lid airfoil was not a standard 240Z feature in all markets.

WINDSHIELD
Steeply raked windshield aided aerodynamic efficiency.

BALANCE
This view shows that the engine was placed forward of the centerline, with the occupants well behind it; yet the Z was noted for its fine balance. The large rear window offered the driver excellent rearward vision.

HOOD
Hood was uncluttered by unnecessary louvers; it later became fussier.

ENGINE
The six-cylinder twin-carb 2.4-liter engine was developed from the four-cylinder unit of the Bluebird sedan range.

DATSUN

WHEELS
Tacky plastic wheel trim is an original fitment.

(see pages 306–09) *(see pages 420–21)* *(see pages 282–85)*

FIRST OF BREED

As with so many long-lived sports cars, the first-of-breed 240Z is seen as the best sporting package—lighter and nimbler than its successors. If you wanted to cut a real dash in a 240Z, the ultimate Samurai performance option had what it takes. Modifications gave six-second 0–60 (96 km/h) figures.

MIXED STYLING CUES

As with the recessed lights at the front, there is an echo of the E-Type Jaguar fixed-head coupe *(see pages 306–09)* at the rear, with a little Porsche 911 *(see pages 420–21)*, Mustang fastback *(see pages 282–85)*, and Aston Martin DBS of 1969.

CAT LIGHTS

Recessed front light treatment is very reminiscent of an E-Type Jaguar.

INTERIOR

Cockpit layout was tailored to American tastes, with hooded instruments and beefy controls. The vinyl-covered bucket seats offered generous rear luggage space.

Z IDENTITY

The model was launched in Japan as the Fairlady Z, replacing the earlier Fairlady line; export versions were universally known as 240Z and badged accordingly. Non-UK and US models were badged as Nissans rather than Datsuns.

SPECIFICATIONS

MODEL Datsun 240Z (1969–73)

PRODUCTION 156,076

BODY STYLE Three-door, two-seater sports hatchback.

CONSTRUCTION Steel monocoque.

ENGINE Inline single overhead-camshaft six, 2393cc.

POWER OUTPUT 151 bhp at 5600 rpm.

TRANSMISSION All-synchromesh four- or five-speed manual gearbox, or auto.

SUSPENSION *Front:* Independent by MacPherson struts, low links, coil springs, telescopic shock absorbers; *Rear:* Independent by MacPherson struts, lower wishbones, coil springs, telescopic dampers.

BRAKES Front discs, rear drums.

MAXIMUM SPEED 125 mph (210 km/h)

0–60 MPH (0–96 KM/H) 8.0 sec

A.F.C. 20–25 mpg (7–9 km/l)

BODY PANELS
Thin, rot-prone body panels were one of the few things that let the 240Z down.

BADGING
The name Datsun —literally son of Dat—first appeared on a small Dat in 1932.

RHX 156L

SUSPENSION
Sophisticated suspension spec was independent with MacPherson struts on all four wheels.

DeLorean *DMC 12*

"The long-awaited transport revolution has begun" bellowed the glossy brochure for John Zachary DeLorean's mold-breaking DMC 12. With a unique brushed stainless-steel body, gullwing doors, and an all-electric interior, the DMC was intended as a glimpse of the future. Today its claim to fame is as one of the car industry's greatest failures, on a par with Ford's disastrous Edsel *(see pages 216–23)*. Despite $130m worth of government aid to establish a specially built factory in West Belfast, DeLorean shut its doors in 1982 with debts of $50m. As for the hapless souls who bought the cars, they were faced with a litany of quality control problems, from doors that would not open, to windows that fell out. Even exposure in the film *Back to the Future* did not help the DeLorean's fortunes. Success depended on American sales, and the company's forecasts were wildly optimistic. After the initial novelty died down, word spread that DeLoreans were dogs, and sales completely evaporated.

BACHELOR WHEELS
The DeLorean was targeted at "the bachelor who's made it" and part of the design brief was that there had to be room behind the front seats for a full set of golf clubs. It was designed by Giugiaro and overseen by Colin Chapman of Lotus fame.

WHEELS
Custom-made spoked alloys were smaller at the front than the back.

LIGHT FRONT
With rear-engined layout, the weight distribution was split 35 percent front to 65 percent rear.

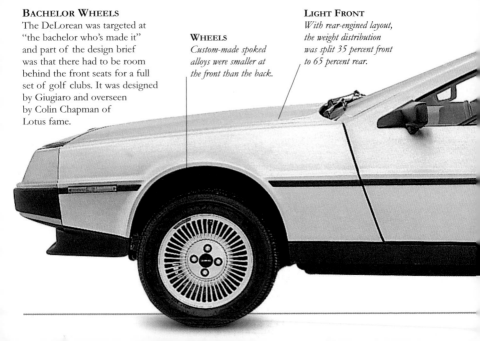

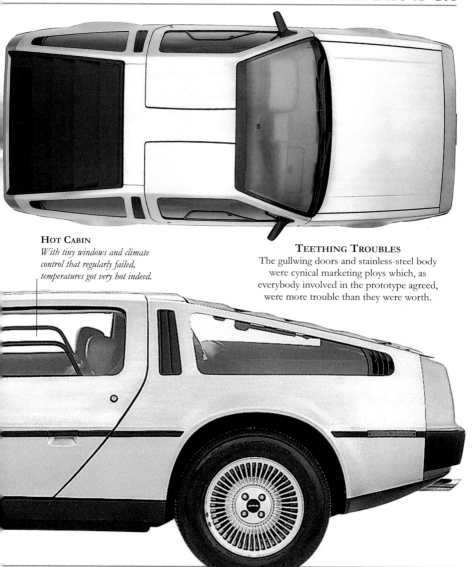

Hot Cabin
With tiny windows and climate control that regularly failed, temperatures got very hot indeed.

Teething Troubles
The gullwing doors and stainless-steel body were cynical marketing ploys which, as everybody involved in the prototype agreed, were more trouble than they were worth.

STARRING ROLE

The 1985 film *Back to the Future* used a DeLorean as a time machine to travel back to 1955; in reality the car was very orthodox. Underpinnings were technically uninspiring and relied heavily on components from other cars. Under the hood, the 145 bhp output was modest.

GULLWINGS

The DeLorean's most celebrated trick was gullwing doors that lea and did not open or close proper

STRUT

Held by a puny single gas strut, it was an act of the purest optimism to expect the doors to work properly.

DATED DELOREAN

By the time of its launch in 1979, the DeLorean was old before its time. '70s styling motifs abound, like the slatted rear window and cubed rear lights.

ENGINE

The overhead-cam, Volvo-sourced 2.8 V6 engine used Bosch K-Jetronic fuel injection. Five-speed manual was standard with three-speed automatic optional.

ELECTRONICS
*Complex electronics were
the result of last-minute
cost-cutting measures.*

HEAVY DOORS
*Overloaded doors were
crammed with locks, glass,
electric motors, mirrors,
stereo speakers, and
ventilation pipery.*

STAINLESS-STEEL BODY
*Brushed stainless-steel was
disliked by Colin Chapman
but insisted upon by DeLorean
himself. Soon owners found
that it was impossible to clean.*

INTERIOR
The leather-clad interior looked
imposing, with electric windows,
tilting telescopic steering column,
double weather seals, air-
conditioning, and a seven-position
climate control function.

SPECIFICATIONS

MODEL DeLorean DMC 12 (1979–82)

PRODUCTION 6,500

BODY STYLE Two-seater rear-engined
sports coupe.

CONSTRUCTION Y-shaped chassis with
stainless-steel body.

ENGINE 2850cc ohc V6.

POWER OUTPUT 145 bhp at 5500 rpm.

TRANSMISSION Five-speed manual
(optional three-speed auto).

SUSPENSION Independent with unequal
length parallel arms and rear trailing arms.

BRAKES Four-wheel discs.

MAXIMUM SPEED 125 mph (201 km/h)

0–60 MPH (0–96 KM/H) 9.6 sec

0–100 MPH (0–161 KM/H) 23.2 sec

A.F.C. 22 mpg (7.8 km/l)

DeSoto *Custom*

THE DeSoto OF 1950 had a glittery glamour that cheered up postwar America. Hailed as "cars built for owner satisfaction," they were practical, boxy, and tough. DeSoto was a longtime taxi builder that, in the steel-starved years of 1946–48, managed to turn out 11,600 cabs, most of which plied the streets of New York. Despite more chrome upfront than any other Chrysler product, DeSotos still labored on with an L-head six-pot 250cid mill. The legendary Firedome V8 wouldn't arrive until 1952. But body shapes for 1950 were the prettiest ever, and the American public reacted with delight buying up 133,854 units in the calendar year, ranking DeSoto 14th in the industry. Top-line Custom Convertibles had a very reasonable sticker price of $2,578 and came with Tip-Toe hydraulic shift with Gyrol fluid drive as standard. The austere postwar years were a sales Disneyland for the makers of these sparkling cars, but DeSoto's roll couldn't last. By 1961 they'd disappeared forever.

MODEL LINE
The top-priced Custom line fielded a Club Coupe, two huge wagons, a six-passenger sedan, a two-door Sportsman, and a convertible. DeSoto's volume sellers were its sedans and coupes, which listed at under $2,000 in De Luxe form.

INNOVATIVE GEARING
Fluid drive gearbox was an innovative semiautomatic pre-selector with conventional manual operation or semiauto kick-down.

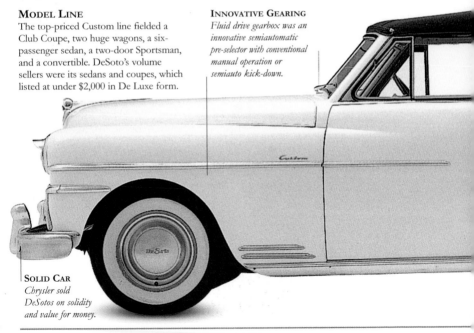

SOLID CAR
Chrysler sold DeSotos on solidity and value for money.

MID-RANGE MODELS

DeSoto's role at Chrysler was much like Mercury's at Ford and Oldsmobile's at GM —to plug the gap between budget models and uptown swankmobiles. '50 DeSotos came in two levels of trim: De Luxe and the plusher Custom, at $200 more.

CHROME INTERIOR

There's more chrome than instruments; by 1952 the dashboard would have chrome dials.

HOOD

Hood is sleek and swish but had to be raised by hand.

DASHBOARD

Direction signals and backup lights were offered as standard on the Custom, while options included heater, electric clock, and two-tone paint.

TIRES

Convertibles came with whitewalls and wheel covers as standard.

REAR FENDER
The DeSoto body shape still carried hints of the separate fenders of prewar cars.

SPLIT WINDSHIELD
Flat glass split windshield was parted with a chromed center rod on which the rearview mirror was positioned.

CHUNKY YET REFINED
The DeSoto's rump was large, round, and unadorned, and trunk space was cavernous. The Custom Convertible was clean and elegant enough to be seen cruising along the most stylish boulevards.

HOOD ORNAMENT
Optional hood ornament was one Hernando DeSoto, a 17th-century Spanish conquistador. The ornament glowed in the dark.

TOOTHY GRILLE

The mammoth-tooth grille dominates the front aspect of the DeSoto but would be scaled down for 1951. 1950 models are easily spotted by their body-color vertical grille divider, unique to this year.

SHARED UNIT
All '50 DeSotos shared the same lackluster straight six.

SPECIFICATIONS

MODEL DeSoto Custom Convertible (1950)
PRODUCTION 2,900 (1950)
BODY STYLE Two-door convertible.
CONSTRUCTION Steel body and box-section chassis.
ENGINE 236.7cid straight-six.
POWER OUTPUT 112 bhp.
TRANSMISSION Fluid drive semiautomatic.
SUSPENSION *Front:* independent coil springs; *Rear:* leaf springs with live axle.
BRAKES Front and rear drums.
MAXIMUM SPEED 90 mph (145 km/h)
0–60 MPH (0–96 KM/H) 22.1 sec
A.F.C. 18 mpg (6.4 km/l)

ENGINE
The side-valve straight six was stodgy, putting out a modest 112 bhp.

ADVERTISEMENT

During the 1950s, car advertising copy became extravagant, relying more on hyperbole than fact. This DeSoto promotion was no exception.

DE TOMASO *Pantera GT5*

AN UNCOMPLICATED SUPERCAR, the Pantera was a charming amalgam of Detroit grunt and Italian glam. Launched in 1971 and sold in North America by Ford's Lincoln-Mercury dealers, it was powered by a mid-mounted Ford 5.7-liter V8 that could muster 159 mph (256 km/h) and belt to 60 mph (96 km/h) in under six seconds. The formidable 350 bhp GT5 was built after Ford pulled out in 1974 and De Tomaso merged with Maserati. With a propensity for the front lifting at high speed, hopeless rear visibility, no headroom, awkward seats, and impossibly placed pedals, the Pantera is massively flawed, yet remarkably easy to drive. Handling is poised and accurate, plus that wall of power which catapults the car to 30 mph (48 km/h) in less time than it takes to pronounce its name.

TRUNK
Lift-up rear panel gave total engine accessibility for maintenance.

HOT BLOCK
Early Panteras would overheat, and owners would often see the temperature gauge creep past 230°F (110°C).

ALL SHOOK UP
Elvis Presley shot his Pantera when it wouldn't start.

EXHAUSTS
Four exhausts were necessary to provide an efficient outlet for all that power.

LIMITED HEADROOM
Do not buy a Pantera if you are over 5 ft 10 in (178 cm) tall—there is no headroom.

CONSTRUCTION
The underside was old-fashioned welded pressed steel monocoque.

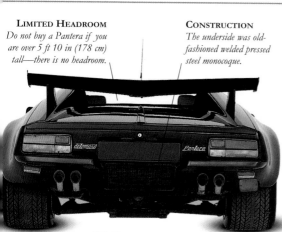

SPECIFICATIONS

MODEL De Tomaso Pantera GT5 (1974–93)

PRODUCTION N/A

BODY STYLE Mid-engined two-seater coupe.

CONSTRUCTION Pressed-steel chassis body unit.

ENGINE 5763cc V8.

POWER OUTPUT 350 bhp at 6000 rpm.

TRANSMISSION Five-speed manual ZF Transaxle.

SUSPENSION All-around independent.

BRAKES All-around ventilated discs.

MAXIMUM SPEED 159 mph (256 km/h)

0–60 MPH (0–96 KM/H) 5.5 sec

0–100 MPH (0–161 KM/H) 13.5 sec

A.F.C. 15 mpg (5.3 km/l)

US RESTRICTIONS
Americans were not able to buy the proper GT5 due to the car's lack of engine-emission controls and had to settle for just the GT5 badges.

STYLING
Shape was penned by Tom Tjaarda, who gave it a clean uncluttered nose.

STUNNING PROFILE
Fat arches, aggressive GT5 graphics down the flanks, 11-in (28-cm) wide wheels, and ground clearance you could not slide an envelope under make the Pantera look evil.

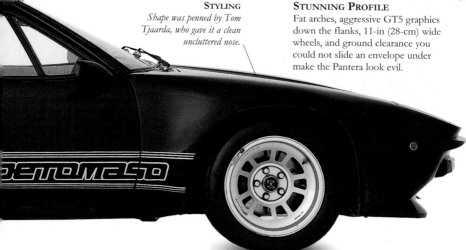

WHEEL ARCH
Wheel arches strained outward to cover 13-in (33-cm) rear tires.

PANTERA AT SPEED
The huge fender helps rear down-force but actually slows the Pantera down. At the General Motors Millbrook proving ground in England, a GT5 with the fender in place made 148 mph (238 km/h); without the fender it reached 151.7 mph (244 km/h).

COCKPIT
With the engine so close to the interior, the cabin temperature could get very hot.

INTERIOR
The Pantera requires a typical Italian driving position—long arms and short legs. Switches and dials are all over the place, but the glorious engine tone is right next to your ears.

TIRES
Giant Pirelli P7 345/45 rear rubber belonged on the track and gave astonishing road traction.

Transaxle
The ZF transaxle was also used in the Ford GT40 (see pages 258–61) and cost more to make than the engine.

Shared Engineering
The Pantera was engineered by Giampaolo Dallara, also responsible for the Lamborghini Miura (see pages 318–21).

Engine

The Pantera is really just a big power plant with a body attached. The monster V8 lives in the middle, mated to a beautifully built aluminum-cased ZF transaxle.

Front-end Scares

Despite a front spoiler, the little weight upfront meant that when the Pantera hit over 120 mph (193 km/h), the nose would lift and the steering would lighten up alarmingly. Generally, though, the car's rear-wheel drive setup made for neat, controllable handling; an expert could literally steer the Pantera on the throttle.

DODGE *Charger R/T*

COLLECTORS RANK THE 1968 Dodge Charger as one of the fastest and best-styled muscle cars of its era. This, the second generation of Charger, marked the pinnacle of the horsepower race between American car manufacturers in the late 1960s. At that time, gasoline was 10 cents a gallon, Americans had more disposable income than ever before, and engine capacity was everything to the aspiring car buyer. With its hugely powerful 7.2-liter engine, the Charger 440 was, in reality, a thinly veiled street racer. The Rapid Transit (R/T) version was a high-performance factory option, which included heavy-duty suspension and brakes, dual exhausts, and wider tires. At idle, the engine produced such massive torque that it rocked the car body from side to side. Buyers took the second generation Charger to their hearts in a big way, with sales outstripping the earlier lackluster model by a factor of six.

HANDSOME BEAST
The Charger was the creation of Dodge's chief of design, Bill Brownlie, and its clean, voluptuous lines gave this car one of the most handsome shapes of the day. It left you in no doubt as to what it was all about: guts and purpose. The mean-looking nose, blacked-out grille, and low hood made drivers of lesser machines move over fast.

INDICATORS
Neat styling features included indicator repeaters built into the hood scoop.

ENGINE
The potent engine had enough power to spin the rear wheels in every gear.

WOODEN WHEEL
Factory options included wood-grained steering wheel and cruise control.

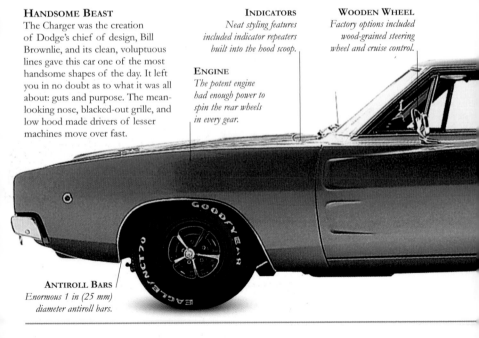

ANTIROLL BARS
Enormous 1 in (25 mm) diameter antiroll bars.

REAR STYLING

"Buttress-backed" styling was America's version of a European 2+2 sports coupe. Ads called the Charger "a beautiful screamer," which was aimed at "a rugged type of individual." Profile is all aggression, with lantern-jawed lines, mock vents on the doors, bumblebee stripes and twin exhausts that roared.

SPECIFICATIONS

MODEL Dodge Charger (1967–70)
PRODUCTION 96,100
BODY STYLE Two-door, four-seater.
CONSTRUCTION Steel monocoque body.
ENGINE 7.2-liter V8.
POWER OUTPUT 375 bhp at 3200 rpm.
TRANSMISSION Three-speed TorqueFlite auto, or Hurst four-speed manual.
SUSPENSION *Front:* heavy duty independent; *Rear:* leaf-spring.
BRAKES Heavy duty, 11 in (280 mm) drums, with optional front discs.
MAXIMUM SPEED 150 mph (241 km/h)
0–60 MPH (0–96 KM/H) 6 sec
0–100 MPH (0–161 KM/H) 13.3 sec
A.F.C. 10 mpg (3.5 km/l)

SEATS
Bucket seats were de rigueur *at the time.*

"SOFT" INTERIOR
Chargers were also for those "who like it soft inside." All had standard clock, heater, and cigarette lighter.

SECURITY
The chrome, quick-fill, racing-style gas cap was attached to the car by wire to stop souvenir hunters.

TIRES
Transferring all the power to the road required ultra-wide 235x14 tires.

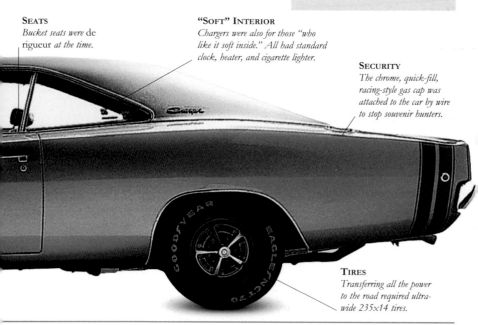

INTERIOR

The standard R/T cockpit is functional to the point of being stark. No distractions here—just a matte black dash with six gauges that included a 150 mph (241 km/h) speedometer.

COLORS
Choices originally included Plum Crazy, Go Mango, and Top Banana.

STEERING WHEEL
Huge steering wheel was essential for keeping all that grunt in a straight line.

FUEL
The gargantuan engine returned just 10 mpg (3.5 km/l).

LIGHTS
Hazard warning lights were groovy features for 1967.

NEVA
00

STAR OF THE SCREEN

A car with star quality, the Charger featured in the classic nine-minute chase sequence in the film *Bullitt*. It also had major roles in the 1970s cult movie *Vanishing Point*, and the television series, *The Dukes of Hazzard*.

ENGINE

The wall-to-wall engine found in the R/T Charger is Dodge's immensely powerful 440 Magnum—a 7.2-liter V8. This stump-pulling power plant produced maximum torque at a lazy 3200 rpm—making it obscenely quick, yet as docile as a kitten in town traffic.

HEADLIGHTS

These were hidden under electric flaps to give the Charger a sinister grin.

EDSEL *Bermuda*

WITHOUT THAT INFAMOUS GRILLE, the Bermuda wouldn't have been a bad old barge. The rest looked pretty safe and suburban, and even those faddish rear lights weren't that offensive. At $3,155 it was the top Edsel wagon, wooing the WASPs with more mock wood than Disneyland. But Ford had oversold the Edsel big time, and every model suffered guilt by association. Initial sales in 1957 were nothing like the predicted 200,000, but weren't disastrous either. The Bermudas, though, found just 2,235 buyers and were discontinued after only one year. By '58, people no longer believed the hype, and Edsel sales evaporated; the company went out of business in November 1959. Everybody knew that the '58 recession killed the Edsel, but at Ford, major players in the project were cruelly demoted or fired.

ODD STYLING

Looking back, one wonders how one of the most powerful corporations in the world could possibly have signed off on such a stylistic debacle. '58 Edsels weren't just ugly, they were appallingly weird. The Bermuda's side view, however, is innocuous enough and no worse than many half-timbered shopping-mall wagons of the period.

ANTENNA

Push-button radio with manual antenna was an expensive $95 option.

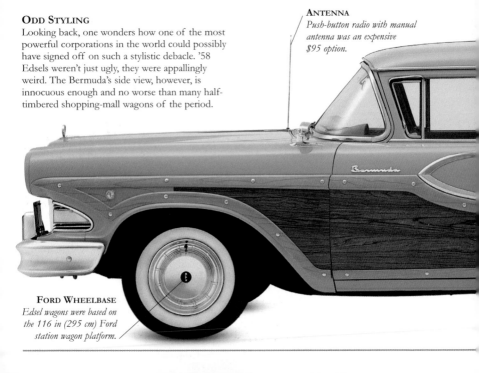

FORD WHEELBASE

Edsel wagons were based on the 116 in (295 cm) Ford station wagon platform.

FRONT ASPECT

The grille was so prominent that it required separate flanking bumpers. The Edsel mascot adorns the front of the hood; the name was chosen from 6,000 possibilities, including Mongoose, Turcotinga, and Utopian Turtletop.

STEERING

49 percent of all Edsels had power steering.

COLOR CHOICE

This Bermuda is painted in Spring Green, but buyers had a choice of 161 different color combinations.

ROOF KINK

Note how the roof is slightly kinked to give the huge panel extra rigidity.

FUEL FIGURES

Not surprisingly for a station wagon this size, fuel consumption wasn't great at 15 mpg (5.3 km/l).

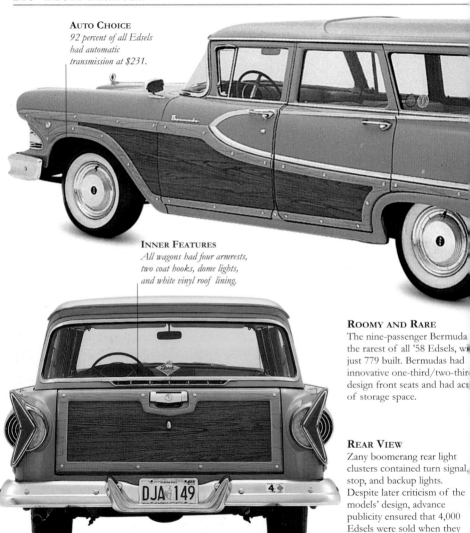

AUTO CHOICE
92 percent of all Edsels had automatic transmission at $231.

INNER FEATURES
All wagons had four armrests, two coat hooks, dome lights, and white vinyl roof lining.

ROOMY AND RARE
The nine-passenger Bermuda the rarest of all '58 Edsels, wi just 779 built. Bermudas had innovative one-third/two-third design front seats and had acr of storage space.

REAR VIEW
Zany boomerang rear light clusters contained turn signal, stop, and backup lights. Despite later criticism of the models' design, advance publicity ensured that 4,000 Edsels were sold when they were launched on "Edsel Day September 4, 1957.

SUSPENSION
*Rear suspension was
by leaf springs.*

SPECIFICATIONS

MODEL Edsel Bermuda (1958)

PRODUCTION 1,456 (1958, six-seater Bermudas)

BODY STYLE Four-door, six-seater station wagon.

CONSTRUCTION Steel body and chassis.

ENGINE 361cid V8.

POWER OUTPUT 303 bhp.

TRANSMISSION Three-speed manual with optional overdrive, optional three-speed automatic with or without Teletouch control.

SUSPENSION *Front:* independent coil springs; *Rear:* leaf springs with live axle.

BRAKES Front and rear drums.

MAXIMUM SPEED 108 mph (174 km/h)

0–60 MPH (0–96 KM/H) 10.2 sec

A.F.C. 15 mpg (5.3 km/l)

TELETOUCH
*Teletouch button
sent a signal
to the car's
"precision brain."*

ENGINE
"They're the industry's newest—and the best," cried the advertising. Edsel engines were strong 361 or 410cid V8s, with the station wagons usually powered by the smaller unit. The E400 on the valve covers indicates the unit's amount of torque.

INTERIOR
Never one of Edsel's strongest selling points, the Teletouch gear selector was operated by push buttons in the center of the steering wheel. It was gimmicky and unreliable.

EDSEL *Corsair*

BY 1959 AMERICA HAD LOST HER confidence; the economy nose-dived, Russia was first in space, there were race riots in Little Rock, and Ford was counting the cost of its disastrous Edsel project—close to 400 million dollars. "The Edsel look is here to stay" brayed the ads, but the bold new vertical grille had become a countrywide joke. Sales didn't just die, they never took off, and those who had been rash enough to buy hid their chromium follies in suburban garages. Eisenhower's mantra of materialism was over, and buyers wanted to know more about economical compacts like the Nash Rambler, Studebaker Lark, and novel VW Beetle. Throw in a confusing 18-model lineup, poor build quality, and disenchanted dealers, and "The Newest Thing on Wheels" never stood a chance. Now famous as a powerful symbol of failure, the Edsel stands as a telling memorial to the foolishness of consumer culture in Fifties America.

A REHASHED FORD

By 1959, the Corsair had become just a restyled Ranger, based on the Ford Fairlane. Corsairs had bigger motors and more standard equipment. But even a sticker price of $3,000 for the convertible didn't help sales, which were a miserable model year total of 45,000. Ford was desperate and tried to sell it as "A new kind of car that makes sense."

DOOR MIRROR
The hooded chrome door mirror was remote-controlled, an extremely rare aftermarket option.

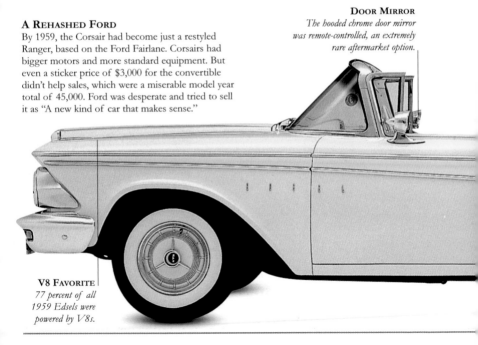

V8 FAVORITE
77 percent of all 1959 Edsels were powered by V8s.

EMPTY ADVERTISING

Ford's Edsel arrived in 1957 on the back of intense TV and magazine coverage. But by the time it hit the showrooms, the market had done a *volte-face* and wanted more than just empty chromium rhetoric.

SPECIFICATIONS

MODEL Edsel Corsair Convertible (1959)

PRODUCTION 1,343 (1959)

BODY STYLE Four-seater coupe.

CONSTRUCTION Steel body and chassis.

ENGINES 332cid, 361cid V8s.

POWER OUTPUT 225–303 bhp.

TRANSMISSION Three-speed manual with optional overdrive, optional two- or three-speed Mile-O-Matic automatic.

SUSPENSION *Front:* independent with coil springs; *Rear:* leaf springs with live axle.

BRAKES Front and rear drums.

MAXIMUM SPEED 95–105 mph (153–169 km/h)

0–60 MPH (0–96 KM/H) 11–16 sec

A.F.C. 15 mpg (5.3 km/l)

DECORATION
The dominating chrome and white sweepspear that runs the entire length of the car makes the rear deck look heavy.

RARE STYLE
Corsair Convertibles are the rarest '59 Edsels, with only 1,343 leaving the Louisville plant.

COLOR
Petal Yellow was one of 17 possible exterior colors.

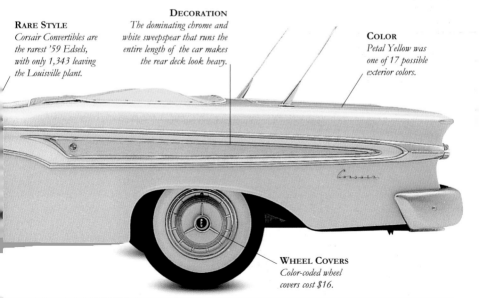

WHEEL COVERS
Color-coded wheel covers cost $16.

Toilet Seat Styling
Roy Brown, the Edsel's designe
claimed that "The front theme
of our newest car combines
nostalgia with modern vertic
thrust." Other pundits wer
not so positive and
compared it to a
horse collar, a man
sucking a lemon, c
even a toilet seat.

Weight
*Weighing in at .
considerable 3,7
lb (1,719 kg) t
convertible was
heavier than
the sedan.*

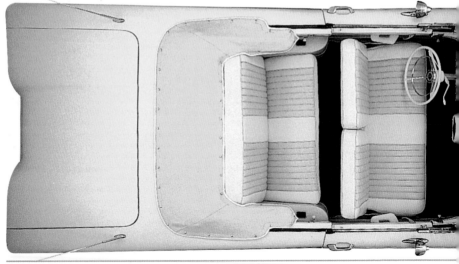

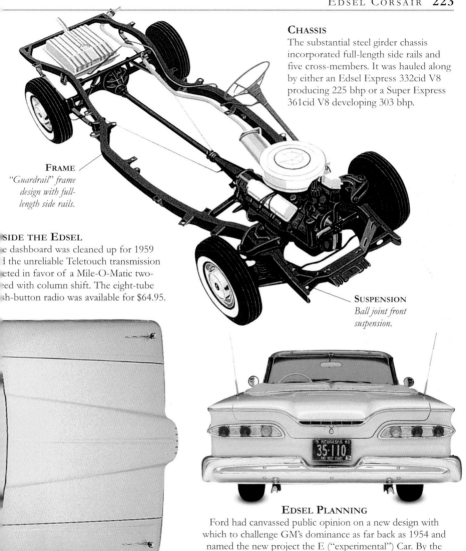

CHASSIS

The substantial steel girder chassis incorporated full-length side rails and five cross-members. It was hauled along by either an Edsel Express 332cid V8 producing 225 bhp or a Super Express 361cid V8 developing 303 bhp.

FRAME

"Guardrail" frame design with full-length side rails.

SIDE THE EDSEL

e dashboard was cleaned up for 1959
d the unreliable Teletouch transmission
eted in favor of a Mile-O-Matic two-
ed with column shift. The eight-tube
sh-button radio was available for $64.95.

SUSPENSION

Ball joint front suspension.

EDSEL PLANNING

Ford had canvassed public opinion on a new design with which to challenge GM's dominance as far back as 1954 and named the new project the E ("experimental") Car. By the time it appeared, it was a ridiculous leviathan.

FACEL *Vega II*

WHEN SOMEONE LIKE PABLO PICASSO chooses a car, it is going to look good. In its day, the Facel II was a poem in steel and easily as beautiful as anything turned out by the Italian styling houses. Small wonder then that Facels were synonymous with the Sixties' jet set. Driven by Ringo Starr, Ava Gardner, Danny Kaye, Tony Curtis, François Truffaut, and Joan Fontaine, Facels were one of the most charismatic cars of the day. Even death gave them glamour; the novelist Albert Camus died while being passengered in his publisher's FVS in January 1960. In 1961, the HK 500 was reskinned and given cleaner lines, an extra 6 in (15 cm) in length, and dubbed the Facel II. At 1.5 tons, the II was lighter than the 500 and could storm to 140 mph (225 km/h). Costing more than the contemporary Aston Martin DB4 *(see pages 32–35)* and Maserati 3500, the Facel II was as immortal as a Duesenberg, Hispano Suiza, or Delahaye. We will never see its like again.

HANDCRAFTED SUPERCAR

In terms of finish, image, and quality, Facel Vegas were one of the most successful handmade supercars. Body joints were perfectly flush, doors closed like heavy vaults, brightwork was stainless steel, and even the roof line was fabricated from five seamlessly joined sections.

REAR SEATING

The leather backseat folded down to make a luggage platform.

BUMPER

Bumper is not chrome but rust-resistant stainless steel.

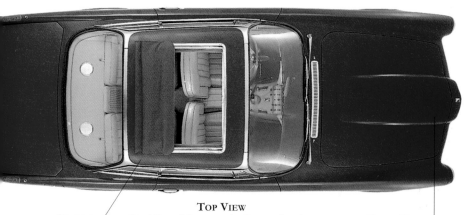

TOP VIEW
Facel II used the same wheelbase and engine
as the HK 500, but the shape was refined to
make it look more modern, losing such
cliches as the dated wraparound windshield.

SUNROOF
*Fabric, roll-back, full-
length sunroof was a period
aftermarket accessory.*

POWER BULGE
*Prodigious hood
bulge cleared air cleaners
and twin carbs.*

GEARBOX
*Manual Pont-a-Mousson
gearbox began life in a truck.*

FUEL CONSUMPTION
*Driven fast, the Facel II
would drink one gallon of
fuel every 10 miles.*

SPINNERS
*Knockoff wheel
spinners.*

REAR VISIBILITY
The enlarged rear window gave a much greater glass area than the H_ 500 and almost 90 percent visibili_ helped by slimmer pillars.

MANUFACTURERS
In the '50s, Facel ma_ motor scooters, jet engines, office furniture_ and kitchen cabinets.

DIMENSIONS
At 1.5 tons (30 cwt), 15 ft (4.57 m) long, 6 ft (1.83 m) wide, and only 4 ft 3 in (1.3 m) high, the Facel II aped the girth and bulk of contemporary American iron.

INTERIOR
Steering wheel points straight to the driver's heart. Note the unmistakable aircraft-type panel layout with center gauges and heater controls like hand throttles.

SUSPENSION
Selectaride shock absorbers provided a comfortable ride.

DOMINATING GRILLE
The intimidating frontage is all grille, because the hot-running V8 engine needed all the cooling air it could get. HK 500 had four round headlights, but the Facel II's voguish stacked lights were shamelessly culled from contemporary Mercedes sedans.

MOOTH LIGHTING

ake-indicator lights are cut out
the rear fenders and help to
hance the Facel's seamless lines.
achieve this stunning one-
ece look, the car's light alloy
dy panels were hand finished
d mated to each other.

BODY STYLING
*Rakish body was
artistically similar to
the Facellia Coupe.*

RARE MOTOR
*By far the rarest Facel with only
184 made, IIs are still fiercely
admired by Facel fanciers.*

SPECIFICATIONS

MODEL Facel Vega Facel II (1962–64)
PRODUCTION 184
BODY STYLE Two-door, four-seater
Grand Tourer.
CONSTRUCTION Steel chassis, steel/light
alloy body.
ENGINE 6286cc cast-iron V8.
POWER OUTPUT 390 bhp at 5400 rpm
(manual), 355 bhp at 4800 rpm (auto).
TRANSMISSION Three-speed TorqueFlite
auto or four-speed Pont-a-Mousson manual.
SUSPENSION Independent front coil
springs, rear live axle leaf springs.
BRAKES Four-wheel Dunlop discs.
MAXIMUM SPEED 149 mph (240 km/h)
0–60 MPH (0–96 KM/H) 8.3 sec
0–100 MPH (0–161 KM/H) 17.0 sec
A.F.C. 15 mpg (5.4 km/l)

HOOD
*Hood lid was
huge, but then so
was the engine.*

BRAKES

*Disc brakes all-
around countered
the Facel's
immense power.*

FERRARI *250 GT SWB*

IN AN ERA WHEN FERRARI WAS turning out some lackluster road cars, the 250 GT SWB became a yardstick, the car against which all other GTs were judged and one of the finest Ferraris ever. Of the 167 made between 1959 and 1962, 74 were competition cars—their simplicity made them one of the most competitive sports racers of the Fifties. Built around a tubular chassis, the V12 3.0 engine lives at the front, along with a simple four-speed gearbox with Porsche internals. But it is that delectable Pininfarina-sculpted shape that is so special. Tense, urgent, but friendly, those smooth lines have none of the intimidating presence of a Testarossa or Daytona. The SWB stands alone as a perfect blend of form and function —one of the world's prettiest cars, and on the track one of the most successful. The SWB won races from Spa to Le Mans, Nassau to the Nürburgring. Which is exactly what Enzo Ferrari wanted. "They are cars," he said, "which the sporting client can use on the road during the week and race on Sundays." Happy days.

DESIGN CREDITS
Soft, compact, and rounded, Pininfarina executed the design, while Scaglietti took care of the sheet metal. The result was one of the most charismatic cars ever produced.

NO CLEANERS
Instead of air cleaners, competition cars used filterless air trumpets.

AIR SCOOPS
Fender air scoops helped to cool the engine.

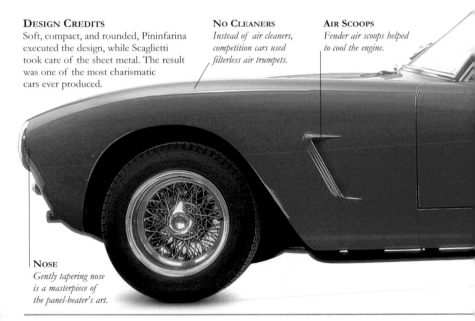

NOSE
Gently tapering nose is a masterpiece of the panel-beater's art.

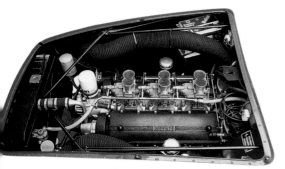

ENGINE

The V12 power unit had a seven-bearing crankshaft turned from a solid billet of steel, single plug per cylinder, and three twin-choke Weber DCL3 or DCL6 carburetors.

SPECIFICATIONS

MODEL Ferrari 250 GT SWB (1959–62)

PRODUCTION 167 (10 RHD)

BODY STYLE Two-seater GT coupe.

CONSTRUCTION Tubular chassis with all-alloy or alloy/steel body.

ENGINE 2953cc V12.

POWER OUTPUT 280 bhp at 7000 rpm.

TRANSMISSION Four-speed manual.

SUSPENSION Independent front coil and wishbones, rear live axle leaf springs.

BRAKES Four-wheel discs.

MAXIMUM SPEED 147 mph (237 km/h)

0–60 MPH (0–96 KM/H) 6.6 sec

0–100 MPH (0–161 KM/H) 16.2 sec

A.F.C. 12 mpg (4.2 km/l)

REAR WINDOW
Expansive rear window sat above enormous 27-gallon (123-liter) fuel tank.

WHEELS
The SWB sat on elegant, chrome-plated Borrani competition wire wheels.

OVERHEAD VIEW

The car has perfect balance. Shape is rounded and fluid, and the first 11 SWBs were built in alloy, though these rare lightweight models suffered from stretching alloy. Road cars had a steel body and aluminum hood and doors.

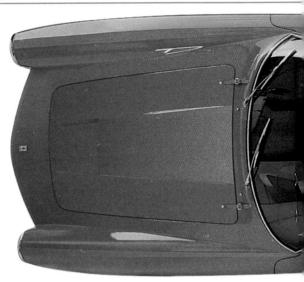

STRAP 'EM IN

The 250's roll cage and modern seat belts were nods to safety, but understandable considering that progressively more power was extracted from the V12 engine.

UNDERSTATED BEAUTY

The 250 GT is a polished gem, hugging the road limpet low. Front combines beauty and threat with steely grin and squat wheel-arch-filling attitude. Nothing is exaggerated for effec[t]

ROAD PROTECTIO[N]

Unlike this race car, cars had vestigial fron[t] bumpers and the pran[cing] horse badge in the gri[ll]

INTERIOR

Despite the movie star exterior, the
interior is a place of work. Functional
dash is basic black with no frills. Sun
visors were notably absent. The cockpit
was snug and airy but noisy when
the key was turned.

GAS CAP

*Huge alloy gas
cap was to allow
fast fill-ups.*

ACING STATEMENT

vo sets of aggressive
ainpipe twin exhausts
ominate the SWB's
mp and declare its
mpetition bloodline.
r many years the 250
T dominated hill climbs
d track meets all over
e world. The SWB 250
T was the ultimate racer.

FERRARI *275 GTB/4*

THE GTB/4 WAS a hybrid made for two short years from 1966 to 1968. With just 350 built, a mere 27 in right-hand drive, it was not one of Ferrari's moneymakers. So named for its four camshafts, the GTB still ranks as the finest road car Ferrari produced before Fiat took control of the company. With fully independent suspension, a five-speed gearbox, and a fetching Pininfarina-designed and Scaglietti-built body, it was the last of the proper Berlinettas. Nimble and compact, with neutral handling and stunning design, this is probably one of the most desirable Ferraris ever made.

SPECIFICATIONS

MODEL Ferrari 275 GTB/4 (1966–68)

PRODUCTION 350

BODY STYLE Two-seater front-engined coupe.

CONSTRUCTION Steel chassis, aluminium body.

ENGINE 3.3-liter twin overhead-cam dry sump V12.

POWER OUTPUT 300 bhp at 8000 rpm.

TRANSMISSION Five-speed all-synchromesh.

SUSPENSION All-around independent.

BRAKES Four-wheel servo discs.

MAXIMUM SPEED 160 mph (257 km/h)

0–60 MPH (0–96 KM/H) 5.5 sec

0–100 MPH (0–161 KM/H) 13 sec

A.F.C. 12 mpg (4.2 km/l)

THE MECHANICS

This was Ferrari's first ever production four-cam V12 engine and their first road-going prancing horse with an independent rear end. The type 226 engine was related to the 330 P2 prototypes of the 1965 racing season. The GTB/4's chassis is made up of a ladder frame built around two oval-tube members.

A MOTORING BEAUT

The GTB/4 is prettier than an E-Type *(see pages 306–09)*, Aston Martin DB4 *(see pages 32–35)*, or Lamborghini Miura *(see pages 318–21)*. The small trunk, small cockpit, and long nose are classic Pininfarina styling—an arresting amalgam of beauty and brawn. The interior, though, is trimm in unluxurious vinyl.

FERRARI *Daytona*

THE CLASSICALLY sculptured and outrageously quick Daytona was a supercar with a split personality. Under 120 mph (193 km/h), it felt like a truck with heavy inert controls and crashing suspension. But once the needle was heading for 140 mph (225 km/h), things started to sparkle. With a romantic flat-out maximum of 170 mph (280 km/h), it was the last of the great front-engined V12 war horses. Launched at the 1968 Paris Salon as the 365 GTB/4, the press immediately named it "Daytona" in honor of Ferrari's success at the 1967 24-hour race. Faster than all its Italian and British contemporaries, the chisel-nosed Ferrari won laurels on the racetrack as well as the hearts and pockets of wealthy enthusiasts all over the world.

POEM IN STEEL
A poem in steel, only a handful of other cars could be considered in the same aesthetic league as the Daytona.

SPECIFICATIONS

MODEL Ferrari 365 GTB/4 Daytona (1968–73)

PRODUCTION 1,426 (165 RHD)

BODY STYLE Two-seater fastback.

CONSTRUCTION Steel/alloy/fiberglass body, separate multitube chassis frame.

ENGINE V12 4390cc.

POWER OUTPUT 352 bhp at 7500 rpm.

TRANSMISSION Five-speed all-synchromesh.

SUSPENSION Independent front and rear.

BRAKES Four-wheel discs.

MAXIMUM SPEED 174 mph (280 km/h)

0–60 MPH (0–96 KM/H) 5.4 sec

0–100 MPH (0–161 KM/H) 12.8 sec

A.F.C. 14 mpg (5 km/l)

INSIDE AND OUT
With hammock-type racing seats, a cornucopia of black-on-white instruments, and a provocatively angled, extralong gear shift, the cabin promises some serious excitement. Beneath the exterior is a skeleton of chrome-molybdenum tube members, giving enormous rigidity and strength.

FERRARI *Dino 246 GT*

PRETTY ENOUGH TO STOP a speeding train, the Dino came not from Enzo Ferrari's head, but from his heart. The Dino was a tribute to the great man's love for his son, Alfredino, who died of a kidney disease. Aimed at the Porsche 911 buyer *(see pages 420–21)*, the 246 Dino engine came with only half the number of cylinders usually found in a Ferrari. Instead of a V12 configuration, it boasted a 2.4-liter V6 engine, yet was nonetheless capable of a very Ferrarilike 150 mph (241 km/h). With sparklir performance, small girth, and mid-engined layout, it handled like a go-kart, and coul be hustled around with enormous aplomb. Beautifully sculpted by Pininfarina the 24 won worldwide acclaim as the high point of 1970s automotive styling. In its day, it was among the most fashionable cars money could buy. The rarest Dino is the GTS, with Targa detachable roof panel. The Dino's finest hour was when it was driven by Tony Curtis in the Seventies' British television series *The Persuaders*.

BODY CONSTRUCTION

Early Dinos were constructed from alloy, later ones from steel, with the bodies built by Italian designer Scaglietti. Unfortunately, little attention was paid to rust protection. Vulnerable interior body joints and cavities were covered with only a very thin coat of paint.

AERODYNAMICS
The sleek aerodynamic shape of the roof line helped to give the car its impressively high top speed.

TIRES
Wide tires were essential to deliver the Dino's lithe handling.

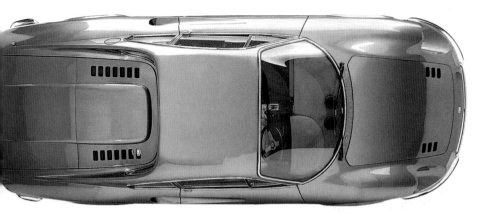

WINDSHIELD
*Windshields do not
come much more
steeply raked than
this one.*

REAR ENGINE

The transversely mounted 2418cc
V6 has four overhead cams, a four-
bearing crankshaft, and breathes
through three twin-choke Weber
40 DCF carburetors. Power output
is 195 bhp. This particular engine's
distinctive throaty roar is
a Ferrari legend.

DINO PRICES
*Prices went crazy in the Eighties,
but are now half that value.*

ENGINE POSITION

The engine is positioned in the middle of the car, which gives mechanics little space to work in. The spare wheel and battery are located under the hood in the front, leaving very little room to carry extras such as luggage. Optional perspex headlight cowls can increase the Dino's top speed by 3 mph (5 km/h).

BADGING

246s wore the Dino badge on the nose, never the Ferrari's prancing horse.

SPECIFICATIONS

MODEL Ferrari Dino 246 GT (1969–74)

PRODUCTION 2,487

BODY STYLE Two-door, two seater.

CONSTRUCTION Steel body, tubular frame.

ENGINE Transverse V6/2.4 liter.

POWER OUTPUT 195 bhp at 5000 rpm.

TRANSMISSION Five-speed, all-synchromesh.

SUSPENSION Independent front and rear.

BRAKES Ventilated discs all around.

MAXIMUM SPEED 148 mph (238 km/h)

0–60 MPH (0–96 KM/H) 7.1 sec

0–100 MPH (0–161 KM/H) 17.6 sec

A.F.C. 22 mpg (7.8 km/l)

CURVY ITALIAN

The sensuous curves are unmistakably supplied by Ferrari. The Ferrari badge and prancing horse were fitted by a later owner. The thin original paint job means that most surviving Dinos will have had at least one body rebuild by now.

INTERIOR

The dashboard is suede and strewn with switches, while the cramped-looking interior is actually an ergonomic triumph. Though the cockpit is hot and noisy, that has not detracted from the car's popularity. Shifting the gearbox though its chrome gate is much like spooning honey.

GEAR LEVER
Five-speed all-synchromesh gearbox.

COLOR
Metallic brown is a rare color—75 percent of Dinos were red.

FIAT LIGHTING
Lights and electrics were supplied by Fiat, which owns Ferrari.

EXHAUSTS
Four exhausts mean the V6 sounds almost as musical as a V12.

FERRARI *365 GT4 Berlinetta Boxer*

THE BERLINETTA BOXER WAS meant to be the jewel in Ferrari's crown—one of the fastest GT cars ever. Replacing the legendary V12 Ferrari Daytona *(see page 233)*, the 365 BB was powered by a flat-12 "Boxer" engine, so named for the image of the horizontally located pistons punching at their opposite numbers. Mid-engined, with a tubular chassis frame and clothed in a peerless Pininfarina-designed body (a mixture of alloy, fiberglass, and steel), the 365 was assembled by Scaglietti in Modena. First unveiled in 1971 at the Turin Motor Show, the formidable 4.4-liter 380 bhp Boxer was so complex that deliveries to buyers did not start until 1973. The trouble was that Ferrari had suggested that the Boxer could top 185 mph (298 km/h), when it could actually only manage around 170 mph (274 km/h), slight slower than the outgoing Daytona. In 1976, Ferrari replaced the 365 with the five-liter Boxer 512, yet the 365 is the faster and rarer model, with only 387 built.

CLASSIC MONEY
In the classic car boom of the mid-Eighties, Boxers changed hands for crazy money. The 512 tripled in value before the stock market crash, with the 365 doubling. Now both machines are back to realistic levels.

FUEL CAPACITY
The Boxer could carry 26 gallons (120 liters) of gasoline.

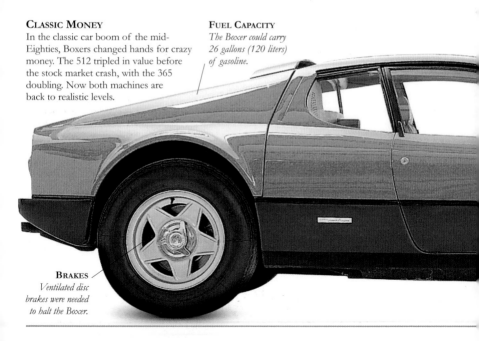

BRAKES
Ventilated disc brakes were needed to halt the Boxer.

ENGINE POSITION
*The entire engine/
drivetrain ensemble was
positioned longitudinally
behind the cockpit.*

EXHAUSTS
*Not many other
production road cars
came with six exhausts.*

FERRARI FIRST
The 365 Boxer was the first mid-engined 12-cylinder
production car to carry the Ferrari name.
Cylinder heads were light alloy, holding two camshafts
each. Fuel was supplied by two electrical pumps into
four triple-throat Weber carburetors.

TIRES
*The Boxer was shod
with ultrawide
Michelin XWX
215/70 tires.*

ANTENNA
*Antenna for the
radio was set in the
windshield.*

BODY SHAPE
*Ferrari's aerodynamic styling
meant that the Boxer had a
very low drag coefficient.*

LOW-SLUNG POSITION
*The Boxer engine layout was
favored because it allowed the whole
car to sit that much lower, giving
better aerodynamics and a lower
center of gravity.*

WHEELS
*Wheels were the same as on
the Daytona—cast alloy.*

PROTOTYPE TESTING

A handful of Boxer prototypes were subject to extensive testing. Preproduction cars were recognizable by a number of differences, one being the roof-mounted radio antenna—factory cars had them enclosed in the windshield. Pininfarina's shape went virtually unchanged from the prototype into the production version.

INTERIOR

An amalgam of racer and grand tourer, the Boxer's cabin was functional yet luxurious, with electric windows and air-conditioning. Switches for these were positioned on the console beneath the gear lever.

CENTER CONSOLE

The rear-mounted gearbox meant that only a small transmission tunnel was needed, saving cabin room.

ENGINE

A magnificent piece of foundry art, the flat-12 has a crankshaft machined from a solid billet of chrome-molybdenum steel. Instead of timing chains, the 365 used toothed composite belts, an innovation in 1973.

CYLINDERS
The Boxer had twin oil filters, one for each bank of six cylinders.

SPECIFICATIONS

MODEL Ferrari 365 GT4 Berlinetta Boxer (1973–76)
PRODUCTION 387 (58 RHD models)
BODY STYLE Two-seater sports.
CONSTRUCTION Tubular space-frame chassis.
ENGINE 4.4-liter flat-12.
POWER OUTPUT 380 bhp at 7700 rpm.
TRANSMISSION Five-speed all synchromesh, rear-mounted gearbox.
SUSPENSION Independent front and rear.
BRAKES Ventilated front and rear discs.
MAXIMUM SPEED 172 mph (277 km/h)
0–60 MPH (0–96 KM/H) 6.5 sec
0–100 MPH (0–161 KM/H) 15 sec
A.F.C. 14 mpg (4.2 km/l)

COOLING VENT
Slatted hood cooling vent helped keep interior cabin temperatures down.

CHASSIS
The Boxer's chassis was derived from the Dino (see pages 234–37), with a frame of steel tubes and doors, oil pan, and nose in aluminum.

LOWER BODYWORK
This was fiberglass, along with the wheel-arch liners and bumpers.

FERRARI *308 GTB*

ONE OF THE best-selling Ferraris ever, the 308 GTB started life with a fiberglass body designed by Pininfarina and built by Scaglietti. Power was courtesy of the V8 3.0 engine and five-speed gearbox inherited from the 308 GT4. With uptown America as the GTB's target market, federal emission regulations made the GTB clean up its act, evolving into a refined and civilized machine with such hi-tech appurtenances as four valves per cylinder and Bosch fuel injection. Practical and tractable in traffic, it became the 1980s entry-level Ferrari, supplanting the Porsche 911 *(see pages 420–21)* as the standard issue yuppiemobile.

SPECIFICATIONS

MODEL Ferrari 308 GTB (1975–85)
PRODUCTION 712 (308 GTB fiberglass); 2,185 (308 GTB steel); 3,219 (GTS)
BODY STYLE Two-door, two-seater sports coupe.
CONSTRUCTION Fiberglass/steel.
ENGINE Mid-mounted transverse dohc 2926cc V8.
POWER OUTPUT 255 bhp at 7600 rpm.
TRANSMISSION Five-speed manual.
SUSPENSION Independent double wishbones/coil springs all around.
BRAKES Ventilated discs all around.
MAXIMUM SPEED 154 mph (248 km/h)
0–60 MPH (0–96 KM/H) 7.3 sec
0–100 MPH (0–161 KM/H) 19.8 sec
A.F.C. 16 mpg (5.7 km/l)

MIXED STYLING CUES
The handsome styling is a blend of Dino 246 and 365 GT4. The Dino provided concave rear windows and conical air intakes, while the 365 brought double bodyshell appearance with a waistline groove. The 2926cc V8 has double overhead cams per bank and four 40 DCNF Weber carburetors.

FRONT ASPECT
With the engine at the back, the wide slatted grille scooped up air for brake and interior ventilation. Retractable flush-fitting pop-up headlights keep wind down on the nose and front wheels. The roof on the GTB was always a tin top; the chic GTS had a Targa top panel.

FERRARI *400 GT*

HE FIRST Ferrari ever offered with automatic
ansmission, the 400 was aimed at the American
arket, and was meant to take the prancing horse
to the boardrooms of Europe and the US. But the
0's automatic box was a most un-Ferrarilike device,
azy three-speed GM Turbo-Hydramatic also used
Cadillac, Rolls-Royce, and Jaguar. It may have been
e best self-shifter in the world, but it was a radical
eparture for Maranello, and met with only modest
ccess. The 400 was possibly the most discreet and
fined Ferrari ever made. It looked awful in Racing
ed—the color of 70 percent of Ferraris—so most
ere finished in dark metallics. The 400 became the
0i GT in 1973 and the 412 in 1985.

SPECIFICATIONS

MODEL Ferrari 400 GT (1976–79)

PRODUCTION 501

BODY STYLE Two-door, four-seater
sports sedan.

CONSTRUCTION Steel/alloy body, separate
tubular chassis frame.

ENGINE 4390cc twin ohc V12.

POWER OUTPUT 340 bhp at 6800 rpm.

TRANSMISSION Five-speed manual
or three-speed automatic.

SUSPENSION Independent double
wishbones with coil springs, rear as front
with hydro-pneumatic self-leveling.

BRAKES Four-wheel ventilated discs.

MAXIMUM SPEED 150 mph (241 km/h)

0–60 MPH (0–96 KM/H) 7.1 sec

0–100 MPH (0–161 KM/H) 18.7 sec

A.F.C. 12 mpg (4.2 km/l)

5 SIMILARITIES
art from the delicate chin
oiler and bolt-on alloys, the
ape was pure 365 GT4 2+2.
e rectangular design of
e body was lightened
a plunging hood line
d a waist-length
dentation running
ng the 400's flanks.

HEADLIGHTS
*Four headlights
ere retracted into
the bodywork
y electric motors.*

FERRARI *Testarossa*

THE TESTAROSSA WAS never one of Modena's best efforts. With its enormous girth and overstuffed appearance, it perfectly sums up the Eighties credo of excess. As soon as it appeared on the world's television screens in *Miami Vice*, the Testarossa, or Redhead, became a symbol of everything that was wrong with a decade of rampant materialism and greed. The Testarossa fell from grace rather suddenly. Dilettante speculators bought them new at $150,000-odd and ballyhooed their values up to a quarter of a million. By 1988, secondhand values were slipping badly, and many an investor saw their car shed three-quarters of its value overnight. Today, used Testarossas are highly prized with rising prices and growing investment potential.

RACING LEGEND

Ferrari bestowed on its new creation one of the grandest names from its racing past—the 250 Testa Rossa, of which only 19 were built for retail customers. Design of the new model was determined with the help of Pininfarina's full-sized wind tunnel, but enthusiasts were initially cool about the Testarossa's size and shape.

STYLING

Striking radiator cooling ducts obviated the need to pass water from the front radiator to the mid-mounted engine, freeing the front luggage compartment.

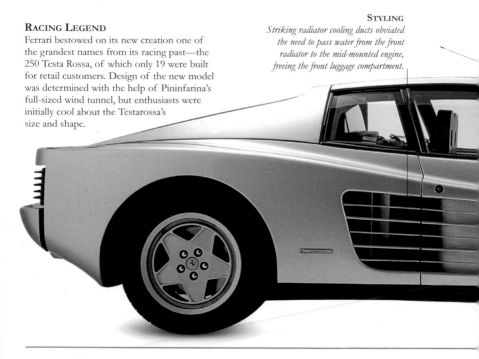

UAE 576

WIDE SUPERCAR

Wider than the Ferrari 512 BB, the Corvette
(see pages 142–45), and the Countach *(see pages 322–25)*,
it measured a portly 6 ft (1.83 m) across. While this
meant a bigger cockpit, the ultrawide door sills
collected mud in wet weather.

SPECIFICATIONS

MODEL Ferrari Testarossa (1988)

PRODUCTION 1,074

BODY STYLE Mid-engined, two-seater sports coupe.

CONSTRUCTION Steel frame with aluminum and fiberglass panels.

ENGINE Flat-12, 4942cc with dry sump lubrication.

POWER OUTPUT 390 bhp at 6300 rpm.

TRANSMISSION Five-speed manual.

SUSPENSION Independent front and rear.

BRAKES *Front:* disc; *Rear:* drums.

MAXIMUM SPEED 181 mph (291 km/h)

0–60 MPH (0–96 KM/H) 5.3 sec

0–100 MPH (0–161 KM/H) 12.2 sec

A.F.C. 12 mpg (4.2 km/l)

TIRES
*Tires were either Goodyear
Eagles or Michelin TRXs.*

AERODYNAMICS
*Front spoiler kept the nose
firmly attached to the road
and channeled cooling air to
the front brakes.*

SPACIOUS INTERIOR
The Testarossa's large body meant plenty of cabin space, with more room for both occupants and luggage. Even so, interior trim was flimsy and looked tired after 70,000 miles (112,000 km).

DOOR MIRRORS
Prominent door mirrors on both sides gave the Testarossa an extra 8 in (20 cm) in width.

REARVIEW MIRROR
The curious, periscopelike rearview mirror was developed by Pininfarina.

COCKPIT
The cockpit was restrained and spartan, with a hand-stitched leather dashboard and little distracting ornamentation. For once a Ferrari's cockpit w accommodating, with electrically adjustable leathe seats and airconditioning as standard.

UAE 576

REAR TREATMEN
Pininfarina's grille treatment was picked on the rear end, givin stylistic continuity.

TRADITIONAL TOUCHES

Despite the modern external styling, traditional touches remained inside the car—the classic Ferrari gearshift, with its chrome gate, and prancing horse steering-wheel boss were ever-present.

STORAGE
Mid-engined format allowed storage space in the front.

REAR FENDER VENTS

Borrowed from Grand Prix racing experience, these cheese-slicer cooling ducts are for the twin radiators, located forward of the rear wheels to keep heat away from the cockpit.

ORIGINAL GRILLES
The Testarossa's distinctive side grilles are now among the most widely imitated styling features.

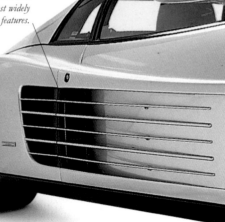

ENGINE
The flat-12 mid-mounted engine had a 4942cc capacity and produced 390 bhp at 6300 rpm. With four valves per cylinder, coil ignition, and fuel injection, it was one of the very last flat-12 GTs.

FERRARI *456 GT*

A USED FERRARI 456 is one of the world's great supercar bargains. For the price of a new, hot Ford Focus you can have a beautiful 186 mph (300 km/h) grand tourer that's also a reliable and practical full four-seater. Strong and capable with a fine ride and a glorious V12 engine, the 456 is a definite neoclassic. Launched in 1992 to replace the unloved Mondial, it was the fastest production 2+2 on the planet and, apart from the F40, the most powerful road car developed by Ferrari. Slippery and handsome with a carbon-fiber hood, pop-up headlamps, a glorious six-speed gearbox plus an automatic option, the 456 looked and felt like a Daytona for a fraction of the price. More importantly, the 456 was that rare thing—a Ferrari with quiet class.

A POEM IN ALLOY

The body was alloy, spot-welded to a steel tubular chassis using "Feran" filler, and was shaped by extensive wind tunnel testing. The rear wing was electronically retractable to give extra down force at speed. Luggage space was generous, and the optional special fitted leather luggage set cost about the same as a small car.

SMART WINDOWS
Electric windows moved down slightly when you opened the doors.

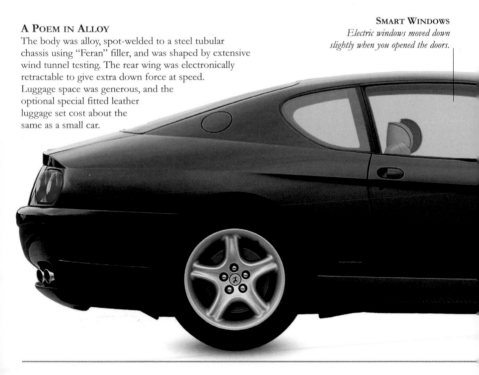

BEAUTY BOX

The six-speed transaxle manual gearbox lived at the rear and was an engineering gem, lubricated by its own pump and radiator. GTA had a hydraulic four-speed automatic managed by twin Bosch computers. Chrome gear gate, alloy shifter, and precise action means that manual 456s are worth more than autos.

SPECIFICATIONS

MODEL Ferrari 456 GT (1992)
PRODUCTION 3,289
BODY STYLE Two-door, four-seater coupe.
CONSTRUCTION Alloy panels, tubular steel chassis, composite hood.
ENGINE 5,474cc, V12.
POWER OUTPUT 436 bhp.
TRANSMISSION Six-speed transaxle manual.
SUSPENSION Independent all around.
BRAKES Four-wheel ventilated discs.
MAXIMUM SPEED 186 mph (300 km/h)
0–60 MPH (0–96 KM/H) 5 sec
0–100 MPH (0–161 KM/H) 11.6 sec
A.F.C. 15 mpg (6.4 km/l)

ELEGANT INTERIOR
Cabin was high quality and much better than previous Ferraris.

V12 WARHORSE
Brilliant alloy 5.5 liter V12 engine cranked out 436 horsepower.

HIGH LIGHTS
456 was the last Ferrari to have retractable headlights.

FERRARI *Enzo*

THE V12 CARBON-FIBER ENZO is a million-dollar wild child and the most flamboyant Ferrari ever. Good for 226 mph (364 km/h) and capable of 0–100 mph (0–161 km/h) in only 6.6 seconds, the initial production run of 349 units was completely sold out before a single car ever got near a showroom. Ferrari was forced to build another 50 just to please a line of desperate buyers. Designed by Ken Okuyama of Pininfarina, some say the Enzo is one of the ugliest cars ever, but its showstopping looks and dramatic doors (similar to the Lamborghini Countach *(see pages 322–25)* have guaranteed it automotive immortality, and used examples often change hands for more than their original new sticker price. As close as you'll get to a road-going F1 car, the Enzo isn't a supercar or a hypercar— it is best described as the original Wonder Car. The last Enzo ever built, the 400th example, was donated to the Vatican in Rome for charity.

EXPENSIVE EXCESS
The Enzo was the most expensive Ferrari ever built at over $1.2 million. An oil change cost $900, and if you were unlucky (or careless) enough to exceed the 8,500 rev limit a ruined engine could set you back $230,000 in repairs! Brake pad and tire replacement could add up to $3,800 per corner.

F1 WHEELS
Wheels are F1 style with single nut.

BASIC ACCOMMODATION
Cabin is stark, simple, and carbon-fiber.

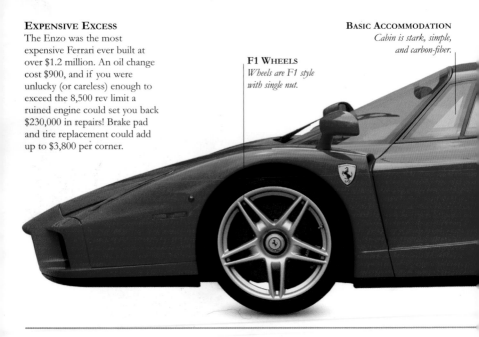

DRAMATIC DOORS
Enormous doors make up most of roof area.

AIR SHOVELS
Massive nostrils cool brakes and keep nose down.

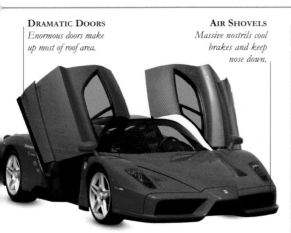

SPECIFICATIONS

MODEL Ferrari Enzo (2002)
PRODUCTION 400
BODY STYLE Two-door, two-seater coupe.
CONSTRUCTION Carbon-fiber composite.
ENGINE 5,998cc V12.
POWER OUTPUT 651 bhp.
TRANSMISSION Six-speed F1 paddle shift.
SUSPENSION Independent with push-rod shockers.
BRAKES Ceramic composite discs.
MAXIMUM SPEED 226 mph (363 km/h)
0–60 MPH (0–96 KM/H) 3.2 sec
0–100 MPH (0–161 KM/H) 6.6 sec
A.F.C. 11 mpg (4.7 km/l)

FEATHER LIGHT

The Enzo was an automotive lesson in weight saving. The body panels and tub are composite and carbon-fiber along with the seats, doors, and even minor switches in the interior. No sound system was available. Only the McLaren F1 is lighter, but not by much.

LIGHT BRAKES
Even brakes are ceramic composite.

ELECTRIC WING
Rear spoiler is computer-controlled.

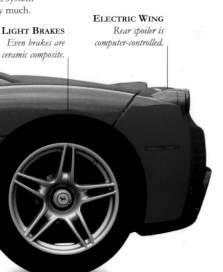

FERRARI *458 Italia*

THE 458 IS THE FINEST Ferrari ever. A narcotic cocktail of blistering performance, smooth ride, low-speed tractability, and gorgeous looks won it *Car of the Year* in 2009. There's a long waiting list, used prices are firm, and it's widely considered to be the coolest prancing horse ever made by the Italian company. The super-quick steering takes just two turns lock-to-lock, the dual-clutch, seven-speed automatic gearbox has no delay, and the 4.5-liter V8 is thunderously fast—hitting 100 mph (161 km/h) in just seven seconds. But the 458's ability to trundle around town at low speeds without any temperament makes it different from every other supercar. This is a Ferrari you don't have to suffer to own and one that can genuinely be used every day.

INCREDIBLE ENGINE
The mid-mounted, direct-injection 4.5 V8 develops 125 bhp per liter—a record for a naturally aspirated piston engine. Maximum horsepower is delivered at a screaming 9,000 rpm, and 80 percent of torque is available at just 3,250 rpm. The Getrag automatic gearbox (shared with the Mercedes SLS) shifts gears in four-tenths of a second. Sixty mph is on the dial in only 3.3 seconds.

COLORED CALIPERS
Carbon ceramic brakes have five caliper color choices.

RACING INTERIOR
Cabin was designed by Grand Prix champion Michael Schumacher.

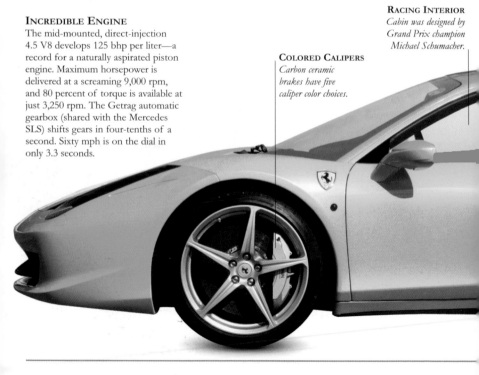

SPECIFICATIONS

MODEL Ferrari 458 Italia (2009)

PRODUCTION N/A

BODY STYLE Mid-engined, two-seater coupe.

CONSTRUCTION Alloy chassis, lightweight panels.

ENGINE 4,499 cc V8.

POWER OUTPUT 562 bhp.

TRANSMISSION Seven-speed, dual-clutch automatic.

SUSPENSION Twin wishbone, double-link.

BRAKES Four-wheel carbon ceramic discs.

MAXIMUM SPEED 202 mph (325 km/h)

0–60 MPH (0–96 KM/H) 3.3 sec

0–100 MPH (0–161 KM/H) 7 sec

A.F.C. 15 mpg (6.4 km/l)

AIR FORCE
Clever vents cool brakes and reduce nose lift.

BEAUTIFUL THING
One of Pininfarina's prettiest designs, the 458 has an alloy chassis bonded using aerospace technology. The underside is flat, and a raft of aerodynamic styling tweaks provide 309 lb (140 kg) of down force at speed. Grip and stability are phenomenal.

LONG HERITAGE
Mid-engined configuration goes back to Dino 246 (see pages 234–37).

UNSPOILED
Aerodynamic design means no rear spoiler is needed.

FIAT *500D*

WHEN THE FIAT 500 NUOVA appeared in 1957, longtime Fiat designer Dante Giacosa defended it by saying, "However small it might be, an automobile will always be more comfortable than a motor scooter." Today though, the diminutive runabout needs no defense, for time has justified Giacosa's faith—over four million 500s and derivatives were produced up to the demise of the Giardiniera estate in 1977. In some senses the Fiat was a mini before the British Mini *(see pages 44–47)*, for the baby Fiat not only appeared two years ahead of its British counterpart, but was also 3 in (7.6 cm) shorter. With its 479cc motor, the original 500 Nuova was rather frantic. 1960 saw it grow to maturity with the launch of the 500D, which was pushed along by its enlarged 499.5cc engine. Now at last the baby Fiat could almost touch 60 mph (96 km/h) without being pushed over the edge of a cliff.

SUNROOF
Some 500s had small fold-back sunroofs. On convertibles, the fabric roof with plastic rear window rolled right back.

"SUICIDE" DOORS
You can tell this Fiat is pre-1965 because of the rear-hinged, so-called "suicide" doors. After that the hinges moved to the front in line with more modern practice.

DOORS
The Giardiniera station wagon kept "suicide" doors until its demise in 1977.

"HOOD"
This houses the gas tank, battery, and spare tire, with a little space left for a modest amount of luggage.

HOT FIAT
Carlo Abarth produced a modified and tuned Fiat-Abarth along the lines of the hot Minis created in Britain by John Cooper.

SPECIFICATIONS

MODEL Fiat 500 (1957–77)

PRODUCTION 4 million plus (all models)

BODY STYLES Sedan, convertible, Giardiniera station wagon.

CONSTRUCTION Unitary body/chassis.

ENGINES Two-cylinder air-cooled 479cc or 499.5cc.

POWER OUTPUT 17.5 bhp at 4400 rpm (499.5cc).

TRANSMISSION Four-speed non-synchromesh.

SUSPENSION *Front:* independent, transverse leaf, wishbones; *Rear:* independent semitrailing arms, coil springs.

BRAKES Hydraulic drums.

MAXIMUM SPEED 59 mph (95 km/h)

0–60 MPH (0–96 KM/H) 32 sec

A.F.C. 53 mpg (19 km/l)

BACK-TO-FRONT
Some rear-engined cars aped front-engined cousins with fake grilles and air intakes. Not the unpretentious Fiat.

CHARMING ITALIAN
This pert little package is big on charm. From any angle the baby Fiat seems to present a happy, smiling disposition. When it comes to parking it is a winner, although accommodation is a little tight. Two average-sized adults can fit up front, but space in the back is a little more limited.

DRIVING THE 500
The baby Fiat was a fine little driver's car that earned press plaudits for its assured and nimble handling. Although top speed was limited, the car's poise meant you rarely needed to slow down on clear roads.

REAR SPACE
Realistic backseat permutations are two kiddies, one adult sitting sideways, or a large shopping bag.

INTERIOR
The Fiat 500's interior is minimal but functional. There is no fuel gauge, just a light that illuminates when three-quarters of a gallon remains—enough for another 40 miles (64 km).

OPEN-TOP VERSION
*Ghia built a Fiat 500-
based open beach car
called the Jolly
which mimicked
prewar roadsters.*

AIR-COOLED REAR
Rear-engined layout, already
employed in the Fiat 600 of
1955, saved space by removing
the need for a transmission
tunnel. The use of an air-
cooled engine and only
two cylinders in the 500
was a completely new
direction for Fiat.

MOTOR
*All engines were feisty
little devils capable of
indefinite flat-out driving.*

FORD *GT40*

TO APPLY THE TERM "SUPERCAR" to the fabled Ford GT40 is to demean it; modern supercars may be uber cool and ferociously fast, but how many of them actually won Le Mans outright? The Ford GT40, though, was not only the ultimate road car but also the ultimate endurance racer of its era, a twin distinction no one else can match. It was so good that arguments are still going on over its nationality. Let us call it a joint design project between the American manufacturer and independent British talent, with a bit of Italian and German input as well. What matters is that it achieved what it was designed for, claiming the classic Le Mans 24-hour race four times in a row. And there is more to the GT40 than its Le Mans legend. You could, if you could afford it, drive around quite legally on public roads in this 200 mph (322 km/h) projectile. Ultimate supercar? No, it is better than that. Ultimate car? Maybe.

CHANGED APPEARANCE
The front section is the easiest way to identify various developments of the GT40. First prototypes had sharp snouts; the squared-off nose, as shown here, first appeared in 1965; the road-going MkIII was smoother, and the end-of-line MkIV rounder and flatter.

SMALL COCKPIT
The cockpit might be cramped, but the GT40's impracticability is all part of its extreme extravagance.

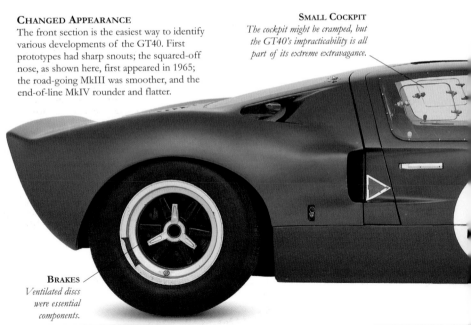

BRAKES
Ventilated discs were essential components.

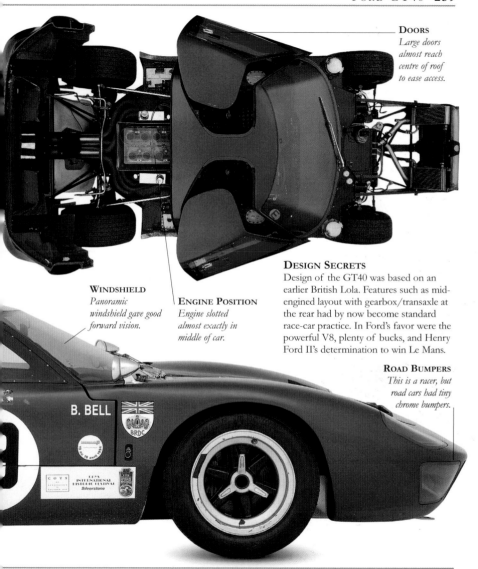

DOORS
Large doors almost reach centre of roof to ease access.

WINDSHIELD
Panoramic windshield gave good forward vision.

ENGINE POSITION
Engine slotted almost exactly in middle of car.

DESIGN SECRETS
Design of the GT40 was based on an earlier British Lola. Features such as mid-engined layout with gearbox/transaxle at the rear had by now become standard race-car practice. In Ford's favor were the powerful V8, plenty of bucks, and Henry Ford II's determination to win Le Mans.

ROAD BUMPERS
This is a racer, but road cars had tiny chrome bumpers.

B. BELL

SPECIFICATIONS

MODEL Ford GT40 MkI, II, III, & IV (1964–68)

PRODUCTION 107

BODY STYLE Two-door, two-seat coupe.

CONSTRUCTION Sheet-steel monocoque (honeycomb MkIV), fiberglass body.

ENGINE Ford V8, 4195cc (MkI), 4727cc (MksI & III), 6997cc (MksII & IV).

POWER OUTPUT From 350 bhp at 7200 rpm (Mk1 4195cc) to 500 bhp at 5000 rpm (MkIV).

TRANSMISSION Transaxle and four- or five-speed ZF gearbox.

SUSPENSION Independent by coil springs and wishbones all around.

BRAKES Ventilated discs all around.

MAXIMUM SPEED 155–200 mph (249–322 km/h, depending on gearing)

0–60 MPH (0–96 KM/H) 4.5 sec

0–100 MPH (0–161 KM/H) 8.5 sec

A.F.C. 12–16 mpg (4.2–5.7 km/l)

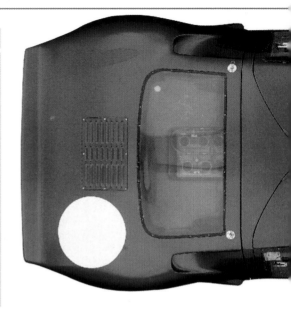

SIDE MIRRORS
Many race cars dispensed with side mirrors.

EXHAUSTS
Exhaust note rises from gruff bellow to ear-splitting yowl.

TAIL
Lip on tail helped high-speed stability.

VITAL STATISTICS
GT, of course, stands for Grand Touring; 40 for the car's height in inches. Overall length was 13 ft 9 in (4.2 m), width 5 ft 10 in (1.78 m), and unladen weight 1,835 lb (832 kg).

WHEELS
Wheel widths varied depending on racing requirements.

WIND EVADER

The graceful and muscular shape was penned in Ford's Dearborn design studios. Requirements included a mid-engined layout and aerodynamic efficiency, vital for burning off Ferraris on the straights of Le Mans.

NO-FRILLS CABIN

The GT40's cabin was stark and cramped. Switches and instruments were pure racer, and the low roof line meant that tall drivers literally could not fit in, with the gullwing doors hitting the driver's head.

REAR VISION

Fuzzy slit above engine cover gives just enough rear vision to watch a Ferrari fade away.

TILL WINNING

T40s can still be en in retrospective ents such as the 94 Tour de France ly, which the atured car won. e British-owned r proudly displays e British Racing rivers' Club badge.

VENTS

cts helped hot air pe from radiator.

FORD *Thunderbird (1955)*

CHEVY'S 1954 CORVETTE may have been a peach, but anything GM could do, Ford could do better. The '55 T-Bird had none of the 'Vette's fiberglass nonsense, but a steel body and grunty V8 motor. Plus it was drop-dead gorgeous and offered scores of options, with the luxury of windup windows. Nobody was surprised when it outsold the creaky Corvette 24-to-one. But Ford wanted volume, and two-seaters weren't everybody's cup of tea, which is why by 1958 the Little Bird became the Big Bird, swollen by four fat armchairs. Nevertheless, as the first of America's top-selling two-seaters, the Thunderbird fired the public's imagination. For the next decade American buyers looking for lively power in a stylish package would greedily devour every Thunderbird going.

NOD TO THE PAST
The styling was very Ford, penned by Bill Boyer and supervised by Frank Hershey. The simple, smooth, and youthful outer wrapping was a huge hit. A rakish long hood and short rear deck recalled the 1940s Lincoln Continental.

POWER BULGE
The hood needed a bulge to clear the large air cleaners. It was stylish too.

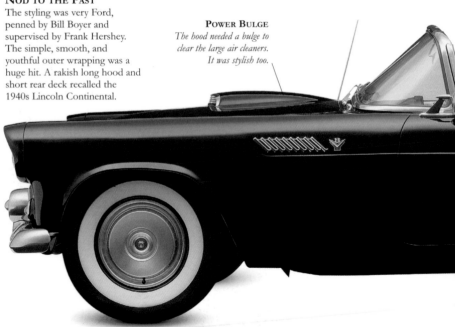

INTERIOR

Luxury options made the Thunderbird an easygoing companion. On the list were power steering, windows, and brakes, automatic transmission, and even electric seats and a power-assisted top. At $100, the push-button radio was more expensive than power steering.

SPECIFICATIONS

MODEL Ford Thunderbird (1955)

PRODUCTION 16,155 (1955)

BODY STYLE Two-door, two-seater convertible.

CONSTRUCTION Steel body and chassis.

ENGINE 292cid V8.

POWER OUTPUT 193 bhp.

TRANSMISSION Three-speed manual with optional overdrive, optional three-speed Ford-O-Matic automatic.

SUSPENSION *Front:* independent coil springs; *Rear:* leaf springs with live axle.

BRAKES Front and rear drums.

MAXIMUM SPEED 105–125 mph (169–201 km/h)

0–60 MPH (0–96 KM/H) 7–11 sec

A.F.C. 17 mpg (6 km/l)

COCKPIT
With the top up, heat from the transmission made for a hot cockpit; ventilation flaps were introduced on '56 and '57 models.

SMOOTH LINES
For 1955, this was an uncharacteristically clean design and attracted 16,155 buyers in its first year of production.

LENGTH
Hardly short, the Little Bird measured 175 in (4.4 m).

CLEARANCE
Road clearance was limited at just 5 in (12.7 cm).

ENGINE
The T-Bird's motor was the new cast-iron OHV 292cid V8 with dual exhausts and four-barrel Holley carb. Compared to the 'Vette's ancient six, the T-Bird's unit offered serious shove. Depending on the state of tune, a very hot T-Bird could hit 60 in seven seconds.

WINDSHIELD
The aeronautical windshield profile is beautifully simple.

SUCCESSFUL BLOCK
The Thunderbird's V8 played a major role in the car's success.

CALIFORNIA
VYD 341

OVERHEAD VIEW
This overhead shot shows that the T-Bird had a bright and spirited personality. Today, the T-Bird is a fiercely prized symbol of American Fifties utopia. The '55–'57 Thunderbirds are the most coveted—the model turned into a four-seater in 1958.

SIMPLE STYLING
Apart from the rather too prominent exhausts, the rear end is remarkably uncluttered. Hardtops were standard fare but soft tops could be ordered as a factory option.

POWER STEERING
*Power steering would only
st the buyer a bargain $98.*

ENGINE OUTPUT
*Power output ranged
from 212 to 300 horses.
Buyers could beautify
their motors with a $25
chrome dress-up kit.*

BIRD NAME
e Thunderbird name was chosen
r a Southwest Native American
d who brought rain and prosperity.
r owners included the movie
resses Debbie Reynolds, Marilyn
nroe, and Jayne Mansfield.

FORD *Fairlane 500 Skyliner*

FORD RAISED THE ROOF IN '57 with their glitziest range ever, and the "Retrac" was a party piece. The world's only mass-produced retractable hardtop debuted at the New York Show of '56, and the first production version was presented to a bemused President Eisenhower in '57. The Skyliner's balletic routine was the most talked-about gadget for years and filled Ford showrooms with thousands of gawking customers. Surprisingly reliable and actuated by a single switch, the Retrac's roof had 610 ft (185 m) of wiring, three drive motors, and a feast of electrical hardware. But showmanship apart, the Skyliner was pricey and had precious little trunk space or leg room. By '59 the novelty had worn off, and division chief Robert McNamara's desire to end expensive "gimmick engineering" led to the wackiest car ever to come out of Dearborn being axed in 1960.

GLASS EXTRA
Options included tinted glass, power windows, power seat, and Styleton two-tone paint.

DECLINING NUMBERS
The Skyliner lived for three years but was never a volume seller. Buyers may have thought it neat, but they were justifiably anxious about the roof mechanism's reliability. Just under 21,000 were sold in '57, less than 15,000 in '58, and a miserly 12,915 found buyers in '59.

ENGINE CHOICE
The Skyliner could be specified with four different V8s ranging from 272 to 352cid.

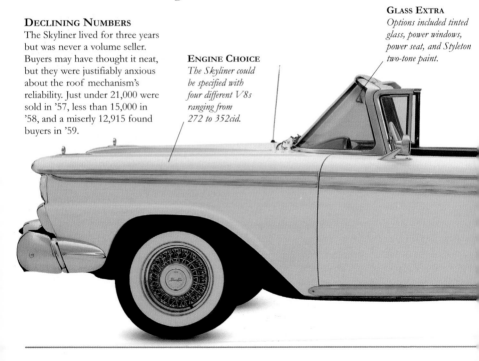

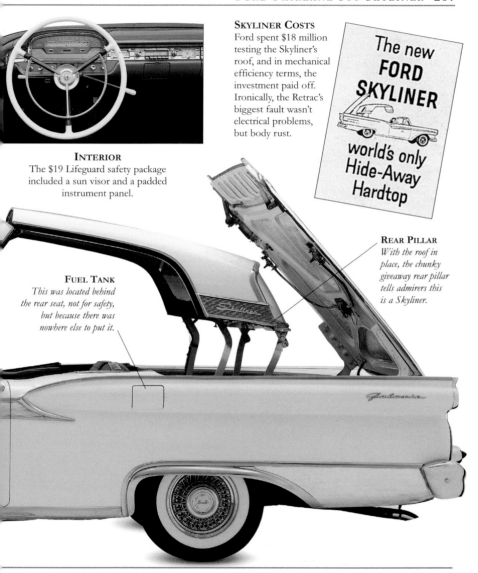

SKYLINER COSTS
Ford spent $18 million testing the Skyliner's roof, and in mechanical efficiency terms, the investment paid off. Ironically, the Retrac's biggest fault wasn't electrical problems, but body rust.

The new
**FORD
SKYLINER**
world's only
Hide-Away
Hardtop

INTERIOR
The $19 Lifeguard safety package included a sun visor and a padded instrument panel.

REAR PILLAR
With the roof in place, the chunky giveaway rear pillar tells admirers this is a Skyliner.

FUEL TANK
This was located behind the rear seat, not for safety, but because there was nowhere else to put it.

WINDSHIELD
Ill-fitting window seals were an all-season annoyance.

CHASSIS
Chassis had to be modified to leave room for the top's control linkage.

SUSPENSION
Though a particularly heavy car, rear suspension was by standard leaf springs.

TOP OF THE PILE

At two tons and $3,138, the Skyliner was the heaviest, priciest, and least practical Ford in the line. The Skyliner's standard power was a 292cid V8, but this model contains the top-spec Thunderbird 352cid Special V8 with 300 bhp.

TRUNK LID
Trunk lid hinged from the rear and folded down over the retracted roof.

STYLING
The trunk sat higher on Skyliners. Large circular taillights were very Thunderbird and became a modern Ford trademark.

REAR VIEW

Fins were down for '59, but missile-shaped pressings on the higher rear fenders were a neat touch to hide all that moving metalwork. Supposedly a midsized car, the Fairlane was the first of the long, low Fords.

TOP UP

With the roof up, the optional Polar-Aire air-conditioning made sense. Other extras that could be specified included tinted glass and, most important for the Retrac, a 70-amp heavy-duty battery. Skyliners came with a comprehensive troubleshooting instruction booklet along with a very slow and ponderous manual backup system.

SPECIFICATIONS

MODEL Ford Fairlane 500 Galaxie Skyliner Retractable (1959)

PRODUCTION 12,915 (1959)

BODY STYLE Two-door hardtop with retractable roof.

CONSTRUCTION Steel body and chassis.

ENGINES 272cid, 292cid, 312cid, 352cid V8s.

POWER OUTPUT 190–300 bhp.

TRANSMISSION Three-speed manual, optional three-speed Cruise-O-Matic automatic.

SUSPENSION *Front:* coil springs; *Rear:* leaf springs.

BRAKES Front and rear drums.

MAXIMUM SPEED 105 mph (169 km/h)

0–60 MPH (0–96 KM/H) 10.6 sec

A.F.C. 15.3 mpg (5.4 km/l)

HOOD PROCEDURE

A switch on the steering column started three motors that opened the rear deck. Another motor unlocked the top, while a further motor hoisted the roof and sent it back to the open trunk space. A separate servo then lowered the rear deck back into place. It all took just one minute, but had to be done with the engine running.

FORD *Galaxie 500XL Sunliner*

IN '62, FORD WAS SELLING its line as "America's liveliest, most carefree cars." And leading the lively look was the bright-as-a-button new Galaxie. This was General Manager Lee Iacocca's third year at the helm, and he was pitching for the young-guy market with speed and muscle. Clean-cut, sleek, and low, the Galaxie line was just what the boys wanted, and it drove Ford into a new era. The new-for-'62 500XL was a real piece, with bucket seats, floor shift, a machine-turned instrument panel, and the option of a brutish 406cid V8. XL stood for "extra lively," making the 500 one of the first cars to kick off Ford's new Total Performance sales campaign. The 500XL Sunliner Convertible was billed as a sporty ragtop and cost an eminently reasonable $3,350. Engines were mighty, rising from 292 through 390 to 406cid V8s, with a Borg-Warner stick-shift four-speed option. Ford learned an important lesson from this car. Those big, in-yer-face engines clothed in large, luxurious bodies would become seriously hip.

BELTS
Front seat belts were an option.

TRENDSETTER
The slab-sided Galaxie body was completely new for '62 and would set something of a styling trend for larger cars. Lines may have been flat and unadorned, but buyers could choose from 13 colors and 21 jaunty two-tones.

PADDED DASH
The dashboard was padded and colormatched the exterior.

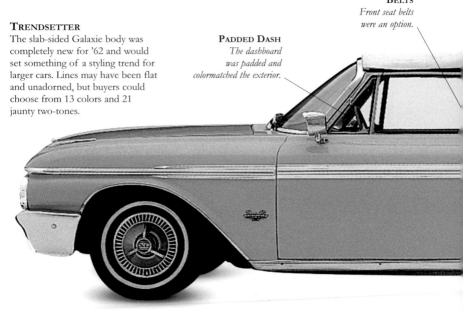

Galaxie 500/XL sunliner

SALES BROCHURE

"This year, more than ever before, Galaxie styling is the
envy of the industry." Subjective sales literature maybe,
but Ford's restyled Galaxies were a real success, and
the new XL series offered peak performance plus
the top trim level of the 500.

SPECIFICATIONS

MODEL Ford Galaxie 500XL Sunliner
Convertible (1962)

PRODUCTION 13,183 (1962)

BODY STYLE Two-door convertible.

CONSTRUCTION Steel body and chassis.

ENGINES 292cid, 352cid, 390cid,
406cid V8s.

POWER OUTPUT 170–405 bhp.

TRANSMISSION Three-speed Cruise-O-
Matic automatic, optional four-speed
manual.

SUSPENSION *Front:* coil springs;
Rear: leaf springs.

BRAKES Front and rear drums.

MAXIMUM SPEED 108–140 mph
(174–225 km/h)

0–60 MPH (0–96 KM/H) 7.6–14.2 sec

A.F.C. 16–18 mpg (5.7–6.4 km/l)

ROOF
*Fiberglass "blankets"
insulated the roof.*

TOP UP
*Unlike this example, the rarest
Sunliners had a wind-evading
Starlift hardtop, which was not
on the options list.*

STYLISH CHROME
*The arrow-straight side flash
is a far cry from the florid
sweepspears that adorned
most Fifties models.*

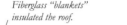

INTERIOR
The interior was plush and palatial, with Mylar-trimmed, deep-pleated buckets flanking the center console. Seats could be adjusted four ways manually and six ways electronically.

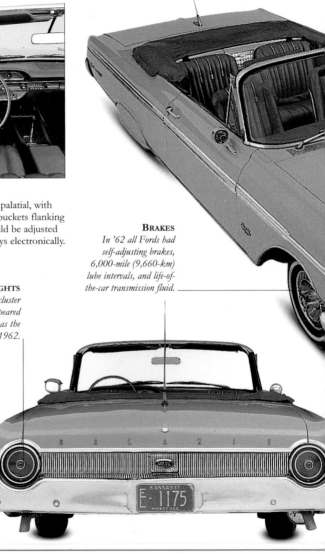

BRAKES
In '62 all Fords had self-adjusting brakes, 6,000-mile (9,660-km) lube intervals, and life-of-the-car transmission fluid.

LIGHTS
Large, round, rear-light cluster copied the T-Bird and appeared on the Falcon as well as the Fairlane, also debuting in 1962.

REAR ASPECT
The fuel filler-cap lurks behind the central hinged section of the anodized beauty panel. The panel itself highlights the car's width. The hardtop version of the 500XL Sunliner was the Club Victoria, $250 cheaper than the convertible and twice as popular, with 28,000 manufactured in '62.

Mirrorlight

The spotlight mirror was a factory option; on a clear night, the light could emit a beam ½ mile (800 meters) ahead.

Body Insulation

The Galaxie had an especially quiet ride because it was soundproofed at various points. Sound-absorbent mastic was applied to the inside surfaces of the doors, hood, trunk lid, fenders, and quarter panels.

Galaxie Performance

The Galaxies of '62 marked Ford boss Lee Iacocca's first sortie into the performance-obsessed youth market, which two years later would blossom into the legendary Mustang *(see pages 278–85)*. It was an inspired marketing gamble that took Ford products through the Sixties with huge success in both showrooms and on the racetrack.

GINE

ck Galaxies lumbered around with a 3cid six or 292cid V8. The 500XL ld choose from a range of underbird V8s that included the cid Special, as here, and a 405 bhp cid V8 with triple Holley carbs, ch could be ordered for $379.

Chassis

Chassis was made up of wide-contoured frame with double-channel side rails.

FORD *Thunderbird* (1962)

IT WAS NO ACCIDENT THAT THE third-generation T-Bird looked like it was fired from rocket silo. Designer Bill Boyer wanted the new prodigy to have "an aircraft and mis like shape," a subtext that wasn't lost on an American public vexed by the Cuban cris and Khrushchev's declaration of an increase in Soviet military spending. The Sports Roadster model was the finest incarnation of the '61–'63 Thunderbird. With Kelsey-Hayes wire wheels and a two-seater fiberglass tonneau, it was one of the most glamorous cars on the block and one of the most exclusive. Virile, vast, and expensi the Big Bird showed that Detroit still wasn't disposed to making smaller, cheaper car GM even impudently asserted that "a good used car is the only answer to America's need for cheap transportation." And anyway, building cars that looked and went like missiles was far more interesting and profitable.

PRETTY CONVERTIBLE

With the hood down, the Big Bird was one of the most attractive and stiffest convertibles Ford had ever made. The heavy unitary-construction body allowed precious few shakes, rattles, and rolls. *Motor Trend* magazine said: "Ford's plush style-setter has plenty of faults... but it's still the classic example of the prestige car."

TILT WHEEL

T-Bird drivers weren't that young, and a Swing-Away steering wheel aided access for the more corpulent driver.

WHEELS

Lesser T-Birds could opt for the Roadster's wire wheels at $343.

CHASSIS
Construction was "dual-unitized,"
with separate front and rear
sections welded together at the cowl.

ROOF FUN
With the top down, the streamlined tonneau made
the Sports Roadster sleek enough to echo the '55
two-seater Thunderbird *(see pages 262–65).*

(see pages 262–65).

SPECIFICATIONS

MODEL Ford Thunderbird Sports
Roadster (1962)
PRODUCTION 455 (1962)
BODY STYLE Two-door, two/four-seater
convertible.
CONSTRUCTION Steel body and chassis.
ENGINE 390cid V8.
POWER OUTPUT 330–340 bhp.
TRANSMISSION Three-speed
Cruise-O-Matic automatic.
SUSPENSION *Front:* upper and
lower A-arms and coil springs;
Rear: leaf springs with live axle.
BRAKES Front and rear drums.
MAXIMUM SPEED 116–125 mph
(187–201 km/h)
0–60 MPH (0–96 KM/H) 9.7–12.4 sec
A.F.C. 11–20 mpg (3.9–7.1 km/l)

DECORATION
Three sets of five cast-chrome
slash marks unmistakably
suggest total power.

BODY CREASE
Odd styling crease ran
from fender to door
and is the model's
least becoming feature.

OVERHANG
Rear overhang was
prodigious, but parking
could be mastered by using
the rear fin as a marker.

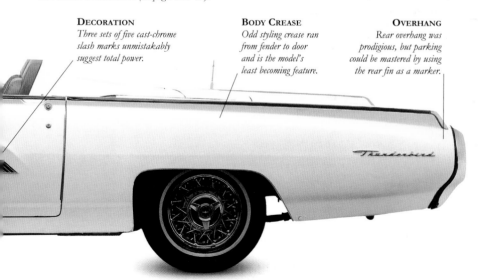

INTERIOR

Aircraft imagery in the controls
is obvious. The interior was
designed around a prominent
center console that split the
cabin into two separate
cockpits, delineating positions
of driver and passenger.

ADDED EXTRAS

*Tinted glass, power seats and
windows, and AM/FM radio
were the most popular options.*

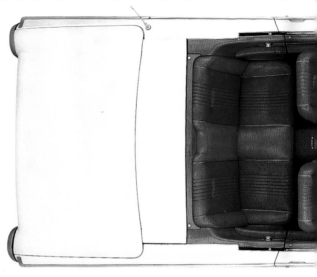

OVERHEAD VIEW

The Sports Roadster could a[l]
be a full four seater. Trouble
there was no space in the tru[nk]
for the tonneau, so it had to [stay]
at home. The large tonneau [panel]
came off easily but require[d]
two people to handle it.

FRONT ASPECT

The front bears an
uncanny resemblance [to]
the British Ford Corsa[ir,]
which is neither surpri[sing]
nor coincidental, since
the Corsair was also
made by Uncle Henry.
This third-generation
T-Bird was warmly
received and sold well.

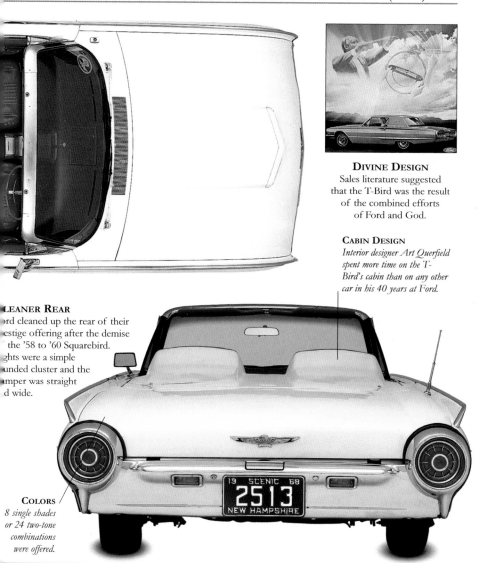

DIVINE DESIGN
Sales literature suggested
that the T-Bird was the result
of the combined efforts
of Ford and God.

CABIN DESIGN
Interior designer Art Querfield
spent more time on the T-
Bird's cabin than on any other
car in his 40 years at Ford.

CLEANER REAR
Ford cleaned up the rear of their
prestige offering after the demise
of the '58 to '60 Squarebird.
Lights were a simple
rounded cluster and the
bumper was straight
and wide.

COLORS
8 single shades
or 24 two-tone
combinations
were offered.

19 SCENIC 68
2513
NEW HAMPSHIRE

FORD *Mustang* *(1965)*

THIS ONE HIT THE GROUND RUNNING—galloping in fact, for the Mustang rewrote the sales record books soon after it burst onto the market in April, 1964. It really broke the mold, for it was from the Mustang that the term "pony car" was derived to describe a new breed of sporty "compacts." The concept of an inexpensive sports car for the masses is credited to dynamic young Ford vice president, Lee Iacocca. In realization, the Mustang was more than classless, almost universal in appeal. Its extensive options list meant there was a flavor to suit every taste. There was a Mustang for moms, sons, daughters, husbands, even young-at-heart grandparents. Celebrities who could afford a ranch full of thoroughbred racehorses and a garage full of Italian exotics were also proud to tool around in Mustangs. Why, this car's a democrat.

MASS APPEAL
The Mustang burst into the history books almost the moment it was unveiled to the public in Spring 1964. At one stroke it revived the freedom of spirit of the early sporting Thunderbirds and brought sports car motoring to the masses.

ANTENNA
Push-button radio and antenna were all part of the options list.

DOORS
Long doors helped entry and exit for rear passengers.

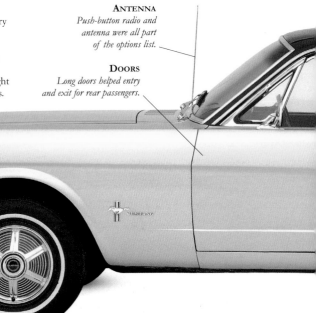

ENGINE

Mustangs were offered with the option of V8 (289cid pictured) or six-cylinder engines; eights outsold sixes two-to-one in 1964–68. Customers could thus buy the car with 100 bhp or have 400 bhp sports car performance.

SPECIFICATIONS

MODEL Ford Mustang (1964–68)

PRODUCTION 2,077,826

BODY STYLES Two-door, four-seat hardtop, fastback, convertible.

CONSTRUCTION Unitary chassis/body.

ENGINES Six-cylinder 170cid to 428cid V8. Featured car: 289cid V8.

POWER OUTPUT 195–250 bhp at 4000–4800 rpm or 271 bhp at 6000 rpm (289cid).

TRANSMISSION Three- or four-speed manual or three-speed automatic.

SUSPENSION Independent front by coil springs and wishbones; semi-elliptic leaf springs at rear.

BRAKES Drums; discs optional at front.

MAXIMUM SPEED 110–127 mph (177–204 km/h) (289cid)

0–60 MPH (0–96 KM/H) 6.1 sec (289cid)

0–100 MPH (0–161 KM/H) 19.7 sec

A.F.C. 13 mpg (4.6 km/l)

PILLARLESS COUPE
*Both front and rear side windows
wound completely out of sight.*

WHEEL OPTIONS
*Myriad options included smaller
wheels, wider tires, wire wheel covers,
and knockoff style hub embellishers.*

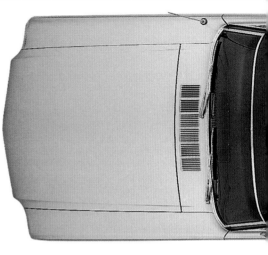

INTERIOR
The first Mustangs shared their
instrument layout with more mundane
Ford Falcons, but in a padded dash.
The plastic interior is a little tacky, but
at the price no one was going to
complain. The sports wheel was
a standard 1965 fixture.

WINDSHIELD
*Banded, tinted
windshield was
another option.*

PROTOTYPE ORIGINS
The Mustang I prototype
of 1962 was a V4 mid-
engined two seater—pret
but too exotic. The four-
seater Mustang II show c
debuted at the US Grand
Prix in 1963, and its
success paved the way for
the production Mustang,
which to this day is still t
fastest selling Ford ever.

BRAKES
*Front discs were
a new option
for 1965.*

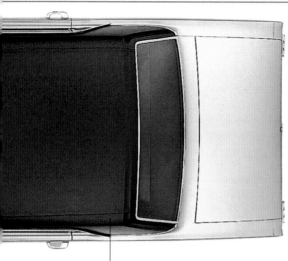

OVERHEAD VIEW

This bird's-eye view of the Mustang shows the sense of its proportions, with a box for the engine, the people, and their luggage. Interior space was maximized by doing away with Detroit's bulging, and often florid, outer panels. The Mustang's almost understated styling was a breath of fresh air.

V-SIGN

The 289 cubic inch, cast-iron V8 engine was a glamorous power unit, seeing service in the iconic AC Cobra, Sunbeam Tiger, and TVR Griffiths.

ROOF

Popular vinyl-covered roof option on the hardtop simulates the convertible.

ONSUMER CHOICE

e Mustang could be as eap or expensive as you ed. "The Mustang is signed to be designed by *u*" gushed an early sales ochure. From a $2,368 try price, you could eck the option boxes to rn your "personal" car o a hot rod costing ore than double that.

SUSPENSION

Harder suspension and handling kits could be ordered as an option.

FORD *Shelby Mustang GT500 (1967)*

LOOKING BACK FROM OUR ERA of environmental sensitivity, it's amazing to remember a time when you could buy this sort of stomach-churning horsepower straight from the showroom floor. What's more, if you couldn't afford to buy it, you could borrow it for the weekend from your local Hertz rent-a-car. The fact is that the American public loved the grunt, the image, and the Carroll Shelby Cobra connection. Ford's advertising slogan went straight to the point—Shelby Mustangs were "*The* Road Cars." With 289 and 428cid V8s, they were blisteringly quick and kings of both street and strip. By '67 they were civilized too, with options like factory air and power steering, as well as lots of gauges, a wood-rim Shelby wheel, and that all-important 225 km/h (140 mph) speedo. The little Pony Mustang had grown into a thundering stallion.

STEERING WHEEL
The wood-rim steering wheel came with the Shelby package.

THE SHELBY IN '67
'67 Shelbys had a larger hood scoop than previous models, plus a custom-built fiberglass front to complement the stock Mustang's new longer hood. Shelbys were a big hit in '67, with 1,175 350s and 2,048 500s sold. Prices were also about 15 percent cheaper than in '66.

500 NAME
GT500 name was arbitrary and did not refer to power.

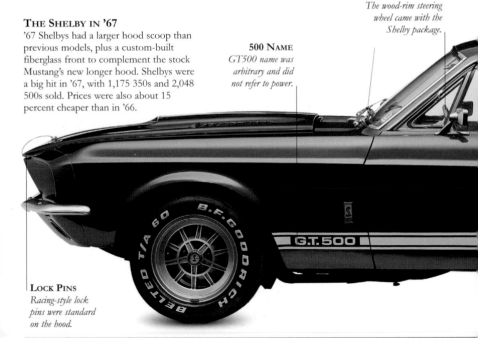

LOCK PINS
Racing-style lock pins were standard on the hood.

SHELBY PLATE

Shelby gave the early Mustangs his special treatment in a factory in Los Angeles. Later cars were built in Michigan. Shelby delivered the first batch to Hertz the day before a huge ice storm. The brakes proved too sharp and 20 cars were written off.

HERTZ FUN

There are tales of rented Shelbys being returned with bald tires and evidence of racing numbers on the doors.

COBRA REBIRTH

At the end of 67, cars were renamed Shelby Cobras, but Ford still handled all promotion and advertising.

SPECIFICATIONS

MODEL Ford Shelby Cobra Mustang GT500 (1967)

PRODUCTION 2,048 (1967)

BODY STYLE Two-door, four-seater coupe.

CONSTRUCTION Steel unitary body.

ENGINE 428cid V8.

POWER OUTPUT 360 bhp.

TRANSMISSION Four-speed manual, three-speed automatic.

SUSPENSION *Front:* coil springs; *Rear:* leaf springs.

BRAKES Front discs, rear drums.

MAXIMUM SPEED 132 mph (212 km/h)

0–60 MPH (0–96 KM/H) 6.8 sec

A.F.C. 13 mpg (4.6 km/l)

SIDE SCOOPS

Scoops acted as interior air extractors for the Shelby.

REAR DECK

Rear deck was made of fiberglass to save weight.

WHEEL OPTION

Wheels are optional Kelsey-Hayes Magstars.

PRACTICAL SEATING
All GT350s and 500s boasted the
standard and very practical Mustang
fold-down rear seat along with Shelby's
own padded roll bar. Shelbys
came in fastback only; there
were no hatchbacks,
and convertibles were
only available from '68.

SUSPENSION
*Shelby's springing
was similar to the
Mustang with front
sway bar, stiff springs,
and Gabriel shocks.*

FUEL CONSUMPTION
*Thirsty 428cid V8 meant
that only 13 mpg
(4.6 km/l) was possible.*

COBRA ORIGINS
*428cid V8 started
life in the original
AC Cobra.*

THE 500'S BLOCK
The GT500 came with the
428 Police Interceptor unit
with two Holley four-barrel
carbs. Oval, finned
aluminum open-element
air cleaner and cast-
aluminum valve covers
were unique to the
big-block Shelby.

CENTER LIGHTS
*The standard center-g
high-beam headlights
were forced to the side
some states because of
federal legislation.*

USA 716
APRIL GEORGIA STATE 1967
SHELBY

TACHOMETER
*The standard
tachometer red-lined
at 8000 rpm.*

INTERIOR
Stewart-Warner oil and amp gauges and a
tachometer were standard fittings. Two interior
colors were available – parchment and black.
Interior decor was brushed aluminum with
molded door panels and courtesy lights.

BRAKES
*The rear drum
brakes were assisted
at the front by more
efficient discs.*

POWER REFINEMENTS
The introduction of power-
assisted steering and brakes
on the '67 model meant
that the once rough-
riding Shelby had
transformed into a
luxury slingshot
that would soon
become an icon.

LIGHTS
*For the Shelby, the
Mustang's rear lights
were replaced with
the '65 T-Bird's
sequential lights.*

GORDON KEEBLE *GT*

IN 1960, THIS WAS THE MOST ELECTRIFYING CAR the British magazine *Autocar & Motor* had ever tested. Designed by Giugiaro in Italy and built in an aircraft hanger in Southampton, England, it boasted good looks, a fiberglass body, and a 5.4-liter, 300 bhp V8 Chevrolet Corvette engine. But, despite plenty of publicity, good looks, epic performance, and a glamorous clientele, the Gordon Keeble was a commercial disaster, with only 104 built. "The car built to aircraft standards," read the advertising copy. And time has proved the Keeble's integrity; a space-frame chassis, rustproof body, and that unburstable V8 has meant that over 90 Gordons have survived, with 60 still regularly used today. Born in an era where beauty mattered more than balance sheets, the Gordon Keeble failed for two reasons. First, the workers could not make enough of them, and second, the management forgot to put a profit margin in the price. How the auto industry has changed...

STYLE
For a '60s' design, the Gordon Keeble is crisp, clean, and timeless.

FEW 555D

SPACE FRAME
The prototype space-frame chassis was a skeleton of square tubes. It was flown to France, then overland to Turin, where Giugiaro supplied the glass-reinforced plastic body.

BARGAIN CLASSIC
Like most classic cars, the Gordon Keeble has fallen in price since the late-'80s. Good examples can be bought for $15,000, or half their 1988 value.

UMPERS
he Keeble's delicate three-piece
rome bumpers were
ecially handmade.

WINDOWS
Electric windows used the
same motors as the Rolls-
Royce Silver Shadow.

ENGINE
The small block
Sting Ray engine
delivered a massive
300 bhp of high-
compression power.

YOUNG DESIGNER

Only 21 when he designed the car,
Giugiaro gave the hood a dummy intake
scoop and fashionably raked twin
headlights. The roof was lengthened and
the slant of the C-pillar decreased to give
wider glass areas and maximum visibility.

HIGH-QUALITY BODY
In its day the Keeble's hand-
finished, glass-reinforced plastic
body was among the best.

SPECIFICATIONS

MODEL Gordon Keeble GT (1964–67)
PRODUCTION 104
BODY STYLE Four-seater fiberglass GT.
CONSTRUCTION Multitubular chassis
frame, grp body.
ENGINE 5.4-liter V8.
POWER OUTPUT 300 bhp at 5000 rpm.
TRANSMISSION Four-speed all-synchro.
SUSPENSION Independent front,
De Dion rear end.
BRAKES Four-wheel disc.
MAXIMUM SPEED 141 mph (227 km/h)
0–60 MPH (0–96 KM/H) 7.5 sec
0–100 MPH (0–161 KM/H) 13.3 sec
A.F.C. 14 mpg (5 km/l)

HOLDEN *FX*

AT THE END OF WORLD WAR II, Australia had a problem—an acute shortage of cars and a newly civilized army with money to burn. Loaded with government handouts, General Motors-Holden came up with a four-door, six-cylinder, six-seater that would become an Australian legend on wheels. Launched in 1948, the 48-215, more generally known as the FX, was Australia's Morris Minor *(see pages 378–81)*. Tubby, conventional, and as big as a Buick, it had a sweet, torquey engine, steel monocoque body, hydraulic brakes, and a three-speed column shift. Light and functional, the FX so impressed Lord Nuffield (of Morris fame) with its uncomplicated efficiency that he had one shipped to England for his engineers to pull apart. The Australians did not care about the FX's humble underpinnings and bought 120,000 with grateful enthusiasm.

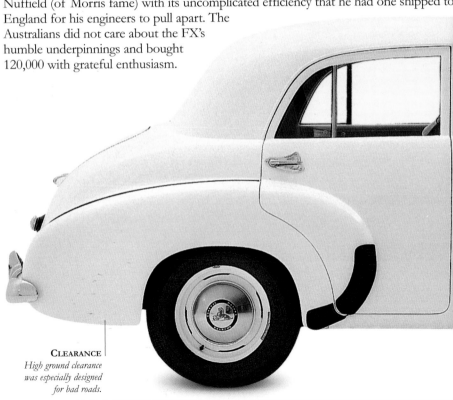

CLEARANCE
High ground clearance was especially designed for bad roads.

S INFLUENCE

ne "Humpy Holden" was a
armed-over prewar design
r a small Chevrolet sedan
at General Motors US had
eated in 1938. A Detroit-
delaide collaboration, the
X eventually emerged as a
in shape that would not
te. Australians still speak of
e FX in hallowed tones,
membering it as one of the
cade's most reliable cars.

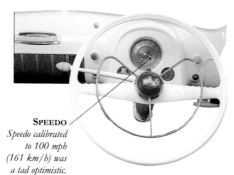

SPEEDO
*Speedo calibrated
to 100 mph
(161 km/h) was
a tad optimistic.*

DASHBOARD

The dash echoes the
Australian culture for
utilitarianism, with
center speedo, two
occasional gauges,
three-speed column
change, and only five
ancillary switches. The
umbrella handbrake and
chrome horn ring were
hangovers from Detroit
design influences.

BODY FLEX
*Taxi drivers complained of
body flexing – doors could
spring open on corners.*

BODY SHELL
*Body was dustproof,
which helped in the hot
Australian climate.*

ECONOMY
*Postwar fuel
shortages meant
that the Holden
was parsimonious.*

LIGHTS
Simple and unadorned, the FX had no indicators or sidelights, just a six-volt electrical system with a single taillight.

REAR FENDER STYLING
The Holden's rear fender line was cut into the rear doors but was much milder than Detroit's styling men would have liked. Rear fender spats were attached to make the car look lower and sleeker. Endlessly practical, the FX had a cavernous luggage compartment.

ENGINE
Power came from a sturdy 2170cc cast-iron straight-six, with an integral block and crankcase, push-rod overhead valves, and a single-barrel downdraught Stromberg carburetor.

FRONT ASPECT
Recumbent lion hood mascot lent the FX an illusion of pedigree. In reality, Holden had no bloodline at all, but that didn't matter since it went on to become the standard transportation of the Australian middle classes.

OUTPUT
The engine developed a modest 60 bhp.

SPECIFICATIONS

MODEL Holden 48-215 FX (1948–53)

PRODUCTION 120,402

BODY STYLE Six-seater, four-door family sedan.

CONSTRUCTION All-steel Aerobilt monocoque body.

ENGINE Six-cylinder cast-iron 2170cc.

POWER OUTPUT 60 bhp at 4500 rpm.

TRANSMISSION Three-speed manual.

SUSPENSION *Front:* coil and wishbone; *Rear:* leaf spring live axle.

BRAKES Four-wheel hydraulic drums.

MAXIMUM SPEED 73 mph (117 km/h)

0–60 MPH (0–96 KM/H) 27.7 sec

A.F.C. 30 mpg (11 km/l)

SUSPENSION
The Holden was too powerful for its suspension and many ended up on their roofs.

BROCHURES
General Motors-Holden started life as a saddlery and leather goods manufacturer, later diversifying into car body builders.

HUDSON *Super Six*

IN 1948, HUDSON'S FUTURE could not have looked brighter. The feisty independent was one of the first with an all-new postwar design. Under the guidance of Frank Spring, the new Hudson Super Six not only looked stunning, it bristled with innovation. The key was its revolutionary "step-down" design, based on a unitary construction, with the floor pan suspended from the bottom of the chassis frame. The Hudson was lower than its rivals, handled with ground-hugging confidence, and with its gutsy six-cylinder engine, outpaced virtually all competitors. In 1951, it evolved into the Hudson Hornet, dominating American stock car racing from 1951 to 1954. But the complex design could not adapt to the rampant demand for yearly revision; the 1953 car looked much like the 1948, and in 1954 Hudson merged with Nash, disappearing for good in 1957.

AERODYNAMIC PROFILE
It is the smooth beauty of the profile that really distinguishes the Hudson. The design team was led by Frank Spring, a longtime Hudson fixture, whose unusual blend of talents combined styling and engineering. His experience in airplane design is evident in the Hudson's aerodynamics.

HEIGHT
Only 60.4 in (1.53 m) high, the Super Six was lower than its contemporaries.

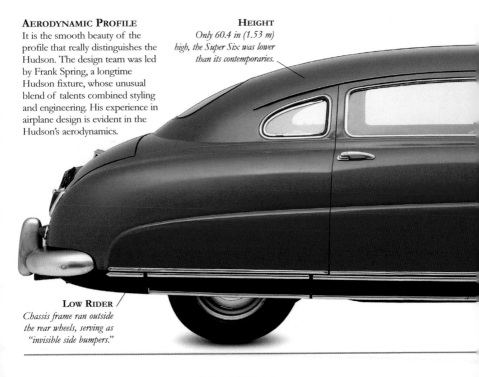

LOW RIDER
Chassis frame ran outside the rear wheels, serving as "invisible side bumpers."

SPECIFICATIONS

MODEL Hudson Super Six (1948–51)

PRODUCTION 180,499

BODY STYLES Four-door sedan, Brougham two-door sedan, Club coupe, hardtop coupe, two-door Brougham convertible.

CONSTRUCTION Unitary chassis/body.

ENGINE 262cid L-head straight six.

POWER OUTPUT 121 bhp at 4000 rpm.

TRANSMISSION Three-speed manual, optional overdrive; semiautomatic.

SUSPENSION *Front:* independent, wishbones, coil springs, telescopic shocks, antiroll bar; *Rear:* live-axle, semi-elliptic leaf springs, telescopic shocks, antiroll bar.

BRAKES Hydraulic drums all round.

MAXIMUM SPEED 90 mph (145 km/h)

0–60 MPH (0–96 KM/H) 14–18 sec (depending on transmission)

A.F.C. 12–18 mpg (4.2–6.4 km/l)

UNDER THE HOOD
The gutsy new 262cid six arrived in 1948 and made the Hudson one of the swiftest cars on America's roads.

SPLIT SCREEN
Each segment of the split screen was well curved for semiwraparound effect and good visibility.

POSTWAR PIONEER
Along with Studebaker, the 1948 Hudson was one of the very first all-new postwar designs.

SUSPENSION
Front suspension was by wishbones, coil springs, and telescopic shocks.

Hudson *Hornet*

Hudson did its best in '54 to clean up the aged 1948 body. Smoother flanks and a lower, wider frontal aspect helped, along with a new dash and brighter fabrics and vinyls. And at long last the windshield was one piece. Mechanically it wasn't bad either. In fact, some say the last Step-Down was the best ever. With the straight six came a Twin-H power option, a hot camshaft, and an alloy head that could crank out 170 bhp; it was promptly dubbed "The Fabulous Hornet." The problem was that everybody had V8s, and by mid-'54 Hudson had hemorrhaged over $6 million. In April of that year, Hudson, which had been around since 1909, was swallowed up by the Nash-Kelvinator Corporation. Yet the Hornet has been rightly recognized as a milestone car and one of the quickest sixes of the era. If Hudson is to be remembered for anything, it should be for its innovative engineers, who could wring the best from ancient designs and tiny budgets.

POWERFUL STEP-DOWNS

These Hudsons were known as Step-Downs because you literally stepped down into the car. Among the fastest cars of the Fifties, they boasted above-average power and crisp handling.

ENGINE

Amazingly, Hudson never offered V8 power, which was to hasten its downfall.

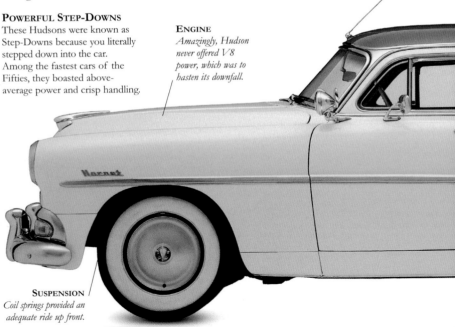

SUSPENSION

Coil springs provided an adequate ride up front.

SPECIFICATIONS

MODEL Hudson Hornet 7D (1954)

PRODUCTION 24,833 (1954 Hornets)

BODY STYLES Two-door coupe or convertible, four-door sedan.

CONSTRUCTION Steel body and chassis.

ENGINE 308cid straight six.

POWER OUTPUT 160–170 bhp.

TRANSMISSION Three-speed manual, optional Hydra-Matic automatic.

SUSPENSION *Front:* coil springs; *Rear:* leaf springs.

BRAKES Front and rear drums.

MAXIMUM SPEED 110 mph (177 km/h)

0–60 MPH (0–96 KM/H) 12 sec

A.F.C. 17 mpg (6 km/l)

RACING HORNETS

NASCAR devotees watched many a Hudson trounce the competition, winning 22 out of 37 major races in '53 alone. Advertising copy made much of Hudson's racing success, and the Hornet was "powered to outperform them all!"

FUEL CONSUMPTION

Despite their aerodynamic styling, Hornets drank a thirsty 17 mpg (6 km/l).

FENDERS

Full-depth fender skirts accentuated the low look.

JAGUAR *XK120*

A CAR-STARVED BRITAIN, still trundling around in perpendicular, prewar hangover cars, glimpsed the future in October of 1948 at the Earl's Court Motor Show in London. The star of the show was the Jaguar Super Sports. It was sensational to look at from any angle, with a purity of line that did not need chrome embellishment. It was also sensationally fast; in production as the Jaguar XK120 it would soon be proven that 120 really did stand for 120 mph (193 km/h), making it the fastest standard production car in the world. The only trouble was that you could not actually buy one. The XK120 was originally planned as a short production run, prestige showstopper, but overwhelming interest at the 1948 show changed all that. Hand-built alloy-bodied cars dribbled out of the Jaguar factory in 1949, and you needed a name like Clark Gable to get your hands on one. Tooling was ready in 1950, and production really took off. Today the XK120 is a platinum-plated investment.

FIXED-HEAD HEAVEN
Many rate the fixed-head coupe as the most gorgeous of all XK120s, with a roof line and teardrop window reminiscent of the beautiful Bugatti Type 57SC Atlantic. The fixed-head model did not appear until March 1951 and is much rarer than the roadster.

COCKPIT
The cockpit was a little cosy—if not downright cramped.

TIRES
Skinny cross-ply tires gave more thrills than needed on hard cornering.

SPECIFICATIONS

MODEL Jaguar XK120 (1949–54)

PRODUCTION 12,055

BODY STYLES Two-seater roadster, fixed-head coupe, and drophead coupe.

CONSTRUCTION Separate chassis, aluminum/steel bodywork.

ENGINE 3442cc twin overhead cam six-cylinder, twin SU carburetors.

POWER OUTPUT 160 bhp at 5100 rpm.

TRANSMISSION Four-speed manual, Moss gearbox with syncromesh on upper three ratios.

SUSPENSION *Front:* independent, wishbones and torsion bars; *Rear:* live rear axle, semi-elliptic.

BRAKES Hydraulically operated 12-in (30-cm) drums.

MAXIMUM SPEED 126 mph (203 km/h)

0–60 MPH (0–96 KM/H) 10 sec

0–100 MPH (0–161 KM/H) 35.3 sec

A.F.C. 17–22 mpg (6.1–7.8 km/l)

EXPORT WINNER
The XK120 was a great success as an export earner, with over 85 percent of all XK120s going to foreign climes.

WHEELS
Standard wheels were the same steel discs as on the Jaguar sedans.

829 JGU

ROADSTER REVIVAL

Even though numbers of roadsters
were trimmed further in the late
Eighties' scrabble to restore them, their
flowing curves and perfect proportions
are now more widely appreciated.

LIMITED VISION

*Fixed-head coupes had
limited rear vision, but
at least you stayed dry
in a British summer.*

MIDAS TOUCH

With the XK120, once again
Jaguar Boss William Lyons had
pulled off his favorite trick:
offering sensational value for
money compared with anything
else in its class. In fact, this time
there was nothing else in its class.

829 JGU

INTERI

Surrounded by leather and thick-
carpet, you feel good just sitting in
XK120—a lush interior, purpos
instruments, and the bark of the exha

SELLING THE DREAM
Beautiful enough as it was, the original sales brochure for the XK120 used airbrushed photographs of the very first car built— the 1948 Motor Show car.

ENGINE
The famed XK six-cylinder engine was designed by Bill Heynes and Wally Hassan, and went on to power the E-Type *(see pages 306–09)* and other Jaguars up until 1986. Even this was "styled"; William Lyons insisted that it have twin camshafts to make it resemble GP cars of the Thirties.

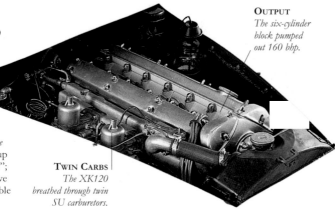

OUTPUT
The six-cylinder block pumped out 160 bhp.

TWIN CARBS
The XK120 breathed through twin SU carburetors.

JAGUAR *C-Type*

THE C-TYPE IS THE CAR that launched the Jaguar racing legend and began a Le Mans love affair for the men from Coventry. In the 1950s, Jaguar boss Bill Lyons was inter on winning Le Mans laurels for Britain, just as Bentley had done a quarter of a century before. After testing mildly modified XK120s in 1950, Jaguar came up with competition version, the XK120C (C-Type) for 1951. A C-Type won that year, failed in 1952, then won again in 1953. By then the C-Type's place in history was assured, for it had laid the cornerstone of the Jaguar sporting legend that blossomed through its successor, the D-Type, which bagged three Le Mans 24-hour wins in four years. C-Types were sold to private customers, most of whom used them for racing rather than road use. They were tractable road cars though, often driven to and from meetings; after their days as competitive racers were over, many were used as high-performance highway tourers.

PRODUCTION-CAR LINK
Jaguar's Bill Lyons dictated that the C-Type racer should bear a strong family resemblance to production Jaguars, and the Malcolm Sayer body, fitted to a special frame, achieved that aim.

FAST FUELING
Quick-release gas cap was another racing feature and could save valuable seconds in a race.

ACCESSIBILITY
It was easier to step over the door than open it; the passenger did not even get one.

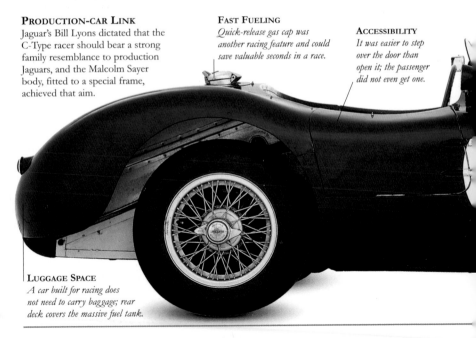

LUGGAGE SPACE
A car built for racing does not need to carry baggage; rear deck covers the massive fuel tank.

SPECIFICATIONS

MODEL Jaguar C-Type (1951–53)

PRODUCTION 53

BODY STYLE Two-door, two-seater sports racer.

CONSTRUCTION Tubular chassis, aluminum body.

ENGINE Jaguar XK120 3442cc, six-cylinder, double overhead camshaft with twin SU carburetors.

POWER OUTPUT 200–210 bhp at 5800 rpm.

TRANSMISSION Four-speed XK gearbox with close-ratio gears.

SUSPENSION Torsion-bars all around; wishbones at front, rigid axle at rear.

BRAKES Lockheed hydraulic drums; later cars used Dunlop discs all around.

MAXIMUM SPEED 144 mph (232 km/h)

0–60 MPH (0–96 KM/H) 8.1 sec

0–100 MPH (0–161 KM/H) 20.1 sec

A.F.C. 16 mpg (5.7 km/l)

NICE AMALGAM
The clever blend of beauty and function retained the pouncing-cat Jaguar "look," while creating an aerodynamically efficient tool for the high-speed Le Mans circuit.

BRAKES
The C-Type introduced disc brakes to road racing in 1952, though most examples used drums.

SUSPENSION
Telescopic shocks smoothed the ride.

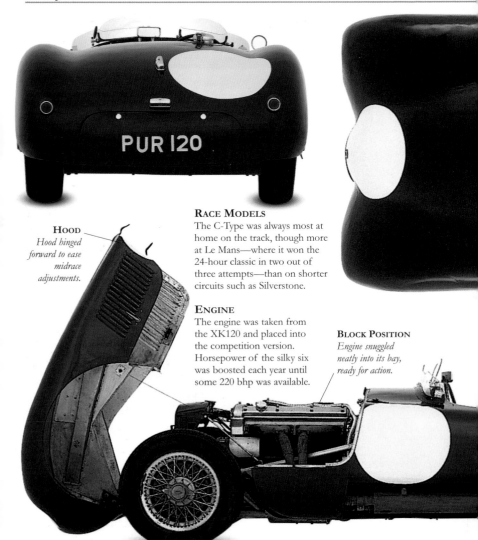

HOOD
Hood hinged forward to ease midrace adjustments.

RACE MODELS
The C-Type was always most at home on the track, though more at Le Mans—where it won the 24-hour classic in two out of three attempts—than on shorter circuits such as Silverstone.

ENGINE
The engine was taken from the XK120 and placed into the competition version. Horsepower of the silky six was boosted each year until some 220 bhp was available.

BLOCK POSITION
Engine snuggled neatly into its bay, ready for action.

AIRCRAFT INFLUENCE
Designer Malcolm Sayer's aircraft industry background shows through in the smooth aerodynamic styling. Louvers on the hood help hot air escape; the engine cover is secured by quick-release handles and leather safety straps.

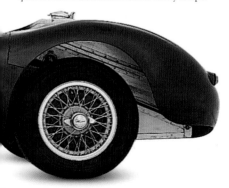

INTERIOR
The cockpit was designed for business, not comfort, but was roomy enough for two adults; passengers were provided with a grab handle in case the driver thought he was at Le Mans. In racing trim, cars ran with a single airshield; this car has an additional full-width windshield.

JAGUAR *XK150*

THE XK150 APPEARED IN the Spring of 1957 and was the most refined of the XK trio. One of the last Jaguars to have a separate chassis, the 150 marked the beginning of the civilization of the Jaguar sports car. With its wider girth and creature comforts, it was to hold the market's interest until the then-secret E-Type project *(see pages 306–09)* was ready for unveiling in 1961. In the late 1950s, the XK150 was a seriously glamorous machine, almost as sleek as an Aston Martin, but cheaper. March 1958 saw more power with the "S" performance package, which brought the 3.4 up to 250 bhp; and in 1959 the 3.8's output soared to 265 bhp. Available as a roadster, drophead, or fixed-head coupe, the 150 sold a creditable 9,400 examples in its four-year run. Despite being eclipsed by the E-Type, the 150 was charismatic enough to be the personal transport for racing ace Mike Hawthorn and startlet Anita Ekberg.

SEDAN REAR
From the rear, the fixed-head has definite sedan lines, with its curved rear window, big wraparound bumper, wide track, and cavernous trunk.

REDUCED PRICE
XK150s have fallen in price and can now be bought for the same price as an Austin Healey 3000 *(see pages 52–55)*, a Daimler Dart *(see pages 190–93)*, or a Sunbeam Tiger *(see pages 438–39)*.

RARE COUPE
*The rarest model is the
XK150S drophead coupe,
with a mere 193 cars built.*

CLASSIC STRAIGHT-SIX
*The classic, twin overhead-cam
design first saw the light of
day in 1949, and was phased
out as recently as 1986.*

PURE CAT PROFILE
The gorgeous curved body sits on a
conventional chassis. Joints and curves
were smoothed off at the factory
using lead. The 1950s' auto industry
paid little thought to rustproofing,
so all Jaguars of the period are
shameful rust-raisers.

SPECIFICATIONS

MODEL Jaguar XK150 FHC (1957–61)

PRODUCTION 9,400

BODY STYLES Two-seater roadster,
drophead, or fixed-head coupe.

CONSTRUCTION Separate pressed-steel
chassis frame with box section
side members.

ENGINES Straight-six, twin overhead-cam
3442cc or 3781cc.

POWER OUTPUT 190 bhp at 5500 rpm
(3.4); 210 bhp at 5500 rpm (3.8);
265 bhp at 5500 rpm (3.8S).

TRANSMISSION Four-speed manual, with
optional overdrive, or three-speed Borg
Warner Model 8 automatic.

SUSPENSION Independent front, rear leaf
springs with live rear axle.

BRAKES Dunlop front and rear discs.

MAXIMUM SPEED 135 mph (217 km/h)

0–60 MPH (0–96 KM/H) 7.6 sec (3.8S)

0–100 MPH (0–161 KM/H) 18 sec

A.F.C. 18 mpg (6.4 km/l)

JAGUAR *E-Type*

WHEN JAGUAR BOSS WILLIAM LYONS, by now Sir William, unveiled the E-Type Jaguar at the Geneva Motor Show in March 1961, its ecstatic reception rekindled memories of the 1948 British launch of the XK120 *(see pages 296–99)*. The E-Type, or XKE as it is known in America, created a sensation. British car magazines had produced road tests of pre-production models to coincide with the launch—and yes, the fixed-head coupe really could do 150.4 mph (242 km/h). OK, so the road-test cars were perhaps fine-tuned a little, and early owners found 145 mph (233 km/h) a more realistic maximum, but the legend was born. It was not just a stunning, svelte sports car though; it was a trademark Jaguar sporting package, once again marrying sensational performance with superb value for money. Astons and Ferraris, for example, were more than double the price.

BEST-OF-BREED
The impact the shape made at its launch on March 15, 1961 at the Geneva Motor Show, is now the stuff of Jaguar lore. Those first E-Type roadsters and fixed-head coupes, produced until June 1962, are now referred to as "flat-floor" models, and they are the most prized of all. In fact, their flat floor was something of a flaw, and recessed foot wells were later incorporated to increase comfort for taller drivers.

HANDLING
Jaguar designed an all-new independent setup at the rear. Handling in the wet and at top speed is often criticized, but for its day the E-Type was immensely capable.

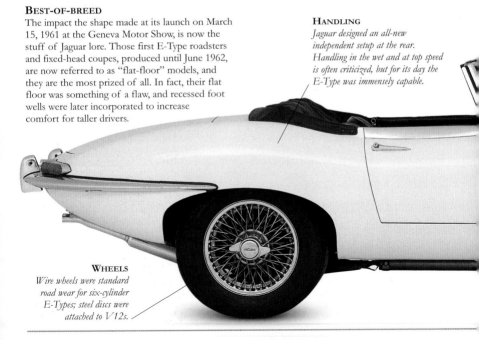

WHEELS
Wire wheels were standard road wear for six-cylinder E-Types; steel discs were attached to V12s.

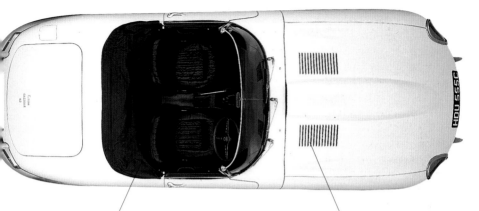

SEATS
*Thin-backed bucket seats
of the 3.8s were criticized.
In the 4.2, as here, they
were greatly improved.*

SIMPLICITY OF LINE
Designer Malcolm Sayer insisted he
was an aerodynamicist and hated to
be called a stylist. He claimed the
E-Type was the first production car
to be "mathematically" designed.

VENTS
*Louvers are not for looks;
E-Types, particularly
early ones, tended to
overheat in hot climates.*

LENS COVERS
*The stylish but
inefficient lens covers
were removed in 1967.*

BRAKES
*All-around disc brakes as
standard were part of the
spec from first E-Types.*

TOP
*Top was neatly tucked
away beneath a fitted
tonneau cover.*

BUMPERS
*Chromed slimline
bumpers were
beautiful but offered
no protection.*

HDU 555C

SPECIFICATIONS

MODEL E-Type Jaguar (1961–74)

PRODUCTION 72,520

BODY STYLES Two-seater roadster and fixed coupe, 2+2 fixed-head coupe.

CONSTRUCTION Steel monocoque.

ENGINES 3781cc straight-six; 4235cc straight-six; 5343cc V12.

POWER OUTPUT 265 to 272 bhp.

TRANSMISSION Four-speed manual, optional automatic from 1966.

SUSPENSION *Front:* independent, wishbones and torsion bar;
Rear: independent, coil and radius arm.

BRAKES Discs all around.

MAXIMUM SPEED 150 mph (241 km/h) (3.8 & 4.2); 143 mph (230 km/h) (5.3)

0–60 MPH (0–96 KM/H) 7–7.2 sec

0–100 MPH (0–161 KM/H) 16.2 sec (3.8)

A.F.C. 16–20 mpg (5.7–7 km/l)

TELL TAIL
The thin bumpers with lights above are an easy giveaway for E-Type spotters. From 1968, with the introduction of the Series 2, bulkier lamp clusters appeared below the bumpers. A detachable hardtop was available as an option.

US MARKET
The E-Type's amazing export success is summed up by the fact that of every three built, two were exported. Fixed-head coupes actually accounted for a little over half of all E-Type production, yet the roadster was the major export winner, with most going to the US. Ironically, though, it was American emission regulations that were increasingly strangling the Cat's performance.

WIPERS
Unusual and sporty-looking triple wipers gave way to a two-blade system with the 1971 V12.

INTERIOR
The interior of this Series 1 4.2 is the epitome of sporting luxury, with leather seats, wood-rim wheel, and an array of instruments and toggle switches—later replaced by less sporting rocker and less injurious rocker switches. The 3.8s had an aluminum-finished center console panel and transmission tunnel.

CLASSY HOOD
This view of the E-Type's bulging, sculptured hood is still the best of any car.

HDU 555C

Jensen *Interceptor*

The Jensen Interceptor was one of those great cars that comes along every decade or so. Built in a small Birmingham, England, factory, a triumph of tenacity over resources, the Interceptor's lantern-jawed looks and tire-smoking power made the tiny Jensen company a household name. A glamorous cocktail of an Italian-styled body, American V8 engine, and genteel British craftsmanship, it became the car for successful Britons of the late 1960s and 1970s. The Interceptor was handsome, fashionable, and formidably fast, but its tragic flaw was a big appetite for fuel—10 mpg (3.5 km/l) if you enjoyed yourself. After driving straight into two oil crises and a worldwide recession, as well as suffering serious losses from the ill-fated Jensen-Healey project, Jensen filed for bankruptcy in 1975 and finally closed its doors in May 1976.

Timeless Styling
The Interceptor's futuristic shape hardly changed over its 10-year life span and was widely acknowledged to be one of the most innovative designs of its decade. The classic shape was crafted by Italian styling house Vignale. From bare designs to running prototype took just three months.

Window
Rear window lifted up to reveal a large luggage compartment.

Bodywork
Bodies were all-steel, with little attention paid to corrosion proofing. Early cars were tragic rust-raisers.

BEAUTIFUL INTERIOR

Road testers complained that the Interceptor's
dash was like the flight deck of a small aircraft,
but the interior was beautifully handmade with
the finest hides and plush Wilton carpets.

SPECIFIC

MODEL Jensen Interceptor (1
PRODUCTION 1,500
BODY STYLE All-steel occasional four-seater coupe.
CONSTRUCTION Separate tubular and platform type pressed steel frame.
ENGINE 6276cc V8.
POWER OUTPUT 325 bhp at 4600 rpm.
TRANSMISSION Three-speed Chrysler TorqueFlite automatic.
SUSPENSION Independent front with live rear axle.
BRAKES Four-wheel Girling discs.
MAXIMUM SPEED 135 mph (217 km/h)
0–60 MPH (0–96 KM/H) 7.3 sec
0–100 MPH (0–161 KM/H) 19 sec
A.F.C. 13.6 mpg (4.9 km/l)

SIMPLE MECHANICS
*With one huge carburetor and
only a single camshaft, the
Interceptor had a simple soul.*

ENGINE
*The lazy Chrysler V8 of
6.2 liters gave drag-strip
acceleration and endless reliability.*

TIRES
*Dunlop SPs
replaced skinny
pre-'68 RS5s.*

rrin

ORLD has been awaiting" was a monster flop. Designed by
n, Kaiser's odd hybrid came about in 1953 as an accident.
nannered chairman of the Kaiser Corporation, had so riled
red into his California studio, spent his own money, and
wo-seater that looked like it wanted to give you a kiss. Its
futuristic fiberglass body rode on a Henry J. chassis and was powered by a Willys six-
pot mill. Alas, the body rippled and cracked, the sliding doors wouldn't slide, and the
weedy 90 bhp flathead was no match for Chevy's Corvette. At a costly $3,668, the
Darrin was in Cadillac territory, and only 435 found buyers. Late in '54, Kaiser-
Willys went under, taking the Darrin with them. Few mourned either's demise.

A TRUE CLASSIC
The Darrin was beautifully
styled and, unlike most visions
of the future, has hardly dated
at all. The Landau top could
be removed and a hardtop
attached, and, with its three-
speed floor shift and
overdrive, it could return
up to 27 mpg (9.6 km/l).

BODY SHELL
*Darrin bodies were made by
boat-builders Glasspar.*

FENDER SHAPE
*Rear fender tapers upward
to create a fine torpedo-
like shape.*

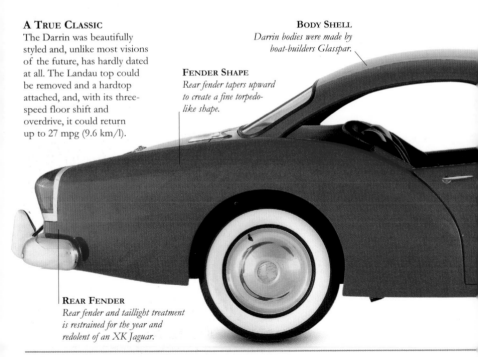

REAR FENDER
*Rear fender and taillight treatment
is restrained for the year and
redolent of an XK Jaguar.*

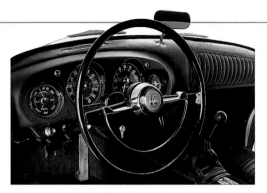

INTERIOR

Standard equipment included electric wipers, tachometer, and a European-style dashboard, with leather trim an optional extra. Whitewall tires and a one-piece windshield were also standard.

SPECIFICATIONS

MODEL Kaiser Darrin 161 (1954)

PRODUCTION 435 (total)

BODY STYLE Two-seater sports.

CONSTRUCTION Fiberglass body, steel frame.

ENGINE 161cid six.

POWER OUTPUT 90 bhp.

TRANSMISSION Three-speed manual with optional overdrive.

SUSPENSION *Front:* coil springs; *Rear:* leaf springs.

BRAKES Front and rear drums.

MAXIMUM SPEED 100 mph (161 km/h)

0–60 MPH (0–96 KM/H) 15.1 sec

A.F.C. 27 mpg (9.6 km/l)

SLIDING DOORS
Howard Darrin first conceived his contentious sliding doors back in 1922. The trouble was that they rattled, jammed, and didn't open all the way.

LIMITED SIX
The six-cylinder unit produced a top speed of only 100 mph (161 km/h).

SLEEK SELL
Ads called it "the outstanding pleasure car of our day."

LATE DELIVERIES
The Darrin took its time coming. It was first announced on September 26, 1952, with 60 initial prototypes eventually displayed to the public on February 11, 1953. Final production cars reached owners as late as January 6, 1954.

RISING ARCH
Undeniably pretty, the fender line slopes down through the door and meets a dramatic kick-up over the rear wheel arch.

CABIN SPACE
Hardtop made the cabin much less claustrophobic and cramped than that of the soft-top model.

SIDE WINDOWS
Swiveling Plexiglas side windows reduced cockpit buffeting.

BELT UP
The Darrin was remarkabl for being only the third US production car to feature seat belts as standard. The other two cars were a Muntz and a Nash.

HEADLIGHTS
The prototype headl height was too low f state lighting laws, s Kaiser stylists hikee up the front fender for the real thing.

CHASSIS
Stock Henry J. chassis and engine didn't do much for the Darrin's bloodline.

ENGINE
Kaiser opted for an F-head Willys version of the Henry J. six-pot motor; but with just one carb, it boasted only 10 more horses than standard. After the company folded, Darrin dropped 300 bhp supercharged Caddy V8s into the remaining cars, which went like the wind.

VW-STYLE
Front aspect looks very much like an early VW Karmann Ghia.

PRICING
The 90 bhp Darrin cost $145 more than the 150 bhp Chevy Corvette.

⌐ UNHAPPY ALLIANCE
nry J. Kaiser was livid that
oward Darrin had worked on the
⌐ without his permission. In the
d, the Darrin was actually
⌐ed by Henry J.'s wife,
⌐o reckoned it was
⌐e most beautiful
⌐ng" she'd ever seen.

BRIT REAR
*Rear aspect is
⌐risingly British-
looking for a
⌐alifornia design.*

KAISER *Henry J. Corsair*

IN THE EARLY 1950s, the major car manufacturers reckoned that small cars meant small profits, so low-priced transportation was left to independent companies like Nash, Willys, and Kaiser-Frazer. In 1951, a streamlined, Frazer-less Kaiser launched "America's Most Important New Car," the Henry J. An 80 bhp six-cylinder "Supersonic" engine gave the Corsair frugal fuel consumption, with Kaiser claiming that every third mile in a Henry J. was free. The market, however, was unconvinced. At $1,561, the Corsair cost more than the cheapest big Chevy, wasn't built as well, and depreciated rapidly. No wonder then that only 107,000 were made. Had America's first serious economy car been launched seven years later during the '58 recession, the Henry J. may well have been a best-seller.

SMALLER MODEL
The stubborn head of Kaiser industries insisted that the Henry J., originally designed as a full-size car by designer Howard "Dutch" Darrin, be scaled down.

FENDERS
Bolt-on front and rear fenders were part of the Henry J.'s money-saving philosophy.

WHEELBASE
The 100 in (2.54 m) wheelbase was short, but the interior space generous.

DASH CONTROLS
*The few controls
included starter,
ignition, light, and
choke switches.*

INSIDE THE CORSAIR
The interior was seriously austere. Apart
from overdrive and auto transmission,
very few options were available.

ROOF LINE
*High roof line owed its
existence to the fact
that Kaiser's chairman
always wore a hat.*

SPECIFICATIONS

MODEL Kaiser Henry J. Corsair Deluxe
(1952)

PRODUCTION 12,900 (1952)

BODY STYLE Two-door, five-seater sedan.

CONSTRUCTION Steel body and chassis.

ENGINES 134cid four, 161cid six.

POWER OUTPUT 68–80 bhp.

TRANSMISSION Three-speed manual with
optional overdrive, optional three-speed
Hydra-Matic automatic.

SUSPENSION *Front:* coil springs;
Rear: leaf springs with live axle.

BRAKES Front and rear drums.

MAXIMUM SPEED 87 mph
(140 km/h)

0–60 MPH (0–96 KM/H) 17 sec

A.F.C. 34 mpg (12 km/l)

COLORS
*Blue Satin was one of
nine colors available.*

TRUNK SPACE
*With the rear seat folded down,
the luggage space was among the
largest of any passenger sedan.*

LAMBORGHINI *Miura*

THE LAUNCH OF THE LAMBORGHINI MIURA at the 1966 Geneva Motor Show was the decade's automotive sensation. Staggeringly beautiful, technically preeminent, and unbelievably quick, it was created by a triumvirate of engineering wizards all in their twenties. For the greater part of its production life the Miura was reckoned to be the most desirable car money could buy, combining drop-dead looks, awesome performance, and unerring stability, as well as an emotive top speed of 175 mph (282 km/h). From its dramatic swooping lines—even Lamborghini thought it was too futuristic to sell—to its outrageously exotic colors, the Miura perfectly mirrored the middle Sixties. But, as the oil crises of the Seventies took hold, the Miura slipped into obscurity, replaced in 1973 by the not so lovely, and some say inferior, Countach *(see pages 322–25)*.

GT40 LINKS

In looks and layout the mid-engined Lambo owes much to the Ford GT40 *(see pages 258–61)* but was engineered by Gianpaolo Dallara. At the core of the Miura is a steel platform chassis frame with outriggers front and rear to support the major mechanicals. The end-of-the-line SV was the most refined Miura, with more power, a stiffer chassis, and redesigned suspension.

INSULATION

In an attempt to silence a violently loud engine, Lamborghini put 4 in (10 cm) of polystyrene insulation between engine and cabin.

REAR FENDER

The rear fender profile was different on the SV than on earlier models.

LIGHTS
Standard Miura dlights were shared by the Fiat 850.

HEIGHT
The Miura only came up to waist height—just 42 in (107 cm).

INTERIOR
Standard interior trim was unimpressive oatmeal vinyl.

ENDURING STYLE
Long, low, and delicate, the Miura is still considered one of the most handsome automotive sculptures ever. The car was so low that headlights had to be "pop-up" to raise them high enough for adequate vision.

RARE SV
Only 150 SVs were built. Very few had a "split sump" that had separate oil for the engine and gearbox.

ACCELERATION
Acceleration still compares well with modern supercars.

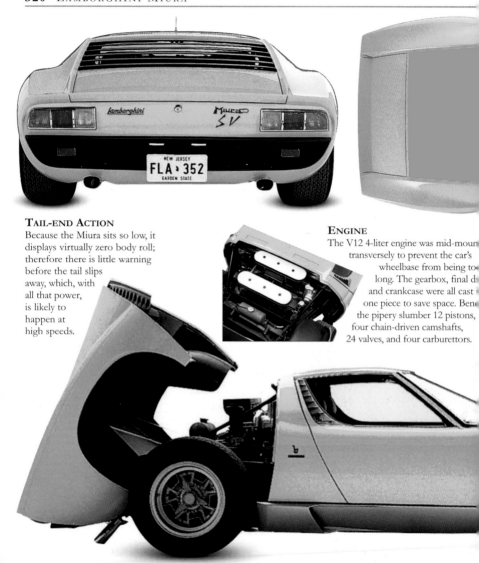

TAIL-END ACTION

Because the Miura sits so low, it displays virtually zero body roll; therefore there is little warning before the tail slips away, which, with all that power, is likely to happen at high speeds.

ENGINE

The V12 4-liter engine was mid-moun transversely to prevent the car's wheelbase from being to long. The gearbox, final d and crankcase were all cast one piece to save space. Ben the pipery slumber 12 pistons, four chain-driven camshafts, 24 valves, and four carburettors.

SPECIFICATIONS

MODEL Lamborghini Miura (1966–72)

PRODUCTION Approx 800

BODY STYLE Two-seater roadster.

CONSTRUCTION Steel platform chassis, light alloy and steel bodywork.

ENGINE Transverse V12 4.0 liter.

POWER OUTPUT P400, 350 bhp at 7000 rpm; P400S, 370 bhp at 7700 rpm; P400SV, 385 bhp at 7850 rpm.

TRANSMISSION Five-speed with trans axle.

SUSPENSION Independent front and rear.

BRAKES Four-wheel ventilated disc.

MAXIMUM SPEED 175 mph (282 km/h) (P400SV)

0–60 MPH (0–96 KM/H) 6.7 sec

0–100 MPH (0–161 KM/H) 15.1 sec

A.F.C. 16 mpg (5.7 km/l)

LIGHT POWERHOUSE
The Miura has a very impressive power-to-weight ratio—it's able to produce 385 bhp, yet it weighs only 2,646 lb (1,200 kg).

FRONT LIFT
Treacherous aerodynamics meant that approaching speeds of 170 mph (274 km/h) both of the Miura's front wheels could actually lift off the ground.

FILLER CAP
The gas filler hid under the hood slat.

GEARBOX
The gearbox was a disappointment, with a trucklike, sticky action that did not do the Miura's gorgeous engine any justice.

INTERIOR
The cockpit is basic but finely detailed, with a huge Jaeger speedo and tacho. Six minor gauges on the left of the console tell the mechanical story. The alloy gear-lever gate is a handmade work of art.

LAMBORGHINI *Countach 5000S*

THE COUNTACH WAS FIRST UNVEILED at the 1971 Geneva Motor Show as the Miura's replacement, engineered by Giampaolo Dallara and breathtakingly styled by Marcello Gandini of Bertone fame. For a complicated, hand-built car, the Countach delivered all the reliable high performance that its swooping looks promised. In 1982, a 4.75-liter 375 bhp V12 was shoe-horned in to give the upcoming Ferrari Testarossa *(see pages 244–47)* something to reckon with. There is no mid-engined car like the Countach. The engine sits longitudinally in a multitubular space frame, with fuel and water carried by twin side-mounted tanks and radiators. On the downside, visibility is appalling, steering is heavy, gear selection recalcitrant, and the cockpit is cramped. Yet such faults can only be considered as charming idiosyncrasies when set against the Countach's staggering performance—a howling 187 mph (301 km/h) top speed and a 0–60 (96 km/h) belt of 5 seconds.

SOUND EFFECTS
Inches away, all occupants were able to hear exactly what this engine had to say.

BREAKING THE RULES
The shape is a riot of creative genius that ignores all established rules of car design. Air scoops under the body's side windows break up the wedge-shaped line and form a ready-made indent for a compact door catch.

AIR SCOOPS
Air scoops provided ideal hand-holds for the huge scissor doors.

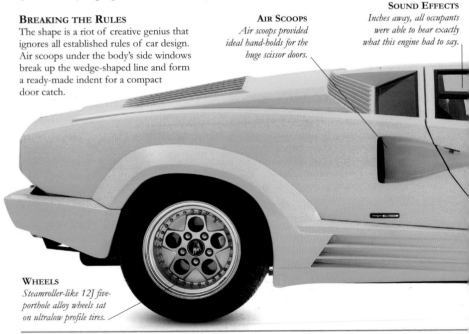

WHEELS
Steamroller-like 12J five-porthole alloy wheels sat on ultralow profile tires.

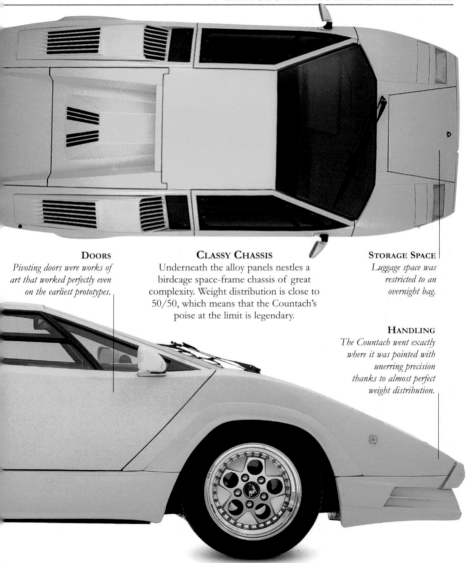

DOORS
Pivoting doors were works of art that worked perfectly even on the earliest prototypes.

CLASSY CHASSIS
Underneath the alloy panels nestles a birdcage space-frame chassis of great complexity. Weight distribution is close to 50/50, which means that the Countach's poise at the limit is legendary.

STORAGE SPACE
Luggage space was restricted to an overnight bag.

HANDLING
The Countach went exactly where it was pointed with unerring precision thanks to almost perfect weight distribution.

INTERIOR
The cabin was crude, with unsubtle interior architecture. Switches and wands were Fiat- and Lancia-sourced. Scant body protection means that most Countach acquire a tapestry of scars.

SUSPENSION
Independent front and rear suspension had double wishbones and coil springs.

CELEBRATIONS
The 25-year anniversary of Lamborghini production in 1985 was celebrated with the 5000S and the elite Quattrovalvole 5000S.

SPECIFICATIONS

MODEL Lamborghini Countach (1973–90)

PRODUCTION Approx 1,000

BODY STYLE Mid-engined, two-seater sports coupe.

CONSTRUCTION Alloy body, space-frame chassis.

ENGINE 4754cc four-cam V12.

POWER OUTPUT 375 bhp at 7000 rpm.

TRANSMISSION Five-speed manual.

SUSPENSION Independent front and rear with double wishbones and coil springs.

BRAKES Four-wheel vented discs.

MAXIMUM SPEED 187 mph (301 km/h)

0–60 MPH (0–96 KM/H) 5.1 sec

0–100 MPH (0–161 KM/H) 13.3 sec

A.F.C. 9 mpg (3.2 km/l)

GRAND AUTO
Everything on the Countach
is built on a grand scale.
Four exhausts, four
camshafts, 12
cylinders, half a
dozen 45DCOE
Webers, and the
widest track
of any car on
the road.

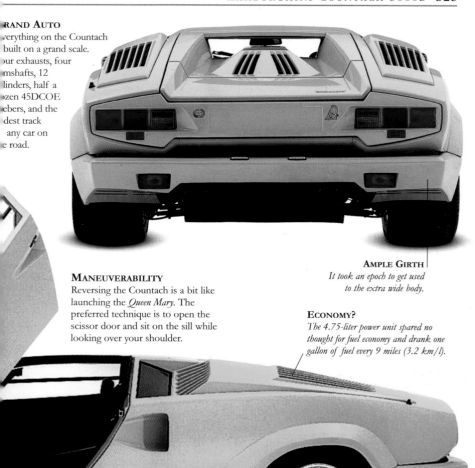

AMPLE GIRTH
*It took an epoch to get used
to the extra wide body.*

MANEUVERABILITY
Reversing the Countach is a bit like
launching the *Queen Mary*. The
preferred technique is to open the
scissor door and sit on the sill while
looking over your shoulder.

ECONOMY?
*The 4.75-liter power unit spared no
thought for fuel economy and drank one
gallon of fuel every 9 miles (3.2 km/l).*

LANCIA *Aurelia B24 Spider*

BEAUTY IS MORE THAN JUST skin deep on this lovely little Lancia, for underneath those lean Pininfarina loins the Aurelia's innards bristle with innovative engineering. For a start there is the compact alloy V6. Designed under Vittorio Jano, the man responsible for the great racing Alfas of the Twenties and Thirties, this free-revving, torquey little lump was the first mass-produced V6. The revolution was not just at the front though, for at the back were the clutch and gearbox, housed in the transaxle to endow the Aurelia with near-perfect weight distribution. These innovations were first mated with the Pininfarina body in 1951, producing the Aurelia B20 GT coupe, often credited as the first of the new breed of modern postwar GTs. And the point of it all becomes clear when you climb behind the wheel, for although the Aurelia was never the most accelerative machine, its handling was so impeccable that 40 years on it still impresses with its masterly cornering poise.

FAMILY RESEMBLANCE
The Spider bears a passing family resemblance to the Aurelia sedan, and even more so to the GT models. Neither of the closed versions had the wrap-around windshield though, or the equally distinctive half-bumpers; the Spider's radiator grille was a slightly different shape, too.

LUGGAGE ROOM
The Aurelia Spider scored well in luggage-carrying capabilities compared with other two-seaters of the time.

DESIGNATIONS
The Spider and convertible were designated B24 Aurelias; B10, 15, 21, and 22 were four-door sedans, and B20 the GT coupe.

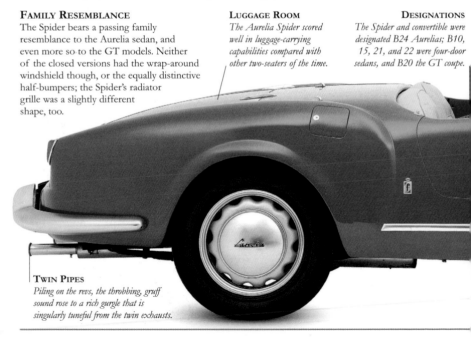

TWIN PIPES
Piling on the revs, the throbbing, gruff sound rose to a rich gurgle that is singularly tuneful from the twin exhausts.

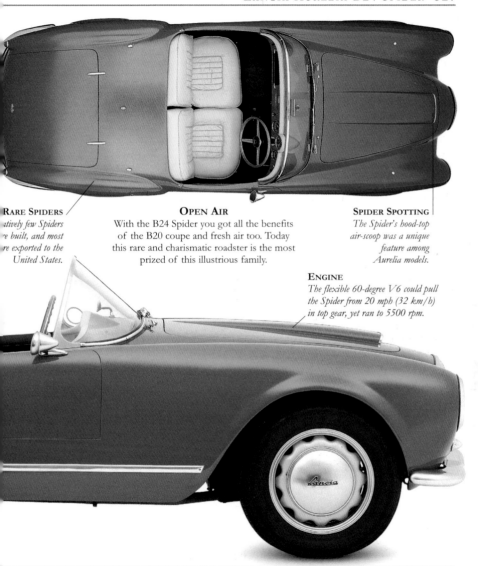

RARE SPIDERS

...atively few Spiders ...e built, and most ...re exported to the United States.

OPEN AIR

With the B24 Spider you got all the benefits of the B20 coupe and fresh air too. Today this rare and charismatic roadster is the most prized of this illustrious family.

SPIDER SPOTTING

The Spider's hood-top air-scoop was a unique feature among Aurelia models.

ENGINE

The flexible 60-degree V6 could pull the Spider from 20 mph (32 km/h) in top gear, yet ran to 5500 rpm.

INTERIOR
The panel has just three major dials and a group of
switches on a painted metal dash. It was devoid of the
walnut-leather trimmings which British carmakers of
the time considered essential for a luxury sports car.
The elegant, adjustable Nardi steering wheel was
standard equipment on the Spider.

ENGINE
Aurelias featured the world's first
mass-production V6, an all-alloy unit
which progressively grew from 1754cc
to 1991cc, to the 2451cc used
in the B24 Spider.

BALANCE
*For perfect balance, the weight
of the engine was offset by
locating clutch and gearbox in a
unit with differential at the rear.*

SWEEPING FENDERS

The curvaceous Pininfarina shape is characterized by the sweeping front fenders and long luggage compartment. The Spider's high-silled monocoque construction meant that the doors were small. Protection from the elements was fairly basic; the B24 had a simple hood with plastic side windows.

FLAG BADGES

These represent the joint input of Lancia, designers and manufacturers of the mechanical parts, and Pininfarina, who styled the body and built the cars.

SPECIFICATIONS

MODEL Lancia Aurelia B24 Spider (1954–56)

PRODUCTION 330

BODY STYLE Two-seater sports convertible.

CONSTRUCTION Monocoque with pressed steel and box-section chassis frame.

ENGINE Twin-overhead-valve aluminum alloy V6, 2451cc.

POWER OUTPUT 118 bhp at 5000 rpm.

TRANSMISSION Four-speed manual.

SUSPENSION Sliding pillar with beam axle and coil springs at front, De Dion rear axle on leaf springs.

BRAKES Hydraulic, finned alloy drums, inboard at rear.

MAXIMUM SPEED 112 mph (180 km/h)

0–60 MPH (0–96 KM/H) 14.3 sec

A.F.C. 22 mpg (7.8 km/l)

RACE PEDIGREE

The B20 GT coupes, from which the B24 Spider was derived, achieved a second overall on the Mille Miglia and a Le Mans class win.

LANCIA *Stratos*

THE LANCIA STRATOS WAS BUILT as a rally winner first and a road car second. Fiat-owned Lancia took the bold step of designing an all-new car solely to win the World Rally Championship, and with a V6 Ferrari Dino engine *(see pages 234–37)* on board, the Stratos had success in 1974, '75, and '76. Rallying rules demanded that at least 500 cars be built, but Lancia needed only 40 for its rally program; the rest lay unsold in showrooms across Europe for years and were even given away as prizes to high-selling Lancia dealers. Never a commercial proposition, the Stratos was an amazing mix of elegance, hard-charging performance, and thrill-a-minute handling.

STUBBY STYLE

Shorter than a Mk II Escort, and with the wheelbase of a Fiat 850, the stubby Stratos wedge looks almost as wide as it is long. The front and back of the car are fiberglass with a steel center-section. The constant radius windshield is cut from a cylindrical section of thin glass to avoid distortion. Whatever the views on the Stratos' styling, though, there is no doubting the fact that the glorious metallic soundtrack is wonderful.

WHEELS
Campagnallo alloys sat on Pirelli P7F rubber— F stands for a soft compound to give a gentler loss of adhesion.

ASSEMBLY
Bertone built the bodies, while Lancia added their sometimes-clumsy finishing touches at the Chivasso factory in Turin.

SHARP END
Flimsy nose section concealed spare wheel, radiator, and twin thermostatically controlled cooling fans.

REAR ASPECT
A 1970s fad, the matte black plastic rear window slats did little for rearward visibility. The raised rear spoiler did its best to keep the rear wheels stuck to the road like lipstick on a collar.

SAFETY BAR
Safety bar was to protect the cabin in case the car rolled.

SUSPENSION
Rear springing was by Lancia Beta-style struts, with lower wishbones.

SPECIFICATIONS

MODEL Lancia Stratos (1973–80)

PRODUCTION 492

BODY STYLE Two-seater mid-engined sports coupe.

CONSTRUCTION Fiberglass and steel unit construction body chassis tub.

ENGINE 2418cc mid-mounted transverse V6.

POWER OUTPUT 190 bhp at 7000 rpm.

TRANSMISSION Five-speed manual in unit with engine and transaxle.

SUSPENSION Independent front and rear with coil springs and wishbones.

BRAKES Four-wheel discs.

MAXIMUM SPEED 143 mph (230 km/h)

0–60 MPH (0–96 KM/H) 6.0 sec

0–100 MPH (0–161 KM/H) 16.7 sec

A.F.C. 18 mpg (6.4 km/l)

INTERIOR

The Stratos was hopeless as a day-to-day machine, with a claustrophobic cockpit and woeful rear vision. The width of 67 in (1.72 m) and the narrow cabin meant that the steering wheel was virtually in the middle of the car. Quality control was dire, with huge panel gaps, mischievous wiring, and ventilation that did not work.

COMFORT
Truncated cabin was cramped, cheap, nasty, and impossibly hot.

RACE UNIT
Factory rally versions had a four-valve V6 engine.

WEIGHT
The Stratos was a two-thirds fiberglass featherweight, tipping the scales at a whisker over 2,000 lb (908 kg).

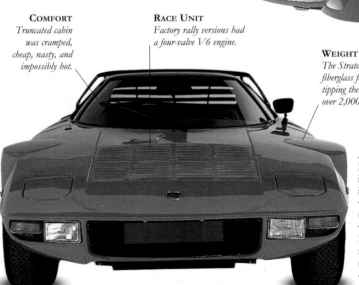

A DRIVER'S CAR

Driving a Stratos hard isn't easy. You sit almost in the middle of the car with the pedals offset to the left and the steering wheel to the right. Ferocious acceleration, monumental oversteer, and lots of heat from the engine make the Stratos a real handful.

RALLY SUCCESS

Lancia commissioned Bertone to build a "take-no-prisoners" rally weapon, and the Stratos debuted at the 1971 Turin Show. Despite scooping three World Championships, sales of Stratos road cars were so slow that they were still available new up until 1980.

REAR COWL

Molded fiberglass rear cowl lifted up by undoing two clips, giving access to midships-mounted power plant.

ENGINE

Lifted straight out of the Dino 246, the 190 bhp transverse, mid-mounted V6 has four chain-driven camshafts spinning in alloy heads, which sit just 6 in (15 cm) from your ear. Clutch and throttle are incredibly stiff, which makes smooth driving an art form.

DEEP WINDOWS

Plexiglas side windows are so deeply recessed within the bodywork that they can be fully opened without causing any wind turbulence.

LEXUS *LFA*

FOR THEIR 20TH BIRTHDAY LEXUS went crazy and built a supercar. But what a car! The LFA is like no other Lexus, with F1 technology, 65 percent carbon-fiber construction, 200 mph (322 km/h) top speed, and one of the best engine notes in the world. The 4.8-liter V10 is so fast-spinning that it can rev from idle to 9,000 rpm in 0.6 seconds—too fast even for a conventional tachometer. The six-speed sequential gearbox has just one clutch for faster changes and a choice of seven different shift speeds. Dry sump lubrication, alloy subframes, and a rear transaxle highlight the LFA's F1 origins. With such cutting-edge technology, Lexus lost money on every LFA they built.

LIMITED EDITION

A team of 175 engineers built the LFA in a dedicated factory, turning out one car a day. Numbers were limited to only 500 units and customers were specially chosen because they would not resell their cars for a profit. The last examples built were Nürburgring spec, good for 562 bhp and the most expensive Japanese road cars ever sold.

SOUND SYMPHONY
Engine note is piped into cabin by twin sound ducts.

EYES FRONT
Engine is front-mounted for perfect weight distribution.

CARBON CAPTURE
Body is special carbon reinforced polymer for extreme lightness.

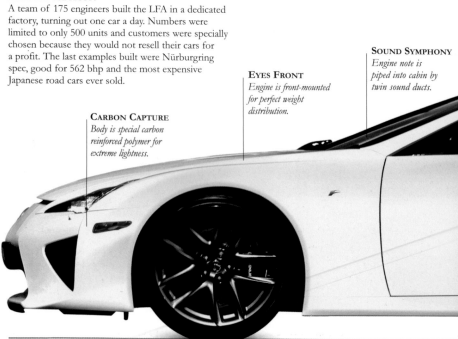

WILD CHILD

The design was hugely radical for traditional Lexus and meant to endow the brand with badly needed sex appeal and glamour. Using carbon-fiber saved 220.5 lb (100 kg) over an alloy body and helped give the LFA a halo of technological modernity.

SPECIFICATIONS

MODEL Lexus LFA (2009)

PRODUCTION 500

BODY STYLE Two-door, two-seater coupe.

CONSTRUCTION Carbon-fiber, aluminium.

ENGINE 4,805cc V10.

POWER OUTPUT 552 bhp.

TRANSMISSION Six-speed sequential.

SUSPENSION Double wishbone, multi-link.

BRAKES Four-wheel ceramic discs.

MAXIMUM SPEED 202 mph (325 km/h)

0–60 MPH (0–96 KM/H) 3.6 sec

0–100 MPH (0–161 KM/H) 7.6 sec

A.F.C. 17 mpg (7.2 km/l)

TOOLED UP
Carbon tub is made using one of only two laser looms in the world.

STOPPING POWER
Rear Brembo brakes have four pistons and ceramic discs.

WING FORCE
Speed-sensitive rear wing rises at over 50 mph (80.5 km/h) to aid down force.

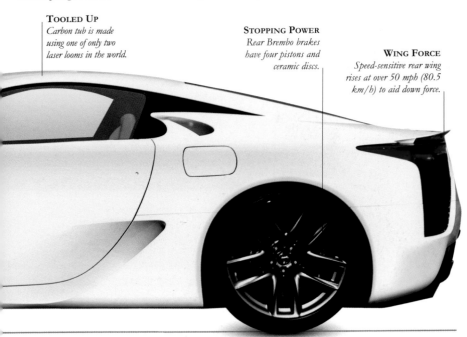

LINCOLN *Continental* (1964)

THERE'S AN UNSETTLING IRONY in the fact that John F. Kennedy was shot in a '61 Lincoln Continental. Like him, the revamped '61 Continental had a new integrity. Substantial and innovative, it was bristling with new ideas and survived for nine years without major change. The car fit for presidents was elegant, restrained, and classically sculptured, perfect for Camelot's new dynasty of liberalism. Ironic, too, that JFK rather liked the Lincoln—he often used a stock White House Continental for unofficial business. Nearly $7,000 bought one of the most influential and best-built American cars of the Sixties. Not only did it carry a two-year, 24,000-mile (39,000-km) warranty, but every engine was bench-tested and each car given a 200-category shakedown. WASP America approved and production doubled in the first year. Even the Industrial Design Institute was impressed, awarding its coveted bronze medal for "an outstanding contribution of simplicity and design elegance."

LINEAR PROFILE

Apart from the gentle dip in the waistline at the back of the rear doors, the roof and fender lines form two uninterrupted, almost parallel lines. Low, wide, and mighty, the '60s Continental was considered the epitome of good taste and discrimination.

ENGINE

Power was supplied by a huge 430cid V8 that generated 320 bhp. Each engine was tested at near maximum revs for three hours and then stripped down for inspection.

INTERIOR

Every Continental had power steering and windows, walnut cappings, a padded dashboard, lush carpets, and vacuum-powered door locks as standard. The locks operated automatically as soon as the car started to move.

SPECIFICATIONS

MODEL Lincoln Continental Convertible (1964)

PRODUCTION 3,328

BODY STYLE Four-door, five-seater convertible.

CONSTRUCTION Steel body and chassis.

ENGINE 430cid V8.

POWER OUTPUT 320 bhp.

TRANSMISSION Three-speed Turbo-Drive automatic.

SUSPENSION *Front:* control arms and coil springs; *Rear:* leaf springs with live axle.

BRAKES Front and rear drums.

MAXIMUM SPEED 115 mph (185 km/h)

0–60 MPH (0–96 KM/H) 11 sec

A.F.C. 14 mpg (5 km/l)

SOLE RAG-TOP

When the revamped Conti was released in '61, Lincoln was the only manufacturer to offer a four-door convertible.

SHARED COSTS

To spread costs, the Continental shared some of its factory tooling with the '61 Thunderbird.

EASY ACCESS
The "suicide" rear-hinged doors hark back to classic prewar construction. On older Continental Convertibles, opening all four doors at once can actually flex the floor and chassis.

CRUISE CONTROL
Even in '64 you could have cruise control, for a mere $96.

STEERING WHEEL
Least popular option in '64 was the adjustable steering wheel.

CONVERTIBLE RARITIES
Rag-top Continentals were really "convertible sedans" with standard power tops. The '64 rag-tops cost only $646 more than the four-door sedans, yet they remain much rarer: only about 10 percent of all '61–'67 Lincolns produced were convertibles.

TIRES
Whitewalls were just one of numerous features that came as standard.

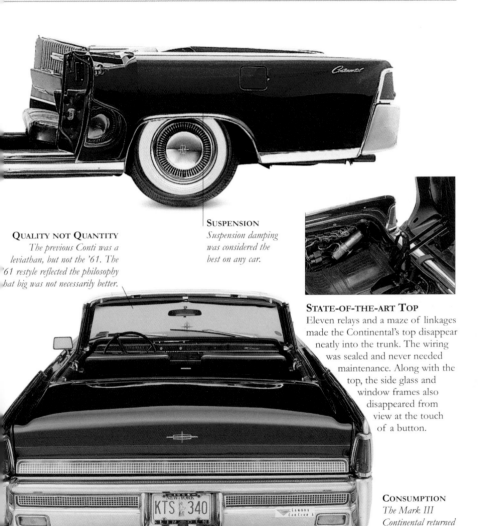

QUALITY NOT QUANTITY
The previous Conti was a leviathan, but not the '61. The '61 restyle reflected the philosophy that big was not necessarily better.

SUSPENSION
Suspension damping was considered the best on any car.

STATE-OF-THE-ART TOP
Eleven relays and a maze of linkages made the Continental's top disappear neatly into the trunk. The wiring was sealed and never needed maintenance. Along with the top, the side glass and window frames also disappeared from view at the touch of a button.

CONSUMPTION
The Mark III Continental returned fuel figures of just 14 mpg (5 km/l).

LOTUS *Elite*

IF EVER A CAR WAS A BRAND landmark, this is it. The Elite was the first Lotus designed for road use rather than outright racing, paving the way for a string of stunning sports and GT cars that, at the least, were always innovative. But the first Elite was much more than that. Its all-fiberglass construction—chassis as well as body—was a bold departure that, coupled with many other innovations, marked the Elite as truly exceptional, and all the more so considering the small-scale operation that created it. What's more, its built-in Lotus race-breeding gave it phenomenal handling and this, together with an unparalleled power-to-weight ratio, brought an almost unbroken run of racing successes. It also happens to be one of the prettiest cars of its era; in short, a superb GT in miniature.

CHAPMAN CREATION

The Elite was the brainchild of company founder and great racing innovator, Anthony Colin Bruce Chapman. The elegant coupe was a remarkable departure for the small company—and, to most, a complete surprise when it appeared at the London Motor Show in October 1957.

FILLER CAP

Quick-release fuel cap was an option many chose.

ᴏᴡ Dʀᴀɢ
ᴏw frontal area, with air intake below
e bumper lip, helped Elite speed and
onomy. Drag coefficient was 0.29,
figure most other manufacturers
uld not match for
years.

Wɪɴᴅsʜɪᴇʟᴅ
*Concealed steel hoop around
windshield added stiffness and
gave some rollover protection.*

Rᴀᴄᴇ Sᴜᴄᴄᴇss
*Elites were uncatchable in
their class, claiming Le Mans
class wins six years in a row
from 1959 to 1964.*

Hᴀɴᴅʟᴇ
*Tiny door handle
was little more
than a hook.*

Wʜᴇᴇʟs
*48-spoke center-lock
Dunlop wire wheels
were standard.*

SPECIFICATIONS

MODEL Lotus Elite (1957–63)

PRODUCTION 988

BODY STYLE Two-door, two-seater sports coupe.

CONSTRUCTION Fiberglass monocoque.

ENGINE Four-cylinder single ohc Coventry Climax, 1216cc.

POWER OUTPUT 75–105 bhp at 6100–6800 rpm.

TRANSMISSION Four-speed MG or ZF gearbox.

SUSPENSION Independent all around by wishbones and coil springs at front and MacPherson-type "Chapman strut" at rear.

BRAKES Discs all around (inboard at rear).

MAXIMUM SPEED 118 mph (190 km/h)

0–60 MPH (0–96 KM/H) 11.1 sec

A.F.C. 35 mpg (12.5 km/l)

AIR EVASION

The Elite's aerodynamic makeup is remarkable considering there were no full-scale wind-tunnel tests, only low-speed air-flow experiments. The height of just 46 in (1.17 m) helped, as did the fully enclosed undertray below.

INTERIOR

Even tall owners were univers in their praise for driving comfort. The award winning interior was crisp and neat, w light, modern materials.

ECONOMY

Contemporary road tests recorded a remarkable 25 mpg (8.8 km/l) at a steady 100 mph (161 km/h).

SUSPENSION

Suspension was derived from the Lotus Formula 2 car of 1956.

LJC322

TRESSED ROOF

he roof was part of the Elite's stressed
ructure, which meant that popular calls
or a convertible—especially from
merica—could not be answered.
he solution came when the Elan
as launched in 1962.

ROOF
*SE (Special
Equipment) models
had silver roof as a
"delete option."*

BUMPERS
*Both front and
rear bumpers hid
body molding seams.*

UNIT ORIGINS
*Engine was developed
from a wartime fire-
pump engine.*

ENGINE
The lightweight 1216cc
four-cylinder engine was
developed by Coventry
Climax from their
successful racing units.
The unit's power rose
from an initial 75 bhp to
83 bhp in the Elite's second
series, but it was possible to
extract over 100 bhp with options.

LOTUS *Elan Sprint*

THE LOTUS ELAN RANKS AS one of the best handling cars of its era. But not only was it among the most poised cars money could buy, it was also a thing of beauty. Conceived by engineering genius Colin Chapman to replace the race-bred Lotus 7, the Elan sat on a steel backbone chassis, clothed in a slippery fiberglass body, and powered by a 1600cc Ford twin-cam engine. Despite a high price tag, critics and public raved and the Elan became one of the most charismatic sports cars of its decade, selling over 12,000 examples. Over an 11-year production life, with five different model series, it evolved into a very desirable and speedy machine, culminating in the Elan Sprint, a 121 mph (195 km/h) banshee with a sub-seven second 0–60 (96 km/h) time. As one car magazine of the time remarked, "The Elan Sprint is one of the finest sports cars in the world." Praise indeed.

RACE ASSOCIATION
The duo-tone paintwork with dividing strip was a popular factory option for the Sprint. The red and gold combination had racing associations—the same look as the Gold Leaf racing team cars. Everybody agreed that the diminutive Elan had an elfin charm.

INTERIOR
The Sprint's interior was refined and upmarket, with all-black trim, wood veneer dashboard, and even electric windows.

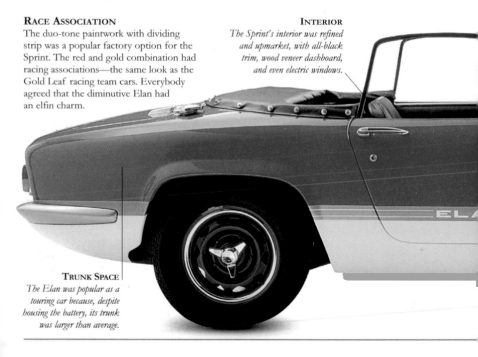

TRUNK SPACE
The Elan was popular as a touring car because, despite housing the battery, its trunk was larger than average.

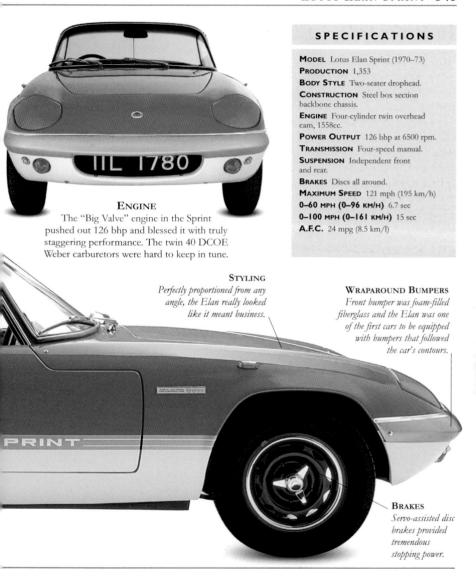

SPECIFICATIONS

MODEL Lotus Elan Sprint (1970–73)

PRODUCTION 1,353

BODY STYLE Two-seater drophead.

CONSTRUCTION Steel box section backbone chassis.

ENGINE Four-cylinder twin overhead cam, 1558cc.

POWER OUTPUT 126 bhp at 6500 rpm.

TRANSMISSION Four-speed manual.

SUSPENSION Independent front and rear.

BRAKES Discs all around.

MAXIMUM SPEED 121 mph (195 km/h)

0–60 MPH (0–96 KM/H) 6.7 sec

0–100 MPH (0–161 KM/H) 15 sec

A.F.C. 24 mpg (8.5 km/l)

ENGINE

The "Big Valve" engine in the Sprint pushed out 126 bhp and blessed it with truly staggering performance. The twin 40 DCOE Weber carburetors were hard to keep in tune.

STYLING

Perfectly proportioned from any angle, the Elan really looked like it meant business.

WRAPAROUND BUMPERS

Front bumper was foam-filled fiberglass and the Elan was one of the first cars to be equipped with bumpers that followed the car's contours.

BRAKES

Servo-assisted disc brakes provided tremendous stopping power.

Maserati *Ghibli*

Many believe the Ghibli is the greatest of all road-going Maseratis. It was the sensation of the 1966 Turin Show, and over 30 years later is widely regarded as Maserati's ultimate front-engined road car—a supercar blend of luxury, performance and stunning good looks that never again quite came together so sublimely on anything with the three-pointed trident. Pitched squarely against the Ferrari Daytona *(see page 233)* and Lamborghini Miura *(see page 318–21)*, it outsold both. Its engineering may have been dated, but it had the perfect pedigree, with plenty of power from its throaty V8 engine and a flawless Ghia design. It is an uncompromised supercar, yet it is also a consummate continent-eating grand tourer with 24-karat cachet. Muscular and perhaps even menacing, but not overbearingly macho, it is well mannered enough for the tastes of the mature super-rich. There will only be one dilemma; do you take the windy back roads or blast along the highways? Why not a little of both.

Racing Stance
The Ghibli's dramatic styling is uncompromised, a sublime and extravagant 15 ft (4.57 m) of attitude that can only accommodate two people. From its bladelike front to its short, bobbed tail, it looks fast even in static pose. It has also aged all the better for its lack of finicky detail; the Ghibli's detail is simple and clean, worn modestly like fine, expensive jewelry.

Wide View
The windshield was huge, but the mighty hood could make the Ghibli difficult to maneuver.

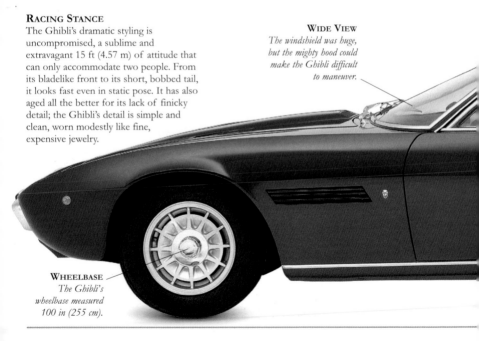

Wheelbase
The Ghibli's wheelbase measured 100 in (255 cm).

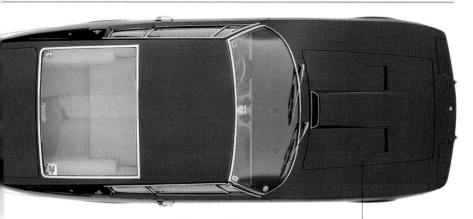

ACCELERATION
The mile (1.61 km) could be reached in just 15.1 seconds.

RAG-TOP CACHET
The most prized of all Ghiblis are the 125 convertible Spiders—out of a total Ghibli production figure of 1,274, only just over 100 were Spiders.

CARB-HEAVY
Four greedy twin-choke Weber carbs sat astride the V8.

THIRSTY
The Ghibli was a gas guzzler, but when was there an economical supercar?

BRAKES
Vented Girling discs with vacuum assist were on all four wheels.

INTERIOR

A cliché certainly, but here you really feel you are on an aircraft flight deck. The high center console houses air-conditioning, which was standard Ghibli equipment. The steering wheel is adjustable and power steering was a later, desirable optional extra.

SPECIFICATIONS

MODEL Maserati Ghibli (1967–73)

PRODUCTION 1,274

BODY STYLES Two-door sports coupe or open Spider.

CONSTRUCTION Steel body and separate tubular chassis.

ENGINES Four-cam 90-degree V8, 4719cc or 4930cc (SS).

POWER OUTPUT 330 bhp at 5000 rpm (4719cc); 335 bhp at 5500 rpm (4930cc).

TRANSMISSION ZF five-speed manual or three-speed Borg-Warner auto.

SUSPENSION Wishbones and coil-springs at front; rigid axle with radius arms/semi-elliptic leaf springs at rear.

BRAKES Girling discs on all four wheels.

MAXIMUM SPEED 154 mph (248 km/h), 168 mph (270 km/h, SS)

0–60 MPH (0–96 KM/H) 6.6 sec, 6.2 sec (SS)

0–100 MPH (0–161 KM/H) 15.7 sec

A.F.C. 10 mpg (3.5 km/l)

UNDER THE HOOD

The potent race-bred quad-cam V8 is even-tempered and undemanding, delivering loads of low-down torque and accelerating meaningfully from as little as 500 rpm in fifth gear. This 1971 Ghibli SS has the 4.9-liter unit.

HEIGH

At 47 in (118 cm *the Ghibli was* *low sports coupe* *the truest sens*

TRIDENT
Masers are instantly recognizable by the three-pointed trident.

EARLY GUIGIARO

Bodywork by Ghia was one of the finest early designs of their brilliant young Italian employee, Giorgetto Giugiaro. He was later to enhance his reputation with many other beautiful creations.

WHAT'S IN A NAME?

Like the earlier Mistral and the Bora, the Ghibli took its name from a regional wind. The Merak, which was introduced in 1972, was named after the smaller star of the constellation of the Plow. Other Maserati names were more race-inspired, including Indy, Sebring, and Mexico.

HIDEAWAY HEADLIGHTS

Pop-up headlights might have improved looks when not needed, but they took their time to pop up. The Ghibli cost nearly $22,000 new in 1971, but buyers could be assured that they were getting a real supercar.

LIFT OFF
Wide front had a tendency to lift above 120 mph (193 km/h).

MASERATI *Kyalami*

THE 1970S PRODUCED some true automotive lemons. It was a decade when barefaced badge engineering and gluttonous V8 engines were all the rage, and nobody cared that these big bruisers cost three arms and a leg to run. The Kyalami is one such monument to excess, a copy of the De Tomaso Longchamp with Maserati's all-alloy V8 on board instead of Ford's 5.8-liter cast-iron lump. The Kyalami was meant to compete with the Jaguar XJS but failed hopelessly. Plagued with electrical gremlins, this was a noisy, bulky, and unrefined machine that was neither beautiful nor poised. Yet despite all that, it still sports that emotive trident on its nose and emits a deep and strident V8 bark. The Kyalami might not be a great car, but most of us, at least while looking at it, find it hard to tell the difference.

DE TOMASO ADAPTATION
Maserati designer Pietro Frua retouched the De Tomaso Longchamp design, turning it into the Kyalami. He gave it a new lower nose with twin lights, full width hood, and new rubber-cap bumpers with integral indicators.

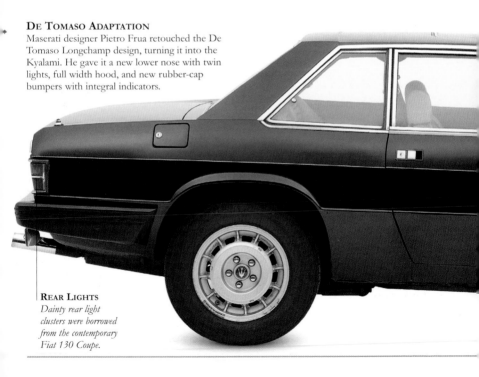

REAR LIGHTS
Dainty rear light clusters were borrowed from the contemporary Fiat 130 Coupe.

SPECIFICATIONS

MODEL Maserati Kyalami 4.9 (1976–82)

PRODUCTION 250 approx.

BODY STYLE Two-door, 2+2 sports saloon.

CONSTRUCTION Steel monocoque body.

ENGINE 4930cc all-alloy V8.

POWER OUTPUT 265 bhp at 6000 rpm.

TRANSMISSION Five-speed ZF manual or three-speed Borg Warner automatic.

SUSPENSION Independent front with coil springs and wishbones. Independent rear with double coils, lower links, and radius arms.

BRAKES Four-wheel discs.

MAXIMUM SPEED 147 mph (237 km/h)

0–60 MPH (0–96 KM/H) 7.6 sec

0–100 MPH (0–161 KM/H) 19.4 sec

A.F.C. 14 mpg (3.6 km/l)

NOT A PRETTY FACE
The frontal aspect is mean but clumsy. The three-part front bumper looks cheap, while the Maserati grille and trident seem to have been bolted on as afterthoughts.

STEERING
Power-assisted steering robbed the car of much needed accuracy and feel.

ENGINE
The engine was a four-cam, five-bearing 4.9 V8, with four twin-choke Weber carbs, propelling the Kyalami to a touch under 150 mph (241 km/h).

TIRES
The Kyalami generated lots of commotion from fat 205/70 Michelins.

MAZDA *RX7*

THE RX7 ARRIVED IN American showrooms in 1978 and sales promptly went crazy. Even importing 4,000 a month, Mazda could not cope with demand and waiting lists were huge. For a while, RX7s changed hands on the black market for as much as $3,000 above retail price. By the time production ceased in 1985, nearly 500,000 had found grateful owners, making the RX7 the best-selling rotary car of all time. The RX7 sold on its clean European looks and Swiss-watch smoothness. Inspired by the woefully unreliable NSU Ro80 *(see pages 382–83)*, Mazda's engineers were not worried about the NSU's ghost haunting the RX7. By 1978 they had completely mastered rotary-engine technology and sold almost a million rotary-engined cars and trucks. These days the RX7 is becoming an emergent classic— the first car to make Felix Wankel's rotary design actually work and one of the more desirable and better made sports cars of the 1970s.

IMPRESSIVE AERODYNAMICS
The RX7's slippery, wind-evading shape cleaved the air well, with a drag coefficient of only 0.36 and a top speed of 125 mph (210 km/h). Smooth aerodynamics helped the RX7 feel stable and composed with minimal body roll.

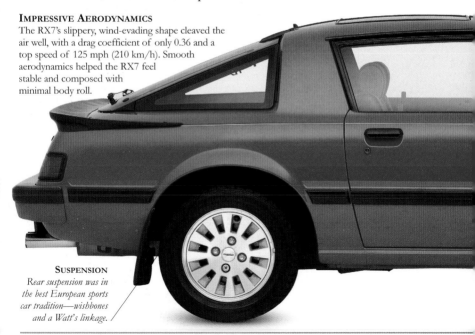

SUSPENSION
Rear suspension was in the best European sports car tradition—wishbones and a Watt's linkage.

SPECIFICATIONS

MODEL Maxda RX7 (1978–85)

PRODUCTION 474,565 (377,878 exported to US)

BODY STYLE All-steel coupe.

CONSTRUCTION One-piece monocoque bodyshell.

ENGINE Twin rotor, 1146cc.

POWER OUTPUT 135 bhp at 6000 rpm.

TRANSMISSION Five-speed all synchromesh/automatic option.

SUSPENSION Independent front. Live rear axle with trailing arms and Watt's linkage.

BRAKES *Front:* ventilated discs; *Rear:* drums.

MAXIMUM SPEED 125 mph (210 km/h)

0–60 MPH (0–96 KM/H) 8.9 sec

0–100 MPH (0–161 KM/H) 24 sec

A.F.C. 21.3 mpg (7.5 km/l)

PERFECT DESIGN
The body design was perfect from the start, and in its seven-year production run few changes were made to the slim and balanced shape.

HANDLING
Fine handling was due to near equal weight distribution and the low center of gravity.

HOOD
The RX7's low hood line could not have been achieved with anything but the compact rotary engine, which weighed only 312 lb (142 kg).

BRAKES
Front discs were ventilated; rear stopping power was by traditional drums.

LEGAL IMPLICATIONS
The RX7 was originally planned as a two-seater, but Mazda was forced to include a small rear seat in the model. The reasoning behind this was that Japanese law stated all cars had to have more than two seats to encourage car sharing.

INTERIOR
Cockpit and dashboard are tastefully orthodox, with a handsome three-spoke wheel and five-gauge instrument binnacle; the two large dials are a speedometer and tachometer.

REAR PLANS
Original design plans for the RX7 favored a one-piece rear tailgate like the Porsche 944, but economics dictated that an all-glass hatch was incorporated instead.

TURBO
The US could enjoy a brisk 135 mph (217 km/h) turbocharged model after 1984.

C418 DYV

ENGINE FLAWS
The Wankel-designed rotary engine had two weak points—low speed pull and fuel economy.

HEADLIGHTS
Pop-up headlights helped reduce wind resistance and add glamour. But, unlike those on the Lotus Esprit and Triumph TR7, the Mazda's always worked.

ENGINE
The twin-rotor Wankel engine gave 135 bhp in later models. Reliable, compact, and easy to tune, there was even a small electric winch on the bulkhead to reel in the choke if owners forgot to push it back in.

EUROPEAN STYLING
For a Japanese design, the RX7 was atypically European, with none of the garish overadornment associated with other cars from Japan. Occasional rear seats and liftback rear window helped in the practicality department.

MERCEDES-BENZ *300SL Gullwing*

WITH ITS GORGEOUS GULLWING doors raised, the 300SL looked like it could fly. And with them lowered shut it really could, rocketing beyond 140 mph (225 km/h) and making its contemporary supercar pretenders look ordinary. Derived from the 1952 Le Mans-winning racer, these mighty coupes were early forebears of modern supercars like the Jaguar XJ220 and McLaren F1 in taking racetrack technology on to the streets. In fact, the 300SL can lay a plausible claim to being the first true postwar supercar. Awkward to enter, and with twitchy high-speed handling, it was sublimely impractical—it is a virtual supercar blueprint. It was a statement, too, that Mercedes had recovered from war-time devastation. Mercedes was back, and at the pinnacle of that three-pointed star was the fabulous 300SL, the company's first postwar sports car.

AERODYNAMICS
Detailed attention to aerodynamics was streets ahead of anything else at the time and helped make the 300SL the undisputed fastest road car of its era. Road cars developed 240 bhp, more than the racing versions of two years earlier.

WHEELS
Some say steel discs were used to keep costs down, but they also look more muscular than wires.

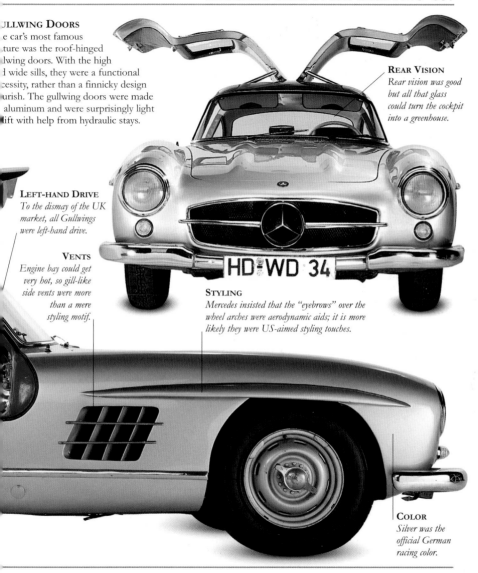

ULLWING DOORS

e car's most famous
ture was the roof-hinged
lwing doors. With the high
d wide sills, they were a functional
cessity, rather than a finnicky design
urish. The gullwing doors were made
aluminum and were surprisingly light
ift with help from hydraulic stays.

REAR VISION
*Rear vision was good
but all that glass
could turn the cockpit
into a greenhouse.*

LEFT-HAND DRIVE
*To the dismay of the UK
market, all Gullwings
were left-hand drive.*

VENTS
*Engine bay could get
very hot, so gill-like
side vents were more
than a mere
styling motif.*

STYLING
*Mercedes insisted that the "eyebrows" over the
wheel arches were aerodynamic aids; it is more
likely they were US-aimed styling touches.*

HD·WD 34

COLOR
*Silver was the
official German
racing color.*

SPECIFICATIONS

MODEL Mercedes-Benz 300SL (1954–57)

PRODUCTION 1,400

BODY STYLE Two-door, two-seat coupe.

CONSTRUCTION Multitubular space-frame with steel and alloy body.

ENGINE Inline six-cylinder overhead camshaft, 2996cc.

POWER OUTPUT 240 bhp at 6100 rpm.

TRANSMISSION Four-speed all synchromesh gearbox.

SUSPENSION Coil springs all around, with double wishbones at front, swinging half-axles at rear.

BRAKES Finned alloy drums.

MAXIMUM SPEED 135–165 mph (217–265 km/h), depending on gearing.

0–60 MPH (0–96 KM/H) 8.8 sec

0–100 MPH (0–161 KM/H) 21.0 sec

A.F.C. 18 mpg (6.4 km/l)

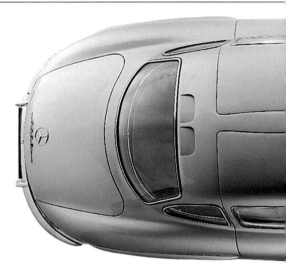

SMOOTH REAR

The Gullwing's smooth styling extended to the clean rear; the trunk lid suggests ample space, but this was not the case. The cockpit became quite hot, but air vents above the rear window helped.

LIMITED SPACE

As this sales illustration shows, with the spare mounted atop the fuel tank there was very little room for luggage in the Gullwing's trunk.

300SL ROADSTER

As Gullwing production wound down, Mercedes introduced the 300SL Roadster, which from 1957 to 1963 sold 1,858, compared to the Gullwing's 1,400. From 1955 to 1963 the 190SL Roadster served as the "poor man's" 300SL.

SLANT SIX

The engine was canted at 50 degrees to give a low hood-line. It was also the first application of fuel injection in a production car.

POWER SOURCE

The engine was originally derived from the 300-Series 3-liter sedans, then developed for the 1952 300SL racer, and two years later let loose in the road-going Gullwing, with fuel injection in place of carburetors.

TILT WHEEL

On some cars, mostly for the US, the wheel tilted to ease access.

BULGES

One hood bulge was for air intakes, the other for aesthetic balance.

STAR IDENTITY

The massive three-pointed star dominated the frontal aspect and is repeated in enamel on the hood edge.

HD·WD·34

MERCEDES-BENZ *280SL*

THE MERCEDES 280SL HAS mellowed magnificently. In 1963, the new SLs took over the sports mantle of the aging 190SL. They evolved from the original 230SL, through the 250SL, and on to the 280SL. The most remarkable thing is how modern they look, for with their simple, clean-shaven good looks, it is hard to believe that the last one was made in 1971. Underneath the timelessly elegant sheet metal, they were based closely on the earlier Fintail sedans, sharing even the decidedly unsporty recirculating-ball steering. Yet it is the looks that mark this car as something special, and the enduring design includes its distinctive so-called pagoda roof. This well-manicured Mercedes is a beautifully built boulevardier that will induce a sense of supreme self satisfaction on any journey.

SUSPENSION
Suspension was on the soft side for driving glove types.

TRADEMARK LIGHTS
So-called "stacked" headlights are unmistakable Mercedes trademarks. Each outer lens concealed one headlamp, indicator, and sidelights.

JBW 62

FRENCH DESIGN

Design of the 280SL was down to Frenchman Paul Bracq. Some macho types may dismiss it as a woman's car, and it is certainly not the most hairy-chested of sporty Mercedes.

GEARING

Relatively few cars were ordered with a manual gearbox.

OPTIONAL THIRD

The SL was essentially a two-seater, although a third, sideways-facing rear seat was available as a (rare) optional extra.

CLAP HANDS

Windshield wipers were of the characteristic "clap hands" pattern beloved of Mercedes.

HORN RING

The D-shaped horn ring allowed an unobstructed view of the instruments.

CHROME BUMPER

The full-width front bumper featured a central recess that was just big enough for a standard license plate; the quality of the chrome, as elsewhere on the car, was first class.

SL MOTIF

In Mercedes-speak, the S stood for Sport or Super, L for Leicht (light) and sometimes Luxus (luxury), although at well over 3,000 lb (1,362 kg) it was not particularly light.

SPECIFICATIONS

MODEL Mercedes-Benz 280SL (1968–71)

PRODUCTION 23,885

BODY STYLE Two-door, two-seat convertible with detachable hardtop.

CONSTRUCTION Pressed-steel monocoque.

ENGINE 2778cc inline six; two valves per cylinder; single overhead camshaft.

POWER OUTPUT 170 bhp at 5750 rpm.

TRANSMISSION Four- or five-speed manual, or optional four-speed auto.

SUSPENSION *Front:* independent, wishbones, coil springs, telescopic dampers; *Rear:* swing axle, coil springs, telescopic dampers.

BRAKES Front discs, rear drums.

MAXIMUM SPEED 121 mph (195 km/h, auto)

0–60 MPH (0–96 KM/H) 9.3 sec

0–100 MPH (0–161 KM/H) 30.6 sec

A.F.C. 19 mpg (6.7 km/l)

SAFE SUSPENSION
Swing-axle rear suspension was tamed to provide natural understeer.

UNDER THE HOOD
The six-cylinder ohc engine saw a process of steady development— the 2281cc 230SL in 1963, the 2496cc 250SL from 1966, and the final 2778cc 280SL shown here from 1968.

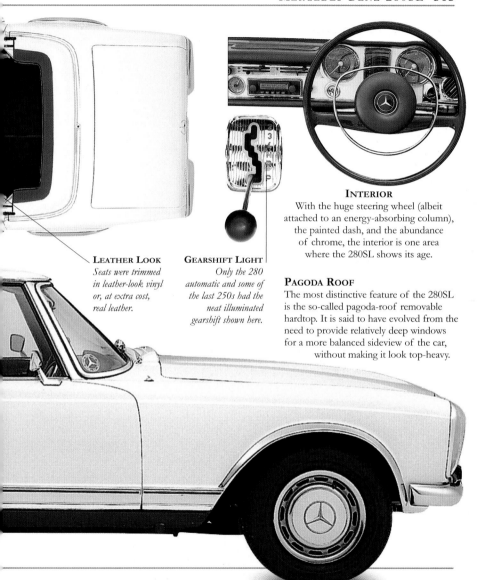

LEATHER LOOK
Seats were trimmed in leather-look vinyl or, at extra cost, real leather.

GEARSHIFT LIGHT
Only the 280 automatic and some of the last 250s had the neat illuminated gearshift shown here.

INTERIOR
With the huge steering wheel (albeit attached to an energy-absorbing column), the painted dash, and the abundance of chrome, the interior is one area where the 280SL shows its age.

PAGODA ROOF
The most distinctive feature of the 280SL is the so-called pagoda-roof removable hardtop. It is said to have evolved from the need to provide relatively deep windows for a more balanced sideview of the car, without making it look top-heavy.

MERCEDES-BENZ *SLS AMG*

THE SLS COUPE REALLY IS ONE of the world's coolest rides, and the car I chose to drive every day. A blisteringly fast, wild hot rod that doesn't rely on electronic gizmos, it looks wonderfully menacing, has the best soundtrack of any V8, and generates universal warm approval. Like the 1954 300SL Gullwing (*see pages 356–59*) that inspired it, the SLS is cramped, hard-riding, and edgy at the limit but intoxicatingly rapid. The best handling and most dramatic Mercedes ever, it is a worthy opponent to the Italian supercar set but looks infinitely more separate and distinctive. Climbing in and out can be a challenge but those crazy doors are the SLS's party piece. This is outrageous automotive mischief at its very finest.

HAND CRAFTED

The 6.3-liter AMG V8 is a masterpiece and each engine is hand assembled in-house by one man. Tuned to deliver 112 bhp more than the standard 6,300cc unit, 0–100 mph (0–161 km/h) is dispatched in an amazing 8 seconds. The Getrag seven-speed automatic has four switchable modes along with paddle-shift manual. Driven carefully, an SLS can return 23 mpg (9.8 km/l).

HERITAGE TOUCH
Twin chrome slashes over brake cooling vent echo original 300SL.

MANUAL DOORS
Doors do not have electric motors to save weight.

LIGHT FANTASTIC
Lightweight body is a mix of aluminium and plastic panels but is extremely rigid.

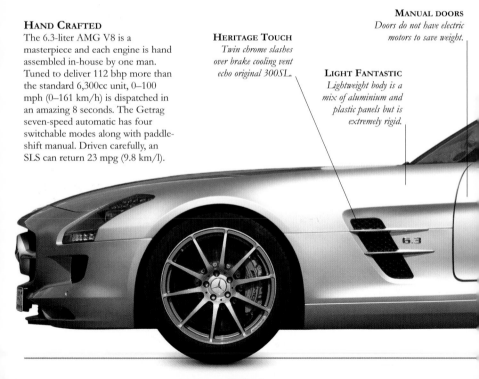

MIND YOUR HEAD
Gullwing doors are heavy and need long arms to close.

SPECIFICATIONS

MODEL Mercedes-Benz SLS AMG (2010)
PRODUCTION N/A
BODY STYLE Two-seater coupe with gullwing doors.
CONSTRUCTION Alloy body panels with plastic boot lid.
ENGINE 6,208cc, V8.
POWER OUTPUT 563 bhp.
TRANSMISSION Seven-speed, dual-clutch semi-automatic.
SUSPENSION Double wishbone, coil spring.
BRAKES Four-wheel discs, optional ceramic.
MAXIMUM SPEED 197 mph (317 km/h)
0–60 MPH (0–96 KM/H) 3.8 sec
0–100 MPH (0–161 KM/H) 8 sec
A.F.C. 21 mpg (9 km/l)

GO CAREFULLY
Wider than an S-Class Mercedes, Jaguar XJ, or Range Rover, the SLS can be hard work driving around town. Delicate AMG alloy wheels are vulnerable to damage from high curbs and costs $3,720 a piece to replace.

STOPPING POWER
Orange caliper ceramic brakes are optional and help reduce fade on the track.

MG *TC Midget*

EVEN WHEN IT WAS NEW, the MG TC was not new. Introduced in September 1945, it displayed a direct lineage back to its prewar forbears. If you were a little short on soul, you might even have called it old fashioned. Yet it was a trailblazer, not in terms of performance, but in opening up new export markets. Popular myth has it that American GIs stationed in England latched on to these quaint sporting devices, and when they got home were eager to take a little piece of England with them. Whatever the reality, it was the first in a long line of MG export successes. There was simply nothing remotely like this TC tiddler coming out of Detroit. It had a cramped cockpit, harsh ride, and lacked creature comforts; but when the road got twisty the TC could show you its tail and leave soft-sprung sofa-cars lumbering in its wake. It was challenging to drive, and all the more rewarding when you did it right.

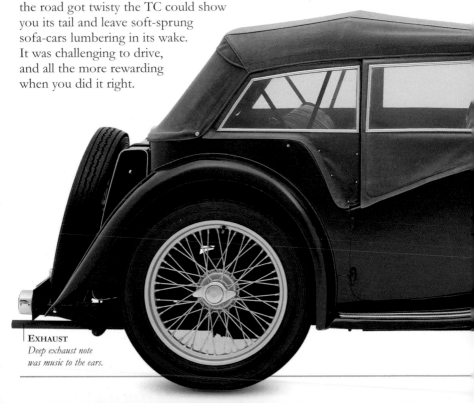

EXHAUST
Deep exhaust note was music to the ears.

TRADITIONAL CLASSIC
With its square-rigged layout, the TC is traditional with a capital T, and certainly a "classic" before the term was applied to cars. With its square front and separate headlights, sweeping front fenders, and cutaway doors, it is a true classic.

RAW MOTORING
While the TC may have been short on sophistication, it contained essential elements, such as wind-in-your-hair driving, that marked it as a true enthusiast's sporting car in the car-starved late 1940s.

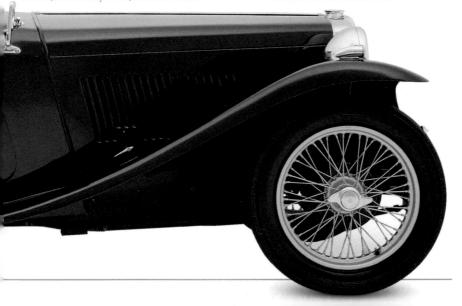

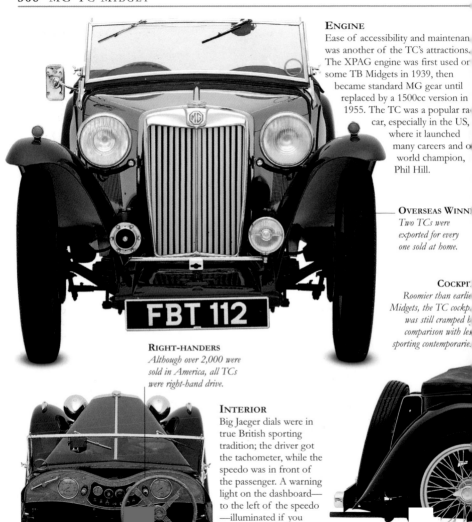

ENGINE
Ease of accessibility and maintenan
was another of the TC's attractions.
The XPAG engine was first used or
some TB Midgets in 1939, then
became standard MG gear until
replaced by a 1500cc version in
1955. The TC was a popular ra
car, especially in the US,
where it launched
many careers and o
world champion,
Phil Hill.

OVERSEAS WINN
*Two TCs were
exported for every
one sold at home.*

COCKPI
*Roomier than earlie
Midgets, the TC cockp
was still cramped b
comparison with le
sporting contemporarie.*

RIGHT-HANDERS
*Although over 2,000 were
sold in America, all TCs
were right-hand drive.*

INTERIOR
Big Jaeger dials were in
true British sporting
tradition; the driver got
the tachometer, while the
speedo was in front of
the passenger. A warning
light on the dashboard—
to the left of the speedo
—illuminated if you
exceeded Britain's
30 mph (48 km/h)
urban speed limit.

SPECIFICATIONS

MODEL MG TC Midget (1947–49)

PRODUCTION 10,000

BODY STYLE Two-door, two-seater sports.

CONSTRUCTION Channel-section ladder-type chassis; ash-framed steel body.

ENGINE Four-cylinder overhead valve 1250cc, with twin SU carburetors.

POWER OUTPUT 54 bhp at 5200 rpm.

TRANSMISSION Four-speed gearbox with synchromesh on top three.

SUSPENSION Rigid front and rear axles on semi-elliptic springs, lever-type shock absorbers.

BRAKES Lockheed hydraulic drums.

MAXIMUM SPEED 73 mph (117 km/h)

0–60 MPH (0–96 KM/H) 22.7 sec

A.F.C. 28 mpg (9.9 km/l)

CONTINUED SUCCESS
The export trend begun so successfully by the TC really took off with the TD, which sold three times the number.

REPLACEMENT TD
The TC was replaced by the TD, which with its smaller disc wheels, chrome hubcaps, and bumpers, some MG aficionados considered less pure.

BRAKES
Lockheed drum brakes balanced the limited power output.

MG*A*

LAUNCHED IN SEPTEMBER 1955, the MGA was the first of the modern sports
MGs. The chassis, engine, and gearbox were all new, as was the smooth, Le Mans-
inspired bodywork. Compared to its predecessor—the TF, which still sported old-
fashioned running boards—the MGA was positively futuristic. Buyers thought so
too, and being cheaper than its nearest rivals, the Triumph TR3 and Austin Healey
100, helped MG sell 13,000 cars in the first year of the MGA's production. The
company's small factory at Abingdon, near Oxford, England, managed
to export a staggering 81,000 MGAs to America. The
car also earned an enviable reputation in competition,
with the Twin Cam being the most powerful of
the MGA engines.

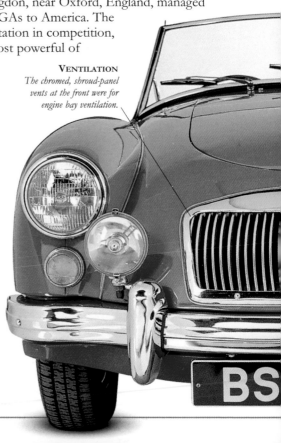

VENTILATION
*The chromed, shroud-panel
vents at the front were for
engine bay ventilation.*

ENGINE
The tough B-Series, push-rod engine went
well and lasted forever. A heater unit in
front of the bulkhead was an optional
extra. The 1600 model pushed out 80 bhp
and featured front-disc brakes.

WHEELS
Perforated steel wheels were standard.

MATERIALS
Door skins, hood, and trunk were light alloy.

RACE ORIGINS

The slippery, wind-evading shape of the MGA was created for racing at Le Mans —an early prototype achieved 116 mph (187 km/h). Production MGAs were very similar and the smooth hood and sloping fenders aid both top speed and fuel consumption.

CONSTRUCTION

MGAs had a separate chassis, with the body bolted on top. The bodies were welded, painted, and trimmed at Morris Bodies in Coventry and then transported to Abingdon for the final fitting of mechanical equipment.

SPECIFICATIONS

MODEL MGA (1955–62)

PRODUCTION 101,081

BODY STYLE Two-door sports coupe.

CONSTRUCTION Steel.

ENGINES Four-cylinder 1489cc, 1588cc, 1622cc (Twin Cam).

POWER OUTPUT 72 bhp, 80 bhp, 85 bhp.

TRANSMISSION Four-speed manual.

SUSPENSION *Front:* independent; *Rear:* leaf-spring.

BRAKES Rear drums, front discs. All discs on De Luxe and Twin Cam.

MAXIMUM SPEED 100 mph (161 km/h); 113 mph (181 km/h) (Twin Cam)

0–60 MPH (0–96 KM/H) 15 sec (13.3 sec, Twin Cam)

0–100 MPH (0–161 KM/H) 47 sec (41 sec, Twin Cam)

A.F.C. 20–25 mpg (7–8.8 km/l)

MG*B*

WIDELY ADMIRED FOR ITS uncomplicated nature, timeless good looks, and brisk performance, the MGB caused a sensation back in 1962. The now famous advertising slogan "Your mother wouldn't like it" was quite wrong. She would have wholeheartedly approved of the MGB's reliability, practicality, and good sense. In 1965 came the even more practical tin-top MGB GT. These were the halcyon days of the MGB—chrome bumpers, leather seats, and wire wheels. In 1974, in pursuit of modernity and American safety regulations (the MGB's main market), the factory burdened the B with ungainly rubber bumpers, a higher ride height, and garish striped nylon seats, making the car slow, ugly, and unpredictable at the limit. Yet the B went on to become the best-selling single model sports car ever, finding 512,000 grateful owners throughout the world.

SIMPLE MECHANICS

All MGBs had the simple 1798cc B-series four-cylinder engine with origins going back to 1947. This Tourer's period charm is enhanced by the rare Iris Blue paintwork and rare pressed-steel wheels—most examples were equipped with optional spoked wire wheels.

TOP

Early cars had a "packaway" top made from ICI Everflex.

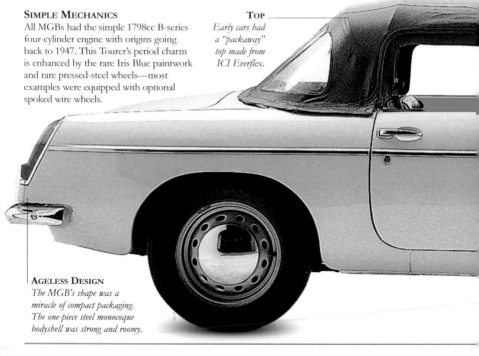

AGELESS DESIGN

The MGB's shape was a miracle of compact packaging. The one-piece steel monocoque bodyshell was strong and roomy.

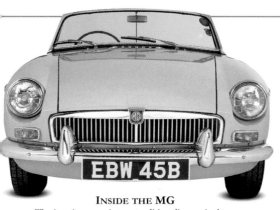

SPECIFICATIONS

MODEL MGB Tourer (1962–1980)

PRODUCTION 512,243

BODY STYLE Steel front-engined two seater with aluminum hood.

CONSTRUCTION One-piece monocoque bodyshell.

ENGINE Four-cylinder 1798cc.

POWER OUTPUT 92 bhp at 5400 rpm.

TRANSMISSION Four-speed with overdrive.

SUSPENSION *Front:* independent coil; *Rear:* half-elliptic leaf springs.

BRAKES Lockheed discs front, drums rear.

MAXIMUM SPEED 106 mph (171 km/h)

0–60 MPH (0–96 KM/H) 12.2 sec

0–100 MPH (0–161 KM/H) 37 sec

A.F.C. 25 mpg (8.8 km/l)

INSIDE THE MG

The interior was vintage traditionalism at its best. Leather seats, crackle black metal dash, nautical-sized steering wheel, and minor controls were strewn about the dash like boulders with scant thought for ergonomics.

MIRROR SUPPORT
The line down the center of the windshield was a mirror support rod.

HOOD
Hood was made out of lightweight aluminum.

SUSPENSION
Front suspension was coil spring with wishbones, and dated back to the MG TF of the 1950s.

MORGAN *Plus Four*

IT IS REMARKABLE THAT MORGANS are still made, but there is many a gent with a cloth cap and corduroys who is grateful that they are. Derived from the first four-wheeled Morgans of 1936, this is the car that buoyed Morgan on after the war while many of the old mainstays of the British auto industry wilted around it. Tweedier than a Scottish moor on the first day of the grouse shooting season, it is as quintessentially English as a car can be. It was a hit in America and other foreign parts, and it has also remained the backbone of the idiosyncratic Malvern-based company, which refuses to move with the times. Outdated and outmoded, Morgans are still so admired they hardly depreciate at all. First introduced in 1951, the Plus Four, with a series of Standard Vanguard and Triumph TR engines, laid the foundations for the modern miracle of the very old-fashioned Morgan Motor Company.

MODERN MORGAN
The second-generation Plus Four was the first of what are generally considered the "modern-looking" Morgans—if that is the right expression for a basic design which, still in production today, dates back to 1936.

"SUICIDE" DOORS
The earlier two-seat drophead coupe retained rear-hinged "suicide" doors; sports models had front-hinged doors.

ON THE RACK
Morgans have limited luggage capacity, so many owners attached external racks.

REAR ILLUMINATION

Rear lights have never been a Morgan strong point. Amber indicators are a good 6 in (15 cm) inboard of the brake lights, and partially obscured by the luggage rack.

SPECIFICATIONS

MODEL Morgan Plus Four (1951–69)

PRODUCTION 3,737

BODY STYLES Two- and four-seater sports convertible.

CONSTRUCTION Steel chassis, ash frame, steel and alloy outer panels.

ENGINES 2088cc overhead-valve inline four (Vanguard); 1991cc or 2138cc overhead-valve inline four (TR).

POWER OUTPUT 105 bhp at 4700 rpm (2138cc TR engine).

TRANSMISSION Four-speed manual.

SUSPENSION *Front:* sliding stub axles, coil springs, and telescopic dampers; *Rear:* live axle, semi-elliptic leaf springs, and lever-arm dampers.

BRAKES Drums front and rear; front discs standard from 1960.

MAXIMUM SPEED 100 mph (161 km/h)

0–60 MPH (0–96 KM/H) 12 sec

A.F.C. 20–22 mpg (7–7.8 km/l)

SUSPENSION
The Plus Four retained simple sliding-pillar front suspension.

INTERIOR
From 1958, Plus Fours had a slightly wider cockpit with a new dash. Speedometer, switches, warning lights, and minor gauges were grouped in a central panel.

TOP
Unlike most convertible cars, the Plus Four has a top which can be partially folded back.

REVISED FEATURES
Major distinguishing features on the second-generation Morgan include the cowled radiator grille and, from 1959, a wider body (as here) to provide more elbow room for driver and passenger. The doors were the only sensible place for external side mirrors.

LIGHT WORK
Headlights are big, bol affairs set in pods on th front fenders, but sideli are about as visible as pair of glowworms.

326 EPW

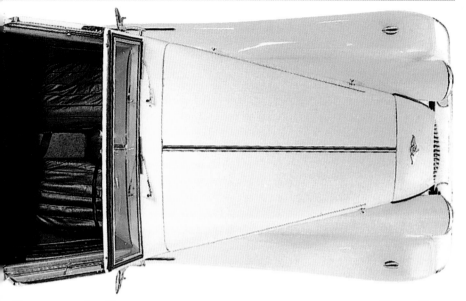

TRADITIONAL ASH FRAME

The current four-cylinder Morgan is built in exactly the same manner as most of its predecessors. The chassis is made from "Z"-section steel members, and on it sits a 94- or 114-piece wooden framework (two- and four-seat cars, respectively) clothed in a mixture of steel and aluminum panels. Today the company builds just two cars: the Plus Four and the Plus Eight.

ENGINE

The later Triumph TR3A 2138cc engine, shown here, provided increased torque. The 2138cc engine was available in the TR3A from summer 1957. The earlier Triumph 1991cc engine was still available for those wishing to compete in sub-two-liter racing classes.

HINGED HOOD

Like all Morgans, the Plus Four has a hinged two-piece hood.

MORRIS *Minor MM Convertible*

THE MORRIS MINOR IS A motoring milestone. As Britain's first million seller it became a "people's car," staple transportation for everyone from nurses to construction workers. Designed by Alec Issigonis, the genius who later went on to pen the Austin Mini *(see pages 44–47)*, the new Series MM Morris Minor of 1948 featured the then novel unitary chassis-body construction. The 918cc sidevalve engine of the MM was rather more antique, a carryover from the prewar Morris 8. Its handling and ride comfort more than made up for the lack of power. With independent front suspension and crisp rack-and-pinion steering it embarrassed its rivals and even tempted the young Stirling Moss into high-speed cornering antics that lost him his license for a month. Of all the 1.5 million Minors the most prized are the now rare Series MM convertibles.

RARE RAGTOPS

Ragtops remained part of the Minor model lineup until 1969, two years from the end of all Minor production. They represent only a small proportion of Minor production. Between 1963 and 1969 only 3,500 soft-tops were produced compared with 119,000 two-door sedans.

SUSPENSION
Morris bean counters dictated old-fashioned live-axle and leaf springs at the rear.

FENDERS
Both front and rear fenders were easily placed, bolt-on items.

IDE WINDOWS
Original MM Tourer had side curtains, placed by glass rear indows in 1952.

MINOR SIGNALING
With no door pillars above waist height, semaphore indicators were mounted lower down on the tourers; flashers eventually replaced semaphores in 1961. Few Minors today have their original semaphores.

SPECIFICATIONS

MODEL Morris Minor (1948–71)

PRODUCTION 1,620,000

BODY STYLES Two- and four-door sedan, two-door convertible (Tourer), wagon (Traveller), van, and pickup.

CONSTRUCTION Unitary body/chassis; steel.

ENGINES Straight-four, 918cc, 803cc, 948cc, and 1098cc.

POWER OUTPUT 28 bhp (918cc); 48 bhp (1098cc).

TRANSMISSION Four-speed manual.

SUSPENSION Torsion bar independent front suspension; live-axle leaf-spring rear.

BRAKES Drums all around.

MAXIMUM SPEED 62–75 mph (100–121 km/h)

0–60 MPH (0–96 KM/H) 50+ sec for 918cc, 24 sec for 1098cc.

A.F.C. 36–43 mpg (12.7–15.2 km/l)

Engine

The original 918cc side-valve engine was replaced progressively in 1952 and 1953 by the Austin A-series 803cc overhead valve engine, then by the A-series 948cc, and finally the 1098cc. Power outputs rose from 28 bhp on the 918 to 48 bhp on the 1098.

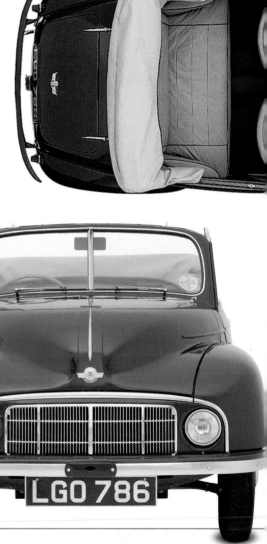

Engine Access
Space and easy engine access make the Minor a do-it-yourself favorite.

"Low Lights"
In 1950, the headlights on all Minors were moved to the top of the fenders. Earlier models such as the car featured here are now dubbed "low lights."

Handling
Even on cross-ply tires the original Minor won praise for its handling; one journalist described it as "one of the fastest slow cars in existence."

LGO 786

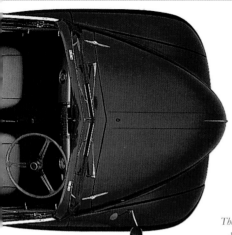

INTERIOR
This simple early dashboard was never really updated, but the speedo was later moved to the central console. The sprung-spoke steering wheel was traditional, but rack-and-pinion steering gave a crisp, light feel.

WINDSHIELD
The split windshield was replaced by a curved screen in 1956.

ADVERTISING
Sales literature described the Minor as "The Best Little Car in the World."

FAKE CONVERTIBLES
o desirable are these open ourers that in recent years there has been a trade in rogue ragtops—chopped sedans masquerading as iginal factory convertibles.

ODEL CHOICE
61 in (155 cm) the oduction car was 4 in cm) wider than the ototype. At its launch e Minor was available a two-door sedan and a convertible (Tourer). four-door, a wagon, a n, and a pickup later mpleted the line.

WIDENED BODY
he fillet in the bumper is another sign of the widening of the body.

NSU *Ro80*

ALONG WITH THE CITROËN DS *(see pages 178–81)*, the NSU Ro80 was 10 years ahead of itself. Beneath that striking, wind-evading shape was an audacious twin-rotary engine, front-wheel drive, disc brakes, and a semi-automatic clutchless gearbox. In 1967, the Ro80 won the acclaimed "Car of the Year" award and went on to be haile by many as "Car of the Decade." Technical preeminence aside, it also handled like a kart—the Ro80's stability, roadholding, ride, steering, and dynamic balance were exceptional, and far superior to most sports and GT cars. But NSU's brave new Wankel power unit was flawed and, due to acute rotor tip wear, would expire after only 15–20,000 miles (24–32,000 km). NSU honored their warranty claims until the bled white and eventually Audi/VW took over, axing the Ro80 in 1977.

PASSENGER SPACE
With no transmission tunnel or propshaft, plenty of headroom, and a long wheelbase, rear passengers found the Ro80 thoroughly accommodating.

ROTARY RELIABILITY
Modern technology has made the troublesome Wankel engine reliable now, and prices of Ro80s have been creeping gently upward.

FUTURISTIC DESIGN
In 1967, the Ro80 looked like a vision of the future with its low center of gravity, huge glass area, and sleek aerodynamics. The high rear end, widely imitated a decade later, held a huge, deep trunk.

SPECIFICATIONS

MODEL NSU Ro80 (1967–77)

PRODUCTION 37,204

BODY STYLE Front-engine five-seater sedan.

CONSTRUCTION Integral chassis with pressed steel monocoque body.

ENGINE Two-rotor Wankel, 1990cc.

POWER OUTPUT 113.5 bhp at 5500 rpm.

TRANSMISSION Three-speed semiautomatic.

SUSPENSION Independent all around.

BRAKES Four-wheel discs.

MAXIMUM SPEED 112 mph (180 km/h)

0–60 MPH (0–96 KM/H) 11.9 sec

0–100 MPH (0–161 KM/H) 25 sec

A.F.C. 20 mpg (7 km/l)

UNDER THE HOOD
Designed by Felix Wankel, the brilliant twin-rotary engine was equivalent to a two-liter reciprocating piston unit. Drive was through a torque converter with a Fichel & Sachs electro-pneumatic servo to a three-speed NSU gearbox.

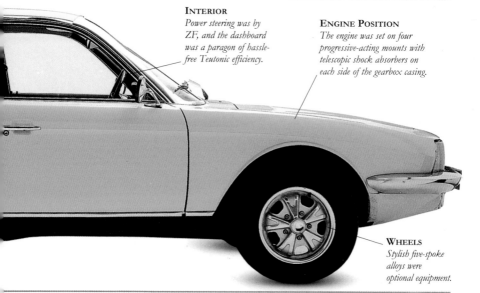

INTERIOR
Power steering was by ZF, and the dashboard was a paragon of hassle-free Teutonic efficiency.

ENGINE POSITION
The engine was set on four progressive-acting mounts with telescopic shock absorbers on each side of the gearbox casing.

WHEELS
Stylish five-spoke alloys were optional equipment.

OLDSMOBILE *Toronado*

THE FIRST BIG FRONT-WHEEL DRIVE land yacht since the Cord 810 of the Thirties, the Toronado was an automotive milestone and the most desirable Olds ever. With a 425cid V8 and unique chain-and-sprocket-drive automatic transmission, it had big-car power, outstanding road manners, and could crack 135 mph (217 km/h). Initial sales weren't great, with sober buyers choosing the more conventional Riviera but by '71 the Riviera's design had lost its way and the Toronado really came into its own, selling up to 50,000 a year until the mid-Seventies. From then on, however, the more glamorous Cadillac Eldorado outsold both the Riviera and the Toronado. Built on an exclusive slow-moving assembly line, Toronados had few faults, which was remarkable for such a technically audacious car. Even so, the press carped about poor rear visibility and lousy gas mileage. But time heals all wounds, and these days there's no greater collector's car bargain than a '66–'67 Toronado.

DISTINCTIVE DESIGN
The Toro was a dream car design. Despite sharing a basic body with other GM models like the Riviera and Eldorado, it still emerged very separate and distinctive. *Automobile Quarterly* called it "logical, imaginative, and totally unique," and *Motor Trade* nominated it Car of the Year in 1966.

ENGINE HEAT
High engine temperatures and the huge Rochester 4GC four-barrel carb caused many under the hood fires.

PRICING
Standard sticker price was $4,585; deluxe versions ran to $4,779.

FRONT DRIVE
Front-wheel drive was a novelty in 1967 and was a break from the past for GM.

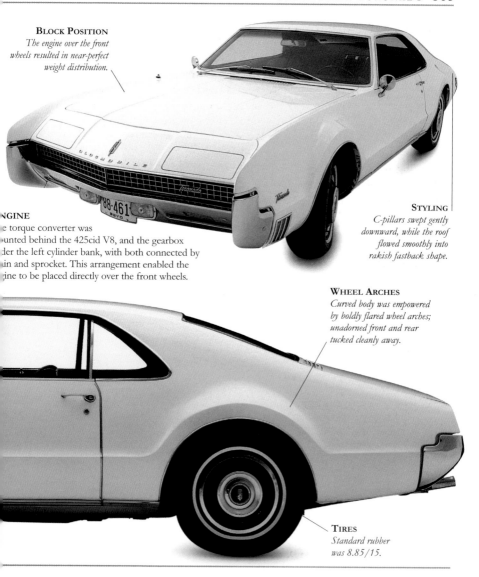

BLOCK POSITION
The engine over the front wheels resulted in near-perfect weight distribution.

NGINE
e torque converter was
unted behind the 425cid V8, and the gearbox
der the left cylinder bank, with both connected by
in and sprocket. This arrangement enabled the
ine to be placed directly over the front wheels.

STYLING
C-pillars swept gently downward, while the roof flowed smoothly into rakish fastback shape.

WHEEL ARCHES
Curved body was empowered by boldly flared wheel arches; unadorned front and rear tucked cleanly away.

TIRES
Standard rubber was 8.85/15.

TOP CREDENTIALS

The Toronado was brisk, poised and accurate. Understeer and front-wheel scrabble were kept t a minimum, and the car handl like a compact. Acceleration w in the Jaguar sedan league, and flat out it could ch the tail feathers of a Hi-Po Mustang.

REAR STYLING

Although an enormo car, the Toronado wa a rakish fastback.

EXHAUSTS
Twin exhausts provided the outlet for the 425cid's grunt.

SPECIFICATIONS

MODEL Oldsmobile Toronado (1967)
PRODUCTION 21,790
BODY STYLE Two-door, five-seater coupe.
CONSTRUCTION Steel body and frame.
ENGINE 425cid V8.
POWER OUTPUT 385 bhp.
TRANSMISSION Three-speed Turbo Hydra-Matic automatic.
SUSPENSION *Front:* torsion bar; *Rear:* leaf springs with solid axle.
BRAKES Front and rear drums.
MAXIMUM SPEED 135 mph (217 km/h)
0–60 MPH (0–96 KM/H) 8.5 sec
A.F.C. 11 mpg (3.9 km/l)

INTERIOR
Standard equipment included Turbo Hydra-Matic tranny, power steering and brakes, Strato-bench front seat, deluxe armrests, rear cigarette lighters, foam seat cushions, and interiors in vinyl, leather, or cloth.

OVEL FRONTAL STYLE

e concealed headlights and horizontal bar grille
ere genuinely innovative but would disappear in
8 for a heavier and less attractive front-end
atment. The Toronado's design arose in a free-
pression competition organized by Olds in 1962.
became the company's top model to date, and the
uivalent of the Buick Riviera. The Toronado was
M's first commitment to front-wheel drive, which
uld become a corporate theology by 1980.

POP-UP LIGHTS
*Unique retractable
headlights were classic
first-generation Toro.*

OLDSMOBILE *4-4-2*

1971 WAS THE LAST OF THE 4-4-2's glory years. A performance package par excellenc it was GM's longest-lived muscle car, tracing its roots all the way back to the heady days of '64 when a 4-4-2 combo was made available for the Oldsmobile Cutlass F-8 Possibly some of the most refined slingshots ever to come from any GM division, 4-4-2s had looks, charisma, and brawn to spare. The 4-4-2 nomenclature stood for a four-barrel carb, four-speed manual transmission, and two exhausts. Olds cleverly raided the store room, using hotshot parts previously only available to police departments. The deal was cheap and the noise on the street shattering. At $3,551, the superswift Hardtop Coupe came with a 455cid V8, Rallye suspension, Strato bucket seats, and a top whack of 125 mph (201 km/h). The 4-4-2 package might have run and run had it not hit the '71 fuel crisis head on. Which proved a shame, because it was to be a long time before power like this would be seen again.

PERFORMANCE ORIGINAL
From 1964 to '67, the 4-4-2 was simply a performance option that could be used on the F-85 line, but its growing popularity meant that in 1968 Olds decided to create a separate series for it in hardtop and convertible guises.

ENGINE BLOCK
Oldsmobile never tired of proclaiming that their 455cid mill was the largest V8 ever placed in a production car.

COLOR CHOICES
In addition to this Viking Blue, Oldsmobile added Bittersweet, Lime Green, and Saturn Gold to their 1971 color range.

MUSCLE LEGACY

Despite legislation that curbed the 4-4-2's power
output and led to the series being deleted after '71,
the 4-4-2 had made its mark and put Oldsmobile
well up there on the muscle-car map.

SPECIFICATIONS

MODEL Oldsmobile 4-4-2 (1971)

PRODUCTION 7,589 (1971)

BODY STYLES Two-door coupe
and convertible.

CONSTRUCTION Steel body and chassis.

ENGINE 455cid V8.

POWER OUTPUT 340–350 bhp.

TRANSMISSION Three-speed manual,
optional four-speed manual, three-speed
Turbo Hydra-Matic automatic.

SUSPENSION *Front:* coil springs;
Rear: leaf springs.

BRAKES Front discs, rear drums.

MAXIMUM SPEED 125 mph
(201 km/h)

0–60 MPH (0–96 KM/H) 6.4 sec

A.F.C. 10–14 mpg (3.5–5 km/l)

REFLECTORS
*Safety reflectors were
evidence of an age where
federal safety regulations
were being introduced.*

EXHAUST
*Apart from the badge, the
twin drain-pipe exhausts
were the only clue that you
were trailing a wild man.*

POWER RESTRAINT
Unleaded fuel meant a drop in engine compression and therefore in speed.

INSIDE EXTRA
The sports console at $77 and Rally pack with clock and tacho at $84 were extras.

SALES PITCH
Advertising literature espoused the 4-4-2's torquey credentials: "A hot new number. Police needed it, Olds built it, pursuit proved it." The 4-4-2 was dropped completely from '81 to '84, but revived in '85, lasting until the final rear-wheel drive Cutlass was rolled out in '87.

MEDIA PRAISE
Motor Trend *said that "despite emission controls the '71 4-4-2 will still churn up plenty of smoke and fury."*

INTERIOR
Despite the cheap-looking, wood-grain vinyl dash, the 4-4-2's cabin had a real race-car feel. Bucket seats, custom steering wheel, and Hurst Competition gear shift came as standard.

MORE OPTIONS

1971 Cutlasses were offered in Convertible or Hardtop Coupe guise. 4-4-2s had bucket seats, wide-louvered hood, heavy-duty wheels, and superwide bias-ply glass-belted tires with white stripes. The hot $369 W-30 option included forced air induction, heavy-duty air cleaner, alloy intake manifold, body striping, sports mirrors, and special "W-car" emblems.

ENGINE

"Factory blue-printed to save you money," screamed the ads. The monster 455cid V8 was stock for 4-4-2s in '71, but it was its swansong year and power output would soon dwindle. By the late-Seventies, the 4-4-2 performance pack had been seriously emasculated.

OLDS FIGURES

In 1971 Olds churned out 558,889 cars, putting them in sixth place in the sales league.

REDUCED POWER

Sales literature pronounced that "4-4-2 performance is strictly top drawer," but in reality, unleaded fuel meant a performance penalty. Sixty could still be reached in under six seconds, though.

PACKARD *Hawk*

DISTINCTIVE, BIZARRE, AND VERY un-American, the '58 Hawk was a pastiche of European styling cues. Inspired by the likes of Ferrari and Mercedes, it boasted tan pleated leather, white-on-black instruments, Jaguaresque fender vents, a turned metal dashboard, gulping hood air-scoop, and a broad fiberglass shovel-nostril that could have been lifted off a Maserati. And it was supercharged. But Packard's attempt to distance itself from traditional Detroit iron failed. At $4,000, the Hawk was overpriced, underrefined, and overdecorated. Packard had merged with Studebaker back in 1954, and although it was initially a successful alliance, problems with suppliers and another buyout in 1956 basically sealed the company's fate. Only 588 Hawks were built, with the very last Packard rolling off the South Bend, Indiana, line on July 13, 1958. Today the Hawk stands as a quaint curiosity, a last-ditch attempt to preserve the Packard pedigree. It remains one of the most fiercely desired of the final Packards.

REAR ASPECT
Despite its European airs, no American car could escape the vogue for fins, and this car has two beauties. Nobody was too sure about the spare wheel impression on the trunk, though.

ENGINE
Flight-O-Matic automatic transmission and a hefty, supercharged 289cid V8 came as standard. The Hawk's blower was a belt-driven McCulloch supercharger.

ATTRACTIVE PROFILE
Uniquely, the Hawk had exterior vinyl armrests running along the side windows and a refreshing lack of chrome gaudiness on the flanks. The roof line and halo roof band are aeronautical, and the belt line is tense.

SPECIFICATIONS

MODEL Packard Hawk (1958)

PRODUCTION 588 (1958)

BODY STYLE Two-door, four-seater coupe.

CONSTRUCTION Steel body and chassis.

ENGINE 289cid V8.

POWER OUTPUT 275 bhp.

TRANSMISSION Three-speed Flight-O-Matic automatic, optional overdrive.

SUSPENSION *Front:* independent coil springs; *Rear:* leaf springs.

BRAKES Front and rear drums.

MAXIMUM SPEED 125 mph (201 km/h)

0–60 MPH (0–96 KM/H) 8 sec

A.F.C. 15 mpg (5.3 km/l)

UNCONVENTIONAL FRONT
Even for the '50s, most buyers found the Hawk's frontal aspect a little too much, preferring instead the more traditional Detroit "million dollar chromium grin." The Hawk's styling was just plain ugly. And that's why it didn't sell.

PANHARD *PL17 Tigre*

PANHARD WAS ONE OF THE world's oldest names in car manufacturing, dating back to 1872. But by 1955 they had lost their upmarket image and had to be rescued by Citroën, who eventually bought them out completely in 1965. The Dyna, produced after World War II in response to a need for a small, practical, and economical machine, had an aluminum alloy frame, bulkhead, and horizontally opposed, air-cooled, twin-cylinder engine. In 1954, the Dyna became front-wheel drive, with a bulbous but streamlined new body. The 848cc flat-twin engine was a gem, and in post-1961 Tigre guise pushed out 60 bhp; this gave 90 mph (145 km/h), enough to win a Monte Carlo Rally. Advertised as "the car that makes sense," the PL17 was light, quick, miserly on fuel, and years ahead of its time.

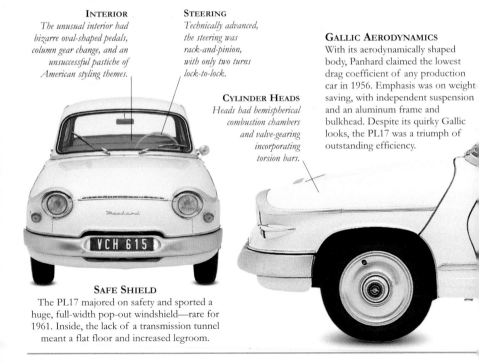

INTERIOR
The unusual interior had bizarre oval-shaped pedals, column gear change, and an unsuccessful pastiche of American styling themes.

STEERING
Technically advanced, the steering was rack-and-pinion, with only two turns lock-to-lock.

CYLINDER HEADS
Heads had hemispherical combustion chambers and valve-gearing incorporating torsion bars.

GALLIC AERODYNAMICS
With its aerodynamically shaped body, Panhard claimed the lowest drag coefficient of any production car in 1956. Emphasis was on weight saving, with independent suspension and an aluminum frame and bulkhead. Despite its quirky Gallic looks, the PL17 was a triumph of outstanding efficiency.

VCH 615

SAFE SHIELD
The PL17 majored on safety and sported a huge, full-width pop-out windshield—rare for 1961. Inside, the lack of a transmission tunnel meant a flat floor and increased legroom.

ENGINE
The engine design dated back to 1940. Cylinders were cast integral with their heads in light alloy, cooling fins and cast-iron liners.

SPECIFICATIONS

MODEL Panhard PL17 Tigre (1961–64)

PRODUCTION 130,000 (all models)

BODY STYLE Four-door, four-seater sports sedan.

CONSTRUCTION Separate chassis with steel and aluminum body.

ENGINE 848cc twin horizontally-opposed air-cooled.

POWER OUTPUT 60 bhp at 5800 rpm.

TRANSMISSION Front-wheel drive four-speed manual.

SUSPENSION Independent front with twin transverse leaf, torsion bar rear.

BRAKES Four-wheel drums.

MAXIMUM SPEED 90 mph (145 km/h)

0–60 MPH (0–96 KM/H) 23.1 sec

A.F.C. 38 mpg (13.5 km/l)

EFFICIENT DESIGN
Simple design meant fewer moving parts, more power, and more miles to the gallon.

PEUGEOT *203*

COMPARED TO THE SCORES OF upright postwar sedans that looked like church pews, Peugeot's 203 was a breath of fresh air. In addition to being one of the French carmaker's most successful products, the 203's monocoque body and revolutionary engine set it apart. In its day, the 1290cc OHV power plant was state-of-the-art, with an aluminum cylinder head and hemispherical combustion chambers, said to be the inspiration for the famous Chrysler "Hemi" unit. With a line that included two- and four-door cabriolets, a family wagon, and a two-door coupe, the French really took to the 203, loving its tough mechanicals, willing progress, and supple ride. By its demise in 1960, the 203 had broken records for Peugeot, with nearly 700,000 sold.

SHOWSTOPPER
Widely acclaimed at the 1948 Paris Motor Show, the 203's slippery shape was wind-tunnel tested in model form and claimed to have a rather optimistic drag coefficient of just 0.36—lower than a modern Porsche 911 *(see pages 420–21)*. Quality touches abound, such as the exterior brightwork in stainless steel.

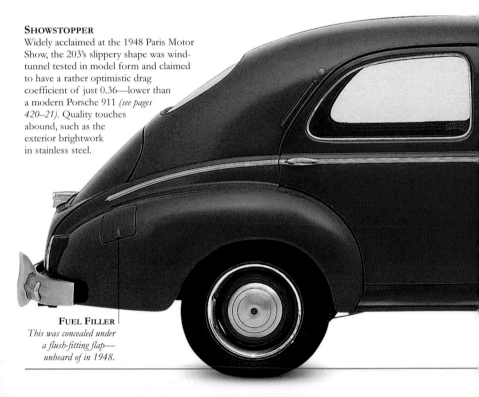

FUEL FILLER
This was concealed under a flush-fitting flap—unheard of in 1948.

WINDSHIELD WIPERS
"Clap hand" windshield wipers may look a period piece, but the motor was so robust that it was still in use 43 years later on the tailgate wiper of the 504 model.

SPECIFICATIONS

MODEL Peugeot 203 (1948–60)

PRODUCTION 685,828

BODY STYLES Two-door coupe, two- or four-door convertible, family wagon.

CONSTRUCTION All-steel monocoque rigid one-piece body shell.

ENGINE Four-cylinder OHV 1290cc.

POWER OUTPUT 42–49 bhp at 3500 rpm.

TRANSMISSION Four-speed column change with surmultiplié overdrive.

SUSPENSION Transverse leaf independent front, coil spring rear with Panhard rod.

BRAKES Drums all around.

MAXIMUM SPEED 73 mph (117 km/h)

0–60 MPH (0–96 KM/H) 20 sec

A.F.C. 20–35 mpg (7–12.4 km/l)

BUDGET INTERIOR
Interior was built to a budget with rubber mats, metal dash, and cloth seat facings.

SMART DESIGN
The hood swung up on counterbalanced springs, and the front grille came away by undoing a butterfly nut.

Badge
Peugeot's lion logo dates back to 1906, when Robert Peugeot started up his own company called Lion-Peugeot.

INTERIOR
With postwar steel in short supply, aluminum was used to good effect in the under-dash handbrake and column gear change. The handsome fastback body gave plenty of cabin room.

ENDURING BLOCK
The basic design was still used in the 1980s for Peugeot's 1971cc 505 model.

ENGINE
The 49 bhp OHV push-rod engine was the 203's most advanced feature. With wet liners, low compression ratio, and alloy head, it was smooth, free-revving, and long-lasting.

GEARBOX
The four-speed gearbox was really a three with overdrive.

Rack Mounts
Integral mounting points for a roof rack were a nice styling touch.

Stylish Butt
These stylish sweeping curves were influenced by the 1946 Chevrolet. A vast trunk with a low-loading sill made the 203 ideal family transportation. Another side to the 203 was racing; many were tuned and campaigned in rallies like the Monte Carlo.

Paintwork
A high gloss finish was achieved by the application of several coats of synthetic lacquer.

Front View
The 203 was modified in 1953 with a curved windshield, revised dashboard, and front quarter lights. This model was registered in 1955. The 203's turning circle was usefully tight—only 14 ft 9 in (5.39 m), with three turns lock-to-lock. Despite its 18 cwt weight and relatively modest power output, the handsome Peugeot's performance was sprightly.

Suspension
Front suspension was by transverse leaf independent springing.

PLYMOUTH *Barracuda (1964)*

THE BIG THREE WEREN'T slow to cash in on the Sixties' youth boom. Ford couldn't keep its Mustang project secret and the Chrysler Corporation desperately wanted a piece of the action. But it had to work fast. It took its existing compact, the Plymouth Valiant, prettied up the front end, added a dramatic wrap-around rear window, and called it the Barracuda. It hit the showroom carpets in April 1964, two weeks before the Mustang. A disarming amalgam of performance, poise, and refinement, Plymouth had achieved a miracle on the scale of loaves and fishes—it made the Barracuda fast, yet handle crisply and ride smoothly. The 273cid V8 made the car quicker than a Mustang, but that bizarre rear window dated fiercely and Mustangs outsold Barracudas 10-to-one. Plymouth believed the long-hood-short-trunk "pony" formula wouldn't captivate consumers like a swooping, sporty fastback. Half a million Mustang buyers told them they'd backed the wrong horse.

HOT INSIDE

The greenhouse interior got hot on sunny days but was well detailed and enormously practical. Standard fare was bucket seats and bucket-shaped rear bench seat. Instruments were matte silver with circular chrome bezels. The padded dash was a $16.35 extra, as was a wood-grain steering wheel.

TRANSMISSION

Optional was Chrysler's new Hurst-linkage manual transmission.

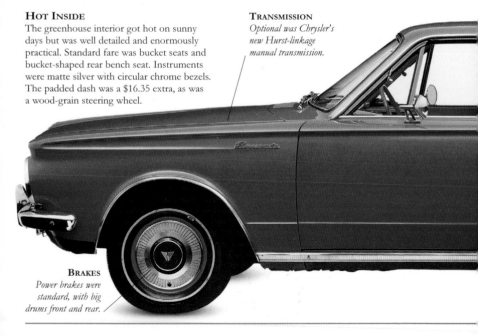

BRAKES

Power brakes were standard, with big drums front and rear.

REAR WINDOW
*Massive window
earned the 'Cuda
top marks for safety.*

SPECIFICATIONS

MODEL Plymouth Barracuda (1964)

PRODUCTION 23,443 (1964)

BODY STYLE Two-door fastback.

CONSTRUCTION Steel body and chassis.

ENGINES 170cid, 225cid sixes,
273cid V8.

POWER OUTPUT 101–235 bhp.

TRANSMISSION Three-speed manual,
optional four-speed manual, and
three-speed TorqueFlite automatic.

SUSPENSION *Front:* torsion bar;
Rear: leaf springs.

BRAKES Front and rear drums, optional
front discs.

MAXIMUM SPEED 100–110 mph
(161–177 km/h)

0–60 MPH (0–96 KM/H) 8–13 sec

A.F.C. 16–22 mpg (5.7–7.8 km/l)

ACRES OF GLASS

The fastback glass wrapped down to the rear fender
line and was developed by the Pittsburgh Plate Glass
Company; it was the largest use of glass in any
production car to date. As a result, visibility was epic.

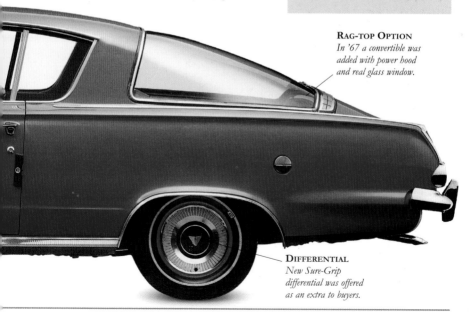

RAG-TOP OPTION
*In '67 a convertible was
added with power hood
and real glass window.*

DIFFERENTIAL
*New Sure-Grip
differential was offered
as an extra to buyers.*

MUSTANG CONTRAST
Compared with the Mustang, the Barracuda's front was busy, cluttered, and lacked symmetry, but it was a brave and bold design. Had the Mustang not been launched in the same month, things might have been very different.

MIRROR
Remote-controlled outside side mirror was a $12 convenience option.

ADJUSTABLE MIRROR
Prismatic day-and-night mirror could be adjusted to deflect annoying headlight glare at night.

SELLING THE WHEEL
The 'Cuda brochure insisted that the optional wood-grain steering wheel "gave you the feel of a racing car."

PLYMOUTH

400th ANNIVERSARY

19 1W166142 65

FLORIDA

MEDIA PRAISE
Road and Track *magazine said, "for sports car performance and practicality, the Barracuda is perfect."*

VALIANT LINKS
The Barracuda was a Plymouth Valiant from the roof line down and shared its power and suspension.

FLEXIBLE SEAT
*Bucket seat could
be adjusted into
six positions.*

COLORS
*Interior colors
available were gold,
blue, black, or this
sharp red.*

TRUNK SPACE
The rear seats folded forward to
produce an astronomical cargo
area that measured 7 ft (2.14 m)
long. Based on the mass-market,
best-selling Valiant, the Barracuda
was aimed at a completely new
market—rich young things with
a desire to look cool.

BUMPERS
*Bumper guards were
an $11.45 option.*

THE FORMULA S OPTION
The 'Cuda's base engine was a
170cid slant six. Other mills were
the 225cid six and two-barrel
273cid V8. Despite the fact that
the Formula S offered a V8
block plus race trimmings, this
was still rather tame by
Plymouth standards. The '61
Fury, for example, had a 318cid
unit that pushed out 230 bhp.

Did you know
that the 1965 Plymouth Barracuda
has an optional Formula 'S' sports package
that includes a Commando 273-cu.-in.
V-8 engine; heavy-duty shocks, springs, and
sway bar; a tachometer; wide-rim (14-in.)
wheels, special Blue Streak tires, and
simulated bolt-on wheel covers?
You do now.

THE ROARING 5½
FURY
BELVEDERE
VALIANT
BARRACUDA

PLYMOUTH *'Cuda (1970)*

THE TOUGH-SOUNDING '70s 'Cuda was one of the last flowerings of America's performance binge. Furiously fast, it was a totally new incarnation of the first '64 Barracuda and unashamedly aimed at psychopathic street-racers. Cynically, Plymouth even dubbed their belligerent model lineup "The Rapid Transit System." '70 Barracudas came in three styles—the 'Cuda was the performance model—and nine engine choices, topped by the outrageous 426cid Hemi. Chrysler's advertising men bellowed that the Hemi was "our angriest body wrapped around ol' King Kong hisself." But rising insurance rates and new emission standards meant that the muscle car was an endangered species. By 1973 Plymouth brochures showed a 'Cuda with a young married couple, complete with a baby in the smiling woman's arms. The party was well and truly over.

NEAT DESIGN
The '70 'Cuda's crisp, taut styling is shared with the Dodge Challenger, and the classic long-hood-short-trunk design leaves you in no doubt that this is a pony car. Government legislation and hefty insurance rates ensured that this was the penultimate year of the big-engined Barracudas; after '71, the biggest block on offer was a 340cid V8.

AIR CLEANER
Unsilenced air cleaners such as this weren't allowed in California because of drive-by noise regulations.

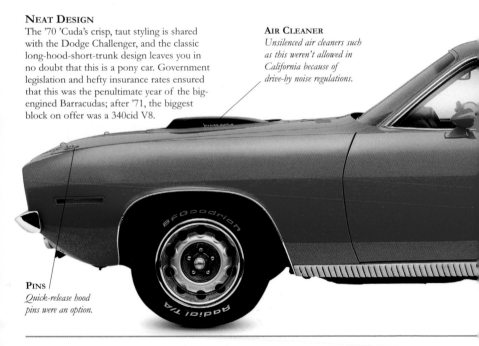

PINS
Quick-release hood pins were an option.

AIR CLEANER
*The air cleaner
~~ated ("shaked")
~~ugh the top of the
hood, a standard
'Cuda feature.*

SALES FIGURES
*Total 1970 'Cuda production
was a healthy 30,267 units.*

SPECIFICATIONS

MODEL Plymouth 'Cuda (1970)

PRODUCTION 30,267 (1970)

BODY STYLES Two-door, four-seater coupe and convertible.

CONSTRUCTION Steel unitary body.

ENGINES 383cid, 426cid, 440cid V8s.

POWER OUTPUT 335–425 bhp.

TRANSMISSION Three-speed manual, optional four-speed manual, and three-speed TorqueFlite automatic.

SUSPENSION *Front:* torsion bars; *Rear:* leaf springs with live axle.

BRAKES Front discs, rear drums.

MAXIMUM SPEED 137–150 mph (220–241 km/h)

0–60 MPH (0–96 KM/H) 5.9–6.9 sec

A.F.C. 12–17 mpg (4.2–6 km/l)

ENGINE
The 440cid "six-pack" Magnum engine cranked out 385 bhp and drank through three two-barrel Holley carbs, explaining the six-pack label. Base engine was a 383cid V8, which pushed out 335 horses.

PERFORMANCE PARTS
*Super Stock springs and
a heavy-duty Dana 60
rear axle were standard
on all 440 'Cudas.*

STRIPING
*Optional inverted
hockey stick graphics
trumpeted engine size.*

OVERHEAD STYLING

Plymouth stylists kept the shape uncluttered, with tapered-in bumpers, concealed wipers, flush door handles, smooth overhangs, and subtly flared wheel arches. Even so, the 'Cuda had ballooned in proportions since the first Barracuda models of the mid-Sixties and, along with the Mustang *(see pages 278–85)*, now started to lose its *raison d'être*. With the energy crisis just around the corner, its days were numbered.

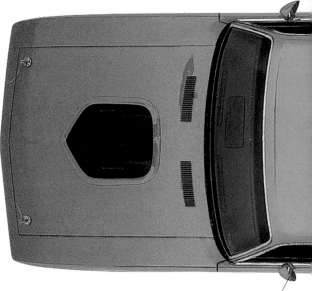

HIDDEN WIPERS
Windshield wipers were neatly concealed behind the rear lip of the hood.

RACING MIRRORS
Color-coded racing mirrors could be ordered for $26.

BIG-BLOCK SPEED
The 440-6 was a $250 'Cuda engine option that allowed the car to hit the quarter mile in 14.44 seconds. Only 652 1970 'Cuda hardtops were equipped with the $871 Street Hemi V8.

CALIFORNIA
595 VNP

TRANSMISSION
Quick manual upshifts were possible with the Slap Stik T-handle.

INTERIOR
'Cuda interiors were flamboyant, with body-hugging bucket seats, Hurst pistol-grip shifter, and wood-grain steering wheel. This model has the Rally instrument cluster, with tachometer and oil pressure gauge.

'CUDA BADGE
'Cuda was a slang name coined by Woodward Avenue cruisers.

COLOR CHOICE
'Cudas came in 18 strident colors, with funky names like In Violet, Lemon Twist, and Vitamin C.

DECLINING FIGURES
Though 'Cuda hardtop models cost $3,164 in 1970, by '74, total Barracuda sales for the year had dipped to just over 1,000, and it was axed before the '75 model year.

TWIN EXHAUSTS
Provocative square exhausts left no doubt about the 'Cuda's grunt.

PONTIAC *GTO*

"THE GREAT ONE" WAS Pontiac's answer to a youth market with attitude and disposable cash. Detroit exploited a generation's rebellion by creating cars with machismo to burn. In 1964, John DeLorean, Pontiac's chief engineer, shoehorned the division's biggest V8 into the timid little Tempest compact with electrifying results. He then beefed up the brakes and suspension, threw in three two-barrel carbs and garnished the result with a name that belonged to a Ferrari. In 1966 it became a model in its own right, and Detroit's first "muscle car" had been born. Pundits believe that the flowing lines of these second-generation GTOs make them the best-looking of all. Engines were energetic performers, with a standard 335 bhp 389cid V8 that could be specified in 360 bhp high-output tune. But by '67 GTO sales had tailed off by 15 percent, depressed by a burgeoning social conscience and federal meddling. The performance era was about to be legislated into the history books.

ORIGINAL MUSCLE

John DeLorean's idea of placing a high-spec engine in the standard Tempest body paved the way for a whole new genre and gave Pontiac immediate success in '64. Had Ford not chosen to release the Mustang in the same year, the GTO would have been the star of '64, and even more sales would have been secured.

BIG BLOCK

Pontiac was the first mainstream manufacturer to combine big-block power with a light body. In tests, a '66 Convertible hit 60 mph (96 km/h) in 6.8 seconds.

WHEELS
Five-spoke Rally II sport wheels were a $72 option.

SALES SUCCESS
Sales peaked in 1966, with over 95,000 GTOs going to power-hungry young drivers whose average age was 25. The convertible was the most aesthetically pleasing of the line.

SPECIFICATIONS

MODEL Pontiac GTO Convertible (1966)

PRODUCTION 96,946 (1966, all body styles)

BODY STYLES Two-door, five-seater hardtop, coupe, and convertible.

CONSTRUCTION Steel unitary body.

ENGINE 389cid V8s.

POWER OUTPUT 335–360 bhp.

TRANSMISSION Three-speed manual, optional four-speed manual, and three-speed Hydra-Matic automatic.

SUSPENSION Front and rear coil springs.

BRAKES Front and rear drums, optional discs.

MAXIMUM SPEED 125 mph (201 km/h)

0–60 MPH (0–96 KM/H) 6.8–9.5 sec

A.F.C. 15 mpg (5.3 km/l)

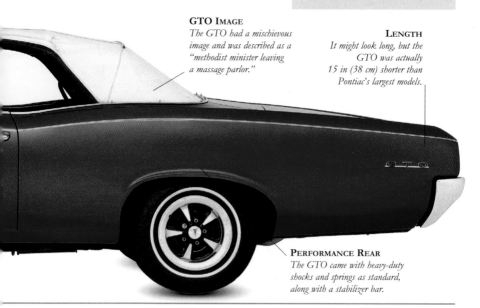

GTO IMAGE
The GTO had a mischievous image and was described as a "methodist minister leaving a massage parlor."

LENGTH
It might look long, but the GTO was actually 15 in (38 cm) shorter than Pontiac's largest models.

PERFORMANCE REAR
The GTO came with heavy-duty shocks and springs as standard, along with a stabilizer bar.

CHOICE EXTRAS
GTOs could be ordered with Rally Cluster gauges, close-ratio four-on-the-floor, center console, and walnut grain dash insert.

SEATS
Reclining front seats could be specified as an extra.

INTERIOR
GTOs were equipped to the same high standard as the Pontiac Tempest Le Mans. Items included ashtray lights, cigarette lighter, carpeting, and a power top for convertibles. Air-conditioning and power steering could be ordered at $343 and $95 respectively.

HEADLIGHTS
The stacked headlights were new for Pontiacs in '65 and were retained on GTOs until the end of the decade.

NICKNAME
Muscle-car buffs dubbed the GTO "The Goat."

ENGINE OPTION
The HO model could do the standing quarter in 14.2 seconds.

GTO BADGE
Road & Track *magazine wrote that the theft of the GTO name from Ferrari was "an act of unforgivable dishonesty."*

ENGINE
The base 335 bhp 389cid block had a high-output Tri-Power big brother that pushed out 360 bhp for an extra $116. The line was expanded in '67 to include an economy 255 bhp 400cid V8 and a Ram-Air 400cid mill that also developed 360 bhp, but at higher revs per minute.

INDICATORS
Turn signals in grille were meant to mimic European-style driving lights.

'66 FACELIFT
First-generation GTOs were facelifted in '66 with a more aggressive split grille and stacked headlight treatment and gently kicked-up rear fenders. 1966 GTOs such as the example here were Pontiac's most popular, with sales nudging close to 100,000 units.

PONTIAC *Trans Am*

IN THE SEVENTIES, FOR THE FIRST TIME in American history, the government intervened in the auto industry. With the 1973 oil crisis, the Big Three were ordered to tighten their belts. Automotive design came to a halt, and the big-block Trans Am became the last of the really fast cars. The muscular Firebird had been around since 1969 and, with its rounded bulges, looked as if its skin had been forced out by the strength underneath. Gas shortage or not, the public liked the '73 Trans Am, and sales quadrupled. The 455 Super Duty V8 put out 310 horsepower and, while Pontiac bravely tried to ignore the killjoy legislation, someone remarked that the High Output 455 was the largest engine ever offered in a pony car. The game was up, and within months modifications to comply with emission regulations had brought power down to 290 bhp. The hell-raising 455 soldiered on until 1976, and that athletic fastback body until '82. But the frenetic muscle years of 1967–73 had irretrievably passed, and those wonderful big-block banshees would never be seen again.

ESTABLISHED MUSCLE
Detroit's oldest warrior, the Firebird is the only muscle car that's been in the brochures for 30 years. Based on the Camaro's F-body, the Firebird debuted in 1967, but the wild Trans Am didn't appear until '69. Surprisingly, there was little fanfare until the hot 1970 restyle.

HOOD SCOOP
The rear-facing "shaker" hood scoop was an indication of the Trans Am's immense power.

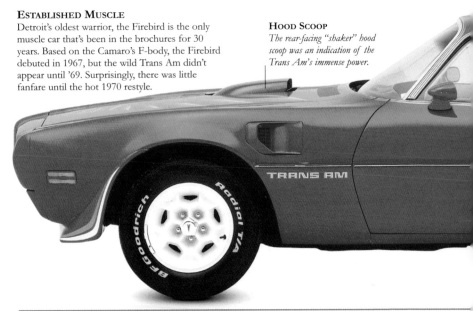

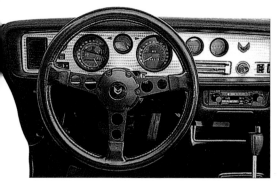

DASHBOARD

Second-edition Trans Ams had a standard engine-turned dash insert, Rally gauges, bucket seats, and a Formula steering wheel. The tachometer was calibrated to a very optimistic 8000 rpm. The speedo was just as untruthful, with a maximum of 160 mph (257 km/h).

SPECIFICATIONS

MODEL Pontiac Firebird Trans Am (1973)

PRODUCTION 4,802 (1973)

BODY STYLE Two-door, four-seater fastback.

CONSTRUCTION Steel unitary body.

ENGINE 455cid V8.

POWER OUTPUT 250–310 bhp.

TRANSMISSION Four-speed manual or three-speed Turbo Hydra-Matic automatic.

SUSPENSION *Front:* coil springs; *Rear:* leaf springs with live axle.

BRAKES Front discs, rear drums.

MAXIMUM SPEED 135 mph (217 km/h)

0–60 MPH (0–96 KM/H) 5.4 sec

A.F.C. 17 mpg (6 km/l)

WHEEL ARCHES
Flared wheel arches made the Trans Am look even tougher.

SPOILER
For 1973 the fastback bodyshell was given a full-width rear-deck spoiler.

DECORATIVE DECAL

The "screaming chicken" graphics gracing the hood were new for 1973. Created by stylist John Schinella, they were a modern rendition of the Native American phoenix symbol. The Trans Am now looked as distinctive as it drove.

BODY BY FISHER

Pontiac wanted to portray that bodies were hand-built by an old-time carriage-maker.

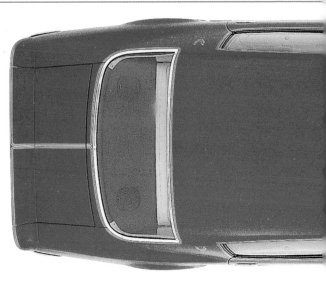

'73 REVIVAL

Steep insurance rates and a national shift away from performance iron didn't help Trans Am sales, but in 1973, the year of the "screaming chicken" hood decal and Super Duty V8, Trans Ams left showroom like heat-seeking missile Nearly killed off by GM, it soldiered on into the emasculated '80s and '90s.

FRONT VALANCE

New front valance panel with small air dam appeared in 197

ENGINE

The big-block Trans Ams were
Detroit's final salute to performance.
The 455 Super Duty could reach 60
(96 km/h) in under six seconds, and
run to 135 mph (217 km/h).

AME IN DISPUTE

e Trans Am name was "borrowed"
m the Sports Car Club of
nerica, and the SCCA threatened
sue unless Pontiac paid a
yalty of $5 per car. The
ans Am was a seriously
acho machine, with
ar & Driver magazine
lling it "a hard-
uscled, lightning-
lexed commando
a car."

EXHAUSTS

*Dual exhausts with
chrome extensions
were standard.*

PORSCHE *356B*

VW BEETLE DESIGNER Ferdinand Porsche may have given the world the "people's car," but it was his son Ferry who, with Karl Rabe, created the 356. These days a Porsche stands for precision, performance, purity, and perfection, and the 356 is the first chapter in that story. Well not quite. The 356 was so named because it was the 356th project from the Porsche design office. It was also the first car to bear the Porsche name. Postwar expediency forced a reliance on Beetle underpinnings, but the 356 is much more than a Bug in butterfly's clothes. Its rear-engined layout and design descends from the father car, but in the athletic son the genes are mutated into a true sports machine. A pert, nimble, tail-happy treat, the pretty 356 is the foundation stone of a proud sports tradition.

INSPIRED ENGINEERING
The first Porsche 356 was a triumph of creative expediency and inspired engineering, taking basic VW Beetle elements to create a new breed of sports car. Aficionados adore the earliest cars, often affectionately dubbed "jelly molds."

ACCESS COVER
Not a covered jacking point but an access cover to allow you to retrieve the torsion bar.

CAB
Seats were wide and fl and the large, alm vertical, steering wheel h a light feel. Passengers g a grab hand

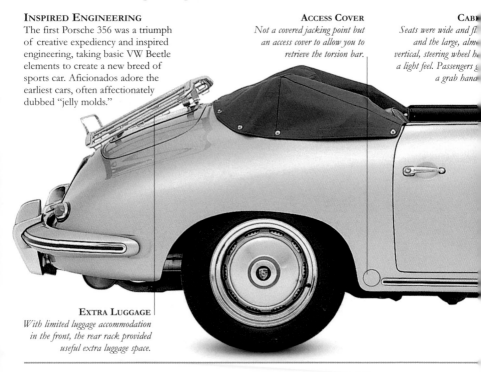

EXTRA LUGGAGE
With limited luggage accommodation in the front, the rear rack provided useful extra luggage space.

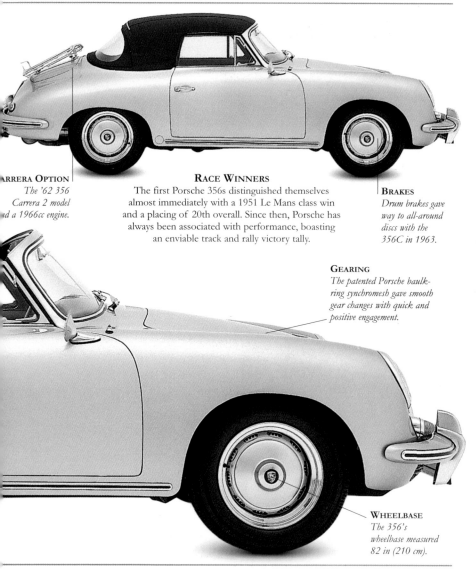

*The '62 356
Carrera 2 model
d a 1966cc engine.*

RACE WINNERS

The first Porsche 356s distinguished themselves
almost immediately with a 1951 Le Mans class win
and a placing of 20th overall. Since then, Porsche has
always been associated with performance, boasting
an enviable track and rally victory tally.

BRAKES
*Drum brakes gave
way to all-around
discs with the
356C in 1963.*

GEARING
*The patented Porsche baulk-
ring synchromesh gave smooth
gear changes with quick and
positive engagement.*

WHEELBASE
*The 356's
wheelbase measured
82 in (210 cm).*

SPLIT-SHIELD DECEIT
On convertibles, the rear-view mirror was attached to a slim chrome bar that gave a deceptive split-windshield appearance from the front.

'62 BLOCK
This is the 1582cc engine of the 1962 356B.

ENGINE
The rear-engined layout was determined by reliance on VW Beetle mechanics and running gear. The flat-four engine, with its so-called "boxer" layout of horizontally opposed cylinders, is not pure Beetle, but a progressive development. Engines grew from 1086cc to 1996cc.

REDESIGN
On the 356B, headlights and bumpers moved higher up the fender.

INTERIOR
The interior is delightfully functional, simple, timeless, and, because of that, enduringly fashionable. Below the padded dash are the classic green-on-black instruments.

DY

911 PRECURSOR

The original incarnation of the 356 had lower wheels and a more bulbous shape. The featured car here is a 1962 356B Super 90, produced just two years before the birth of the 911 *(see pages 420–21)* which, although a very different beast, is still an evolution of the original shape.

REAR VIEW

On the 356B twin exhausts exit on each side through bumper overriders. The busy air-cooled thrum is an unmistakeable trademark sound that was appreciated by thousands of buyers.

SPECIFICATIONS

MODEL Porsche 356B (1959–63)

PRODUCTION 30,963

BODY STYLES Two-plus-two fixed-head coupe, convertible, and Speedster.

CONSTRUCTION Unitary steel body with integral pressed-steel platform chassis.

ENGINE Air-cooled, horizontally opposed flat-four 1582cc with twin carbs.

POWER OUTPUT 90 bhp at 5500 rpm (Super 90).

TRANSMISSION Four-speed manual, all synchromesh, rear-wheel drive.

SUSPENSION *Front:* independent, trailing arms with transverse torsion bars and anti-roll bar; *Rear:* independent, swing half-axles, radius arms, and transverse torsion bars. Telescopic shocks.

BRAKES Hydraulic drums all around.

MAXIMUM SPEED 110 mph (77 km/h)

0–60 MPH (0–96 KM/H) 10 sec

A.F.C. 30–35 mpg (10.6–12.5 km/l)

PORSCHE *Carrera 911 RS*

AN INSTANT LEGEND, THE CARRERA RS became the classic 911 and is hailed as one of the ultimate road cars of all time. With lighter body panels and stripped out interior trim, the RS is simply a featherweight racer. The classic, flat-six engine was bored out to 2.7 liters and boasted uprated fuel injection and forged flat-top pistons—modifications that helped to push out a sparkling 210 bhp. Porsche had no problem selling all the RSs it could make, and a total of 1,580 were built and sold in just 12 months. Standard 911s were often criticized for tail-happy handling, but the Carrera RS is a supremely balanced machine. Its race-bred responses offer the last word in sensory gratification. With one of the best engines ever made, an outstanding chassis, and 150 mph (243 km/h) top speed, the RS can rub bumpers with the world's finest. Collectors and Porsche buffs consider this the preeminent 911, with prices reflecting its cultlike status. The RS is the original air-cooled screamer.

LIGHTWEIGHT COUPE
The polyester bumpers, thin steel bodywork, and lightweight "Glaverbell" glass help the RS to weigh in at just over 1,984 lb (900 kg). Standard Porsches tip the scales at 2,194 lb (995 kg). In addition, the weight distribution and rear engine layout demand some very gentle treatment of the throttle. Handle the 911 roughly and it will understeer.

WINDSHIELD
Steeply raked windshield helped the 911's wind-evading shape.

GoldStar

17

LIGHTS
Classic slanted headlights betrayed the 911's VW Beetle origins.

REAR-ENGINED

The bored-out, air-cooled 2.7-liter "Boxermotor" produces huge reserves of power. Externally, it is identifiable only by extra cylinder cooling fins.

SPECIFICATIONS

MODEL Porsche Carrera 911 RS (1972–73)

PRODUCTION 1,580

BODY STYLE Two door, two seater coupe.

CONSTRUCTION Thin-gauge steel panels.

ENGINE Flat-six, 2687cc.

POWER OUTPUT 210 bhp at 5100 rpm.

TRANSMISSION Close-ratio, five-speed manual.

SUSPENSION Front and rear torsion bar.

BRAKES Ventilated discs front and rear, with aluminum calipers.

MAXIMUM SPEED 150 mph (243 km/h)

0–60 MPH (0–96 KM/H) 5.6 sec

0–100 MPH (0–161 KM/H) 12.8 sec

A.F.C. 23 mpg (8.1 km/l)

WHEEL ARCHES
Rear wheel arches were flared to accommodate 7-in (18-cm) rims.

REAR SPOILER
The RS had a fiberglass Burzel rear spoiler, employed to reduce tail-end lift at high speeds.

RANGE ROVER

DESCRIBING THE RANGE ROVER AS THE BEST CAR in the world is no exaggeration. The sheer breadth of the capabilities of the third-generation Rangie (as it is affectionately known) was truly awesome. Developed by BMW in the late '90s, it set new SUV standards with air suspension, voice-activated satellite navigation, the heave of a hot hatch, and the mountain-climbing tenacity of Sherpa Tenzing. The most expensive and popular Range Rover ever, the L322 was a 4x4 that felt like a Bentley and was the car that helped make Jaguar Land Rover one of the most admired and innovative car companies on the planet.

THE FRUGAL 4x4
4.4 TDV8 versions could better 30 mpg (12.7 km/l).

MAGIC CARPET
On-road ride was serenely smooth.

INTERIOR

Lush leather, cooled seats, a heated steering wheel, touch-screen TV, virtual instruments, and an eight-speed automatic gearbox all came as standard. The interior on top Autobiography models was as palatial as a Rolls Royce.

BIG SCREEN
Massive heated screen had automatic rain-sensitive wipers.

STYLING FLOURISH
Decorative side grilles broke up the huge slab-sided flanks.

SPECIFICATIONS

MODEL Range Rover (2002–12)

PRODUCTION More than 200,000

BODY STYLE Five-door SUV.

CONSTRUCTION Monocoque.

ENGINE 3.0–5.0-liter, straight-six V8.

POWER OUTPUT 286–503 bhp.

TRANSMISSION Five- to eight-speed automatic.

SUSPENSION Independent/air.

BRAKES Four-wheel discs.

MAXIMUM SPEED 130 mph (209 km/h) (supercharged)

0–60 MPH (0–96 KM/H) 6.5 sec (supercharged)

0–100 MPH (0–161 KM/H) 14.2 sec (supercharged)

A.F.C. 19–30 mpg (8.0–12.7 km/l)

A SUPERCHARGED SUV

Supercharged versions gave fierce performance and the title of "The Fastest 4x4 by Far." Jaguar-sourced alloy V8s were 4.2 liter at first, giving 395 bhp, and later enlarged to 5.0 liter, pushing out over 500 horsepower. Different grille and side vents told everyone you had a supercharger up front.

BIG BRAKES
Brakes were Brembo four-wheel discs.

RENAULT-*Alpine A110 Berlinette*

THE RENAULT-ALPINE A110 may be diminutive in its proportions but it has a massive and deserved reputation, particularly in its native France. Although wearing the Renault badge, this pocket rocket is a testimony to the focused dedication of one man—Jean Redélé, a passionate motor sport enthusiast and son of a Dieppe Renault agent. As he took over his father's garage he began to modify Renault products for competition, then develop his own machines based on Renault engines and mechanicals. The A110, with its fiberglass body and backbone chassis, was the culmination of his effort, and from its launch in 1963 it went on to rack up a huge list of victories in the world's toughest rallies. On the public roads, it had all the appeal of a thinly disguised racer, as nimble as a mountain goat, with sparkling performance and just about the most fun you could have this side of a Lancia Stratos *(see pages 330–33)*.

MEAN MACHINE
Squat, nimble, and slightly splay-footed on its wide tires, the Alpine looks purposeful from any angle. Climb into that tight cockpit and you soon feel part of the car; start it up and there is a delicious barrage of noise. On the move, the sting in the Alpine's tail is exhilarating as it buzzes behind you like an angry insect.

COMPACT SIZE
It is a compact little package just 44.5 in (1.16 m) high, 60 in (1.5 m) wide, and 151.5 in (3.85 m) in length.

GT4 OPTION
A short-lived 2+2 version never had the sporty attraction of the Berlinette.

GO-KART HANDLING

The steering is light and the grip limpetlike, but when it does let go that tail wags the dog in a big way. Its singular appearance remained intact through its production life, with only detail changes to the trim, which these days is rare.

SPECIFICATIONS

MODEL Renault-Alpine A110 Berlinette (1963–77)

PRODUCTION 8,203

BODY STYLE Two-seater sports coupe.

CONSTRUCTION Fiberglass body integral with tubular steel backbone chassis.

ENGINES Various four-cylinders of 956 to 1796cc.

POWER OUTPUT 51–66 bhp (956cc) to 170 bhp (1796cc)

TRANSMISSION Four- and five-speed manual, rear-wheel drive.

SUSPENSION Coil springs all around. *Front:* upper/lower control arms; *Rear:* trailing radius arms & swing-axles.

BRAKES Four-wheel discs.

MAXIMUM SPEED 132 mph (212 km/h) (1595cc)

0–60 MPH (0–96 KM/H) 8.7 sec (1255cc), 10 sec (1442cc)

A.F.C. 27 mpg (7.6 km/l) (1296cc)

TRUNK AJAR
Competition versions had engine covers fixed slightly open to aid cooling.

ENGINE

Myriad engine options mirrored Renault's offerings, but in Alpine tune—by Gordini or Mignotet—it really flew. First models used Dauphine engines, progressing through R8 and R16 to R12. This 1967 car sports the 1442cc unit. Engines were slung behind the rear axle, with drive taken to the gearbox in front of the axle.

LEFTIES

Sadly for British enthusiasts, the Alpine A110 was only available in left-hand drive.

RALLY SUCCESSES

Among the many rally successes for Alpine were two Monte Carlo victories and the 1973 World Championship.

EXTERNAL CUTOUT

External cutout switches are a competition requirement, allowing outsiders to switch off the engine to prevent fire in an accident. The Alpine's are on the rear fender.

INSIDE THE CAR
Instrument layout is typical of sports cars of the period, and the stubby gearshift is handily placed for ease of operation. Examples built for road rather than race use lacked the racing seats but were better trimmed and were still fun cars to drive. Getting in and out was not easy though, because of the low roofline and high sills.

NAME
Cars were known at first as Alpine-Renaults, then became Renault-Alpines as Renault influence grew.

ASSEMBLY
Even though only a little over 8,000 A110s were built, they were assembled in Spain, Mexico, Brazil, and Bulgaria, as well as France.

DEALER OPTION
Alpines were sold through Renault dealers—with Renault warranty—from 1969 onward.

ROLLS-ROYCE *Silver Cloud III*

IN 1965, $20,000 BOUGHT A seven-bedroomed house, 11 Austin Minis, or a Rolls-Royce Silver Cloud. The Rolls that everybody remembers was the ultimate conveyance of landed gentry and captains of industry. But, by the early Sixties, Britain's social fabric was shifting. Princess Margaret announced she was to marry a divorcé, and aristocrats were so short of old money that they had to sell their mansions to celebrities and entrepreneurs. Against such social revolution the Cloud was a resplendent anachronism. Each took three months to build, weighed two tons, and had 12 coats of paint. The body sat on a mighty chassis and drum brakes were preferred because discs made a vulgar squealing noise. Beneath the hood slumbered straight-six or V8 engines, whose power output was never declared, but merely described as "sufficient." The Silver Cloud stands as a splendid monument to an old order of breeding and privilege.

MODEL HISTORY

The Cloud I was launched in 1955 and survived until the end of the decade, when Rolls exchanged their six for a V8 and made power steering standard. Cloud IIs ran until 1962, when the car enjoyed its first major facelift—a lowered hood line and the use of voguish twin headlamps.

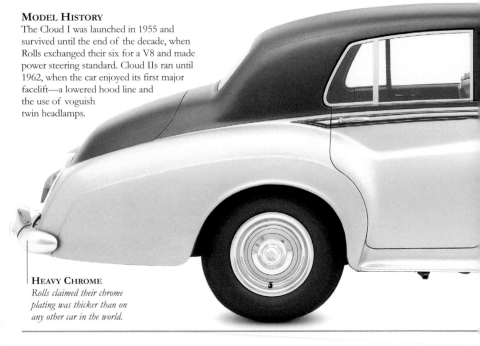

HEAVY CHROME
Rolls claimed their chrome plating was thicker than on any other car in the world.

SPECIFICATIONS

MODEL Rolls-Royce Silver Cloud III (1962–65)

PRODUCTION 2,044 Standard Steel

BODY STYLE Five-seater, four-door sedan.

CONSTRUCTION Girder chassis with pressed-steel body.

ENGINE 6230cc five-bearing V8.

POWER OUTPUT 220 bhp (estimate).

TRANSMISSION Four-speed automatic.

SUSPENSION Independent front with coils and wishbones, rear leaf springs, and hydraulic dampers.

BRAKES Front and rear drums with mechanical servo.

MAXIMUM SPEED 116 mph (187 km/h)

0–60 MPH (0–96 KM/H) 10.8 sec

0–100 MPH (0–161 KM/H) 34.2 sec

A.F.C. 12.3 mpg (4.4 km/l)

INTERIOR

A haven of peace in a troubled world, the Silver Cloud's magnificent interior was a veritable throne room, with only the finest walnut, leather, and Wilton carpeting. The gear selector sat behind the steering wheel.

ENGINE

Cloud IIs and IIIs—aimed at the American market—had a 6230cc five-bearing V8 power unit, squeezed into a cramped engine bay.

MAX HEADROOM
The roof line was high in the best limousine tradition—passengers had enough room to wear top hat The wide rear three-quarter panel was designed so rear occupants could be obscured from prying ey

TOP SECURITY
Doors were secured by the highest quality Yale locks.

TOOLKIT
Every Cloud had a complete toolkit in the trunk.

SCRIPT
Roman numerals w chosen for the Clou III script to lend an air of dignity.

ANTIQUE STYLING

Everything about the Cloud's styling was antique, looking more like a piece of architecture than a car. Standard steel bodies were made by the Pressed Steel Co. of Oxford, England, with the doors, hood, and trunk lid hand-finished in aluminum to save weight.

LEATHER COMFORT

The rear compartment might have looked accommodating, but Austin's little 1100 actually had more legroom. Standard walnut picnic tables were ideal for Champagne and caviar picnics. Rear leaf springs and hydraulic shock absorbers kept the ride smooth.

FRONT ASPECT

The 150-watt 5¾-in (14-cm) Lucas double headlights were necessitated by onerous North American safety requirements. Turn signals were moved from the fog light to the front fender on the Cloud III.

ORNAMENT

The Spirit of Ecstasy graced a silver radiator shell that took several en five hours to polish.

EEL 800C

ROLLS ROYCE *Phantom Drophead*

ROLLS ROYCE CONVERTIBLES have always been the choice of high rollers, but when the first Phantom drop-top was auctioned, it sold for four times its list price. Like the Corniche convertible before it, this is one of the world's most expensive and desirable rag-tops. Despite weighing nearly three tons, it can whisper to 60 mph (96 km/h) in 5.7 seconds thanks to an all-alloy construction and a 435 bhp V12 engine. In fact the sheer speed and fingertip agility of the Phantom are what make it totally unique. Handmade in the RR factory in Goodwood, and available in 44,000 different colors, it's a gorgeous mix of art deco and techno modern. Several examples were used in the 2012 London Olympics closing ceremony. No car is more British than the Phantom and no convertible is more rock 'n' roll.

REAR DECK

The rear tonneau cover is made from wood and echoes the nautical wood colors used in Italian Riva car launches of the '50s and '60s. The interior also has acres of timber, available in hundreds of different colors and finishes.

DETAIL PERFECTION
*Cabin is full of leather,
chrome, alloy, wood,
and crystal.*

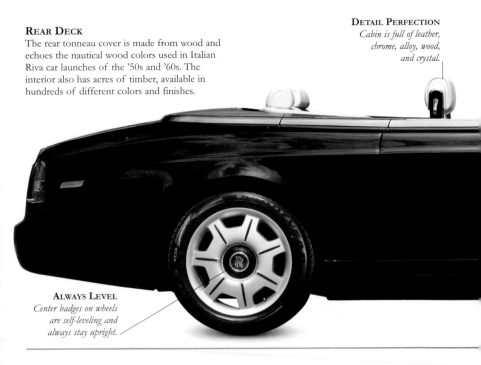

ALWAYS LEVEL
*Center badges on wheels
are self-leveling and
always stay upright.*

MOVING MASCOT
Spirit of Ecstasy falls and rises automatically when the car is locked or unlocked.

SPECIFICATIONS

MODEL Rolls Royce Phantom Drophead (2007)

PRODUCTION N/A

BODY STYLE Two-door, four-seater convertible.

CONSTRUCTION All-alloy.

ENGINE 6,749cc V12.

POWER OUTPUT 435 bhp.

TRANSMISSION Six-speed automatic.

SUSPENSION Self-leveling air suspension.

BRAKES Four-wheel discs.

MAXIMUM SPEED 145 mph (233 km/h) (limited)

0–60 MPH (0–96 KM/H) 5.7 sec

0–100 MPH (0–161 KM/H) 14 sec

A.F.C. 15 mpg (6.4 km/l)

ROLLS REINVENTED
When BMW bought Rolls Royce, many experts believed the brand was beyond saving. The German firm's reinvention of RR has made it the most powerful and desirable it has ever been, attracting a much more fashionable and younger customer.

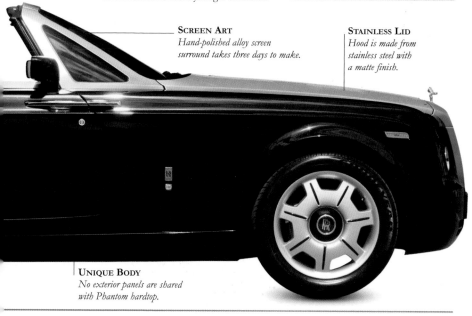

SCREEN ART
Hand-polished alloy screen surround takes three days to make.

STAINLESS LID
Hood is made from stainless steel with a matte finish.

UNIQUE BODY
No exterior panels are shared with Phantom hardtop.

SAAB *99 Turbo*

EVERY DECADE OR SO, one car comes along that overhauls accepted wisdom. In 1978 the British automotive magazine *Autocar* wrote, "this car was so unpredictably thrilling that the adrenalin started to course again, even in our hardened arteries." They had just road tested a Saab 99 Turbo. Saab took all other car manufacturers by surprise when they announced the world's first turbocharged family car, which promptly went on to be the first "blown" car to win a World Championship rally. Developed from the fuel-injected EMS model, the Turbo had Bosch K-Jetronic fuel injection, a strengthened gearbox, and a Garrett turbocharger. A hundred prototypes were built, and between them they covered 2.9 million miles (4.8 million km) before Saab was happy with its prodigy. Although it was expensive, there was nothing to equal its urge. Rare, esoteric, and historically significant, the mold-breaking 99 Turbo is an undisputed card-carrying classic.

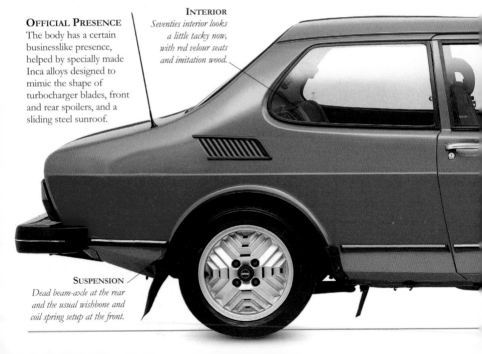

OFFICIAL PRESENCE
The body has a certain businesslike presence, helped by specially made Inca alloys designed to mimic the shape of turbocharger blades, front and rear spoilers, and a sliding steel sunroof.

INTERIOR
Seventies interior looks a little tacky now, with red velour seats and imitation wood.

SUSPENSION
Dead beam-axle at the rear and the usual wishbone and coil spring setup at the front.

ENGINE

The five-bearing, chain-driven single overhead cam engine was an 1985cc eight-valve, water-cooled, four cylinder unit, with low-compression pistons.

SPECIFICATIONS

MODEL Saab 99 Turbo (1978–80)

PRODUCTION 10,607

BODY STYLES Two/three/five-door, four-seater sports sedan.

CONSTRUCTION Monocoque steel bodyshell.

ENGINE 1985cc four-cylinder turbo.

POWER OUTPUT 145 bhp at 5000 rpm.

TRANSMISSION Front-wheel drive four/five-speed manual with auto option.

SUSPENSION Independent front double wishbone and coil springs, rear beam axle, coil springs, and Bilstein shock absorbers.

BRAKES Four-wheel servo discs.

MAXIMUM SPEED 122 mph (196 km/h)

0–60 MPH (0–96 KM/H) 8.2 sec

0–100 MPH (0–161 KM/H) 19.8 sec

A.F.C. 26 mpg (9.3 km/l)

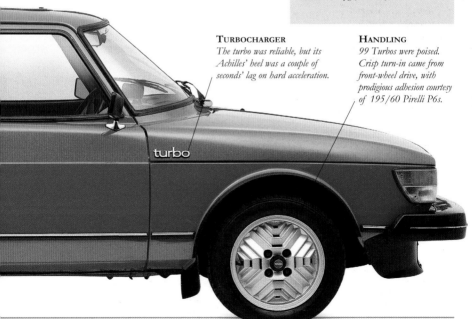

TURBOCHARGER
The turbo was reliable, but its Achilles' heel was a couple of seconds' lag on hard acceleration.

HANDLING
99 Turbos were poised. Crisp turn-in came from front-wheel drive, with prodigious adhesion courtesy of 195/60 Pirelli P6s.

STUDEBAKER *Avanti*

THE AVANTI WAS A BIG DEAL for Studebaker and the first all-new body style since 1953. The last car design of the legendary Raymond Loewy, it rode on a shortened Lark chassis with a stock Studey 289cid V8. The Avanti's striking simplicity of shape was just one of Loewy's celebrated confections. From his voguish Coca-Cola dispenser to the chaste Lucky Strike cigarette pack, Loewy's creations were instant classics, and the brilliant Avanti was a humdinger. Studebaker's prodigy was fairly audacious too, with a fiberglass body, antisway bars, and wind-evading aerodynamics. Dealers, however, could not meet the huge wave of orders and this, combined with other niggles like flexing of the fiberglass shell, resulted in impatient buyers defecting to the Corvette camp instead. Fewer than 4,650 Avantis were made, and production ceased in December 1963, the Avanti concept being sold to a couple of Studebaker dealers. They went on to form the Avanti Motor Corporation, which successfully churned out Avantis well into the Eighties.

EUROPEAN LINES

More European than American, the Avanti had a long neck, razor-edged front fenders, and no grille. Early sketches show Loewy's inspiration, with tell-tale annotations scribbled on the paper that read "like Jaguar, Ferrari, Aston Martin, Mercedes." Lead time for the show Avanti was a hair-raising 13 months, with a full-scale clay model fashioned in only 40 days.

ENGINE

The 289cid was the best Studebaker V8 ever made, developing 240 bhp in standard R1 tune. Supercharged R2 and R3 boasted 290 and 335 bhp respectively.

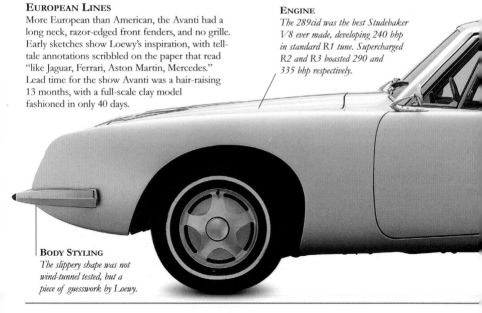

BODY STYLING

The slippery shape was not wind-tunnel tested, but a piece of guesswork by Loewy.

FRONT VIEW
Unmistakable from any angle, early '63
Avantis had round headlights, but most later
'64 models sported square ones.

SPECIFICATIONS

MODEL Studebaker Avanti (1963)
PRODUCTION 3,834 (1963)
BODY STYLE Two-door, four-seater coupe.
CONSTRUCTION Fiberglass body, steel chassis.
ENGINES 289cid, 304cid V8s.
POWER OUTPUT 240–575 bhp (304cid R5 V8 fuel-injected).
TRANSMISSION Three-speed manual, optional Power-Shift automatic.
SUSPENSION *Front:* upper and lower A-arms, coil springs; *Rear:* leaf springs.
BRAKES Front discs, rear drums.
MAXIMUM SPEED 120 mph (193 km/h)
0–60 MPH (0–96 KM/H) 7.5 sec
A.F.C. 17 mpg (6 km/l)

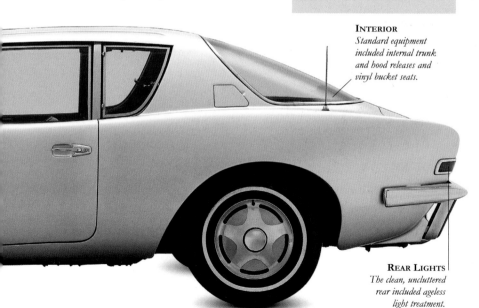

INTERIOR
Standard equipment included internal trunk and hood releases and vinyl bucket seats.

REAR LIGHTS
The clean, uncluttered rear included ageless light treatment.

SUNBEAM *Tiger*

THERE WAS NOTHING NEW ABOUT popping an American V8 into a pert English chassis. After all, that is exactly what Carroll Shelby did with the AC Ace to create the awesome Cobra *(see pages 16–19)*. When Rootes in Britain decided to do the same with their Sunbeam Alpine, they also commissioned Shelby to produce a prototype; and although Rootes already had close links with Chrysler, the American once again opted for a Ford V8. To cope with the 4.2-liter V8, the Alpine's chassis and suspension were beefed up to create the fearsome Tiger late in 1964. In 1967, the Tiger II arrived with an even bigger 4.7-liter Ford V8, but this was a brief swansong as Chrysler took control of Rootes and was not going to sanction a car powered by rivals Ford. Once dubbed "the poor man's Cobra," these days Tiger prices are only for the rich.

ENGINE
The first Tigers used 4.2-liter Ford V8 engines, replaced later—as shown here —by a 4727cc version, the famous 289, but not in the same state of tune as those used in the Shelby Cobras.

DISTINGUISHING FEATURES
The MkII Tiger had an eggcrate grille to distinguish it from the Alpine. Earlier cars were less easy to tell apart: a chrome strip along the side of the Tiger was the giveaway, together with discreet badging on the body.

ADAPTING THE ALPINE
The Alpine's chassis and suspension had to be beefed up to cope with the weight and power of the V8. Resulting modifications included a heavy-duty back axle, sturdier suspension, and chassis stiffening.

RACE HOOD
Race and rally Tigers had improved air-flow with a slightly raised hood.

HOT HOUSE
Tigers often suffered from overheating.

SPECIFICATIONS

MODEL Sunbeam Tiger (1964–67)

PRODUCTION 6,496 (Mk1, 1964–67); 571 (MkII)

BODY STYLE Two-plus-two roadster.

CONSTRUCTION Steel monocoque.

ENGINES Ford V8 4261cc or 4727cc (260 or 289cid).

POWER OUTPUT 164 bhp at 4400 rpm (4261cc), 200 bhp at 4400 rpm (4727cc).

TRANSMISSION Four-speed manual.

SUSPENSION Coil springs and wishbones at front, rigid axle on semi-elliptic leaf springs at rear.

BRAKES Servo-assisted front discs, rear drums.

MAXIMUM SPEED 117 mph (188 km/h) (4261cc), 125 mph (201 km/h) (4727cc)

0–60 MPH (0–96 KM/H) 9 sec (4261cc), 7.5 sec (4727cc)

A.F.C. 20 mpg (7 km/l)

TESLA *Roadster*

THE TESLA WAS THE WORLD'S FIRST sexy electric car. Fast enough to worry a Porsche 911 Turbo or Ferrari 599, the neck-jerking torque and devastating, silent acceleration felt uncanny. Brainchild of PayPal founder Elon Musk, it used a Lotus Elise chassis, stored power in 6,800 laptop batteries, and was the first electric vehicle (EV) to have a range of more than 200 miles (322 km) on a three-and-a-half hour charge. With zero tailpipe emissions and a theoretical fuel consumption of 120 mpg (51 km/l), its green credentials were unimpeachable, but it also gave the struggling EV market glamour and desirability. Without the ferociously fast Tesla, electric cars wouldn't have come as far as they have. This sparky little roadster remains one of the great technological landmark cars of the 21st century.

SMOOTH FEATHERWEIGHT
Slippery aerodynamics and lightweight construction make it as fast as a Lamborghini Gallardo.

ENVIABLE RANGE
The biggest barrier to volume electric car sales has always been "range anxiety," or the fear of running out of battery power. But in 2010 Tesla cleverly and successfully drove a roadster round the world, and owners often achieved over 300 miles (482 km) to one charge.

LOTUS BACKBONE
The Lotus Elise chassis and suspension gives scalpel-sharp handling.

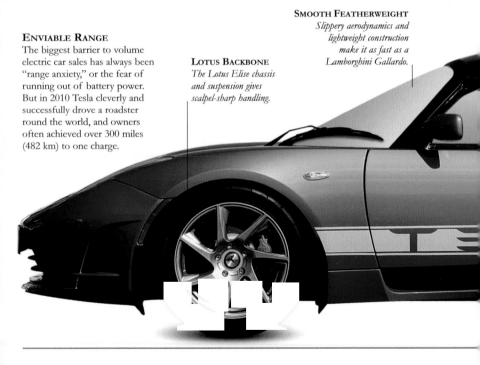

QUICK POWER
Fast charging system is twice as quick as most other EVs.

COOL RIDE
Wing ducts help cool batteries and brakes.

EASY ELECTRICITY
Owners have a home charging unit that simply plugs in, and can also top up at the office or at a street charger, if they can find one.

ROOFLESS
Removable roof panel makes a quick convertible.

STOPPING POWER
Drilled, ventilated four-wheel discs are extremely powerful.

SPECIFICATIONS

MODEL Tesla Roadster (2007)
PRODUCTION 2,450
BODY STYLE Two-door, two-seater.
CONSTRUCTION Steel chassis, carbon-fiber panels.
ENGINE 185-kw electric motor.
POWER OUTPUT 248 hp.
TRANSMISSION Single-speed Borg Warner.
SUSPENSION Independent.
BRAKES Four-wheel discs.
MAXIMUM SPEED 125 mph (53 km/h) (limited)
0–60 MPH (0–96 KM/H) 3.9 sec
0–100 MPH (0–161 KM/H) 12 sec
A.F.C. Theoretical 120 mpg (51 km/l)

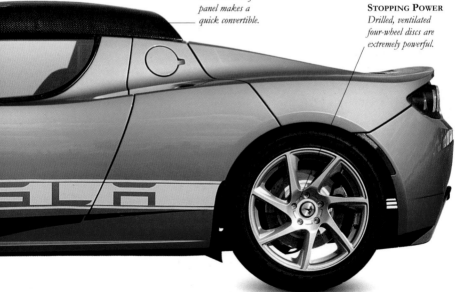

Toyota *2000GT*

Toyota's 2000GT is more than a "might have been"—it's a "should have been."
A pretty coupe with performance and equipment to match its good looks, it
predated the rival Datsun 240Z *(see pages 196–99)*, which was a worldwide sales
success. The Toyota failed to reach much more than 300 sales partly because
of low capacity, but even more because the car was launched before Japan was
geared to export. That left only a domestic market, largely uneducated in the
finer qualities of sports cars, to make what they could of the
offering. As a design exercise, the 2000GT proved that
the Japanese auto industry had reached the stage where
its products rivaled the best in the world. It is just
a pity not more people were able to appreciate
this fine car first hand.

BEEMER LINKS
The design of the Toyota 2000GT is based on
an earlier prototype penned by Albrecht Goertz,
creator of the BMW 507 *(see pages 64–67)* and
the Datsun 240Z. When Nissan rejected the
design, it was offered to Toyota and evolved
into the 2000GT.

GEAR LEVER
*Short-throw wooden-
top gear lever.*

INTERIOR
The 2000GT's snug cockpit featured a
walnut-veneer instrument panel, sporty
wheel, stubby gear-lever, form-fitting
seats, and deep footwells. The eight-
track stereo is a nice period touch.

BRAKES
*Discs on all
four wheels.*

LIGHTING
*Unusual combination
of high-tech pop-up and
fixed headlights gave the
front a cluttered look.*

HOOD PROFILE

The panel on the right concealed the
GT's battery; the one on the lefthand
side of the body was the air cleaner.
This arrangement enabled the hood to
be kept low. The engine was a triple-
carb six-cylinder Yamaha, which
provided 150 bhp. A competition
version boosted output to 200 bhp.

SPECIFICATIONS

MODEL Toyota 2000GT (1966–70)
PRODUCTION 337
BODY STYLE Two-door sports coupe.
CONSTRUCTION Steel body on
backbone frame.
ENGINE Yamaha inline DOHC six, 1988cc.
POWER OUTPUT 150 bhp at 6600 rpm.
TRANSMISSION Five-speed manual.
SUSPENSION Fully independent by coil
springs and wishbones all around.
BRAKES Hydraulically operated discs
all around.
MAXIMUM SPEED 128 mph (206 km/h)
0–60 MPH (0–96 KM/H) 10.5 sec
0–100 MPH (0–161 KM/H) 24 sec
A.F.C. 31 mpg (11 km/l)

TRIUMPH *TR2*

IF EVER THERE WAS A SPORTS CAR that epitomized the British bulldog spirit it must be the Triumph TR2. It is as true Brit as a car can be, born in the golden age of British sports cars, but aimed at the lucrative American market. At the 1952 Earl's Court Motor Show in London, the new Austin-Healey stole the show, but the "Triumph Sports" prototype's debut at the same show was less auspicious. It was a brave attempt to create an inexpensive sports car from a company with no recent track record in this market sector. With its dumpy *derriere*, the prototype was no oil painting; as for handling, chief tester Ken Richardson described it as a "bloody deathtrap." No conventional beauty certainly, but a bluff-fronted car that was a worthy best-of-breed contender in the budget sports car arena, and the cornerstone of a stout sports tradition.

UNCONVENTIONAL STYLING
The design, by Walter Belgrove, was a far cry from the razor-edged Triumph Renown and Mayflower sedans that he had previously styled. If not beautiful, the TR2 has chunky good looks with a bluff, honest demeanor.

TOP
The TR2 had a foldaway top; the later TR3 had the option of a lift-off hardtop.

RACING HOLES
The TR2 came with small holes drilled in the scuttle to attach aero-screens for racing.

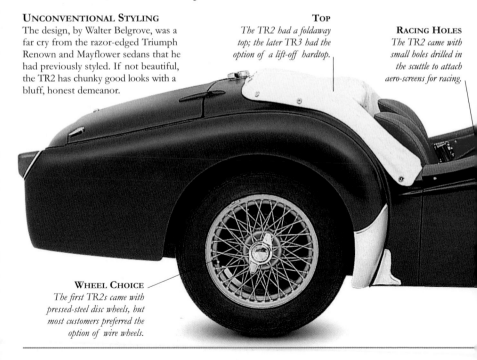

WHEEL CHOICE
The first TR2s came with pressed-steel disc wheels, but most customers preferred the option of wire wheels.

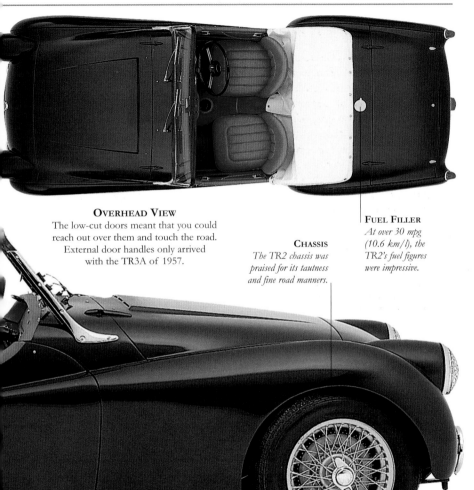

OVERHEAD VIEW
The low-cut doors meant that you could reach out over them and touch the road. External door handles only arrived with the TR3A of 1957.

CHASSIS
The TR2 chassis was praised for its tautness and fine road manners.

FUEL FILLER
At over 30 mpg (10.6 km/l), the TR2's fuel figures were impressive.

WINDSHIELD
The windshield had a slight curve to prevent it from bowing at high speed, which is what the prototype's flat windshield did.

SPORTING SUCCESS
TR2s came in first and second in the 1954 RAC Rally.

NEW REAR
A revised rear, all-new chassis, and other modifications saw Standard-Triumph's new TR2 become a winner at the Geneva Motor Show in March 1953. While the prototype had a stubby tail, the production model had a real opening trunk.

SPECIFICATIONS

MODEL Triumph TR2 (1953–55)

PRODUCTION 8,628

BODY STYLE Two-door, two-seater sports car.

CONSTRUCTION Pressed-steel chassis with separate steel body.

ENGINE Four-cylinder, overhead valve, 1991cc, twin SU carburetors.

POWER OUTPUT 90 bhp at 4800 rpm.

TRANSMISSION Four-speed manual with Laycock overdrive option, initially on top gear only, then on top three (1955).

SUSPENSION Coil-spring and wishbone at front, live rear axle with semi-elliptic leaf springs.

BRAKES Lockheed hydraulic drums.

MAXIMUM SPEED 105 mph (169 km/h)

0–60 MPH (0–96 KM/H) 12 sec

A.F.C. 30+ mpg (10.6+ km/l)

RONT VIEW
e unusual recessed grille may present a ghtly grumpy disposition, but the low front ped the car to a top speed of 105 mph 9 km/h). Fixtures on the TR2 were spartan you did not even get external door handles.

AXLE
Like the Austin-Healey's, the TR chassis ran under the axle at the rear.

STOCK DESIGN
There is nothing revolutionary in the design of the pressed-steel chassis; a simple ladder with X-shaped bracing. It was a transformation, though, from the prototype's original chassis.

INTERIOR
Stubby gear lever and full instrumentation gave TR a true sports car feel; the steering wheel was large, but the low door accommodated "elbows out" driving style.

T<small>RIUMPH</small> *TR6*

T<small>O MOST</small> TR <small>TRADITIONALISTS</small> this is where the TR tale ended, the final flourishing of the theme before the TR7 betrayed an outstanding tradition. In the mid-Sixties, the TR line was on a roll and the TR6 continued the upward momentum, outselling all earlier models. It was a natural progression from the original TR2; the body evolved from the TR4/5, the power unit from the TR5. Crisply styled, with chisel-chin good looks and carrying over the 2.5-liter six-cylinder engine of the TR5, the TR6 in early fuel-injected form heaved you along with 152 galloping horses. This was as hairy chested as the TR got, and a handful too, with some critics carping that, like the big Healeys, its power outstripped its poise. But that just made it more fun to drive.

K<small>ARMANN</small> S<small>TYLING</small>
There is an obvious difference between the TR4/5 and the later TR6, restyled by Karmann; sharper, cleaner lines not only looked more modern, but also gave more luggage space. The chopped off tail was an aerodynamic aid.

T<small>OP</small> O<small>PTION</small>
One-piece hardtop was available as an option, and more practical than the two-piece job seen on earlier models.

S<small>TATESIDE</small> S<small>ALES</small>
Some 78,000 TR6s went to the US even though emission regulations emasculated it.

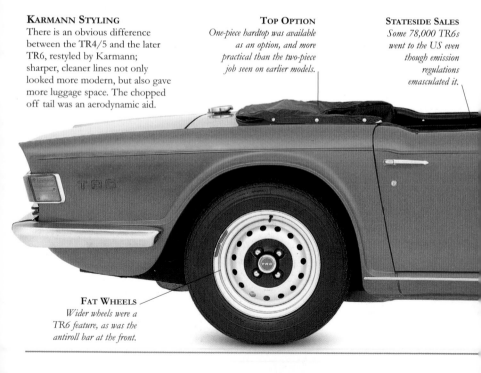

F<small>AT</small> W<small>HEELS</small>
Wider wheels were a TR6 feature, as was the antiroll bar at the front.

ROOMY COCKPIT

The cockpit was more spacious than earlier TRs, providing excellent driving position from comfortable seats. Big, wide-opening doors gave easy access to the TR6, a long cry from the tiny doors of the TR2 and 3.

SMOOTH TR6
Virtually all bulges, like the TR5's hood "power bulge" and cowled headlights, have been ironed out.

POWER DROP
Revised injection metering and reprofiled camshaft reduced power from 1973; US carburetor versions were more sluggish and thirstier.

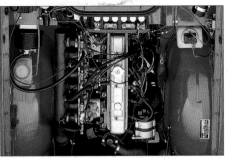

BEST SELLER

The TR6's good looks, and a long production run, made this model the biggest selling of all TR models. British sales stopped in February 1975, but continued in the US until July 1976. The US model may have been slower than the UK model by 12 mph (19 km/h), but 10 times as many TR6s were exported as remained in Britain.

ENGINE

The first engines, as on this 1972 car, produced 152 bhp, but public pressure for something more well mannered resulted in a 125 bhp version in 1973. Americans had to make do with just over 100 bhp and no fuel injection.

STEERING WHEEL

Steering wheel size was reduced at the time of other mid-model changes in 1973.

INTERIOR

The interior is still traditional but more refined than earlier TRs. Yet with its big dials, wooden dash, and short-throw gear knob, its character is still truly sporty.

MERGER

The TR6 was launched just after the 1968 merger of Leyland and BMC, which produced Triumph motors. Hence the badge on the side of the TR6's bodywork.

ENGINE NOISE

Deep-throated burble is still a TR6 come-on.

LONG-TAILED

The TR6's squared-off tail was longer than earlier TRs. Even so, there was only space in the trunk for a set of golf clubs and an overnight bag.

SPECIFICATIONS

MODEL Triumph TR6 (1969–76)

PRODUCTION 94,619

BODY STYLE Two-seat convertible.

CONSTRUCTION Ladder-type chassis with integral steel body.

ENGINE Inline six-cylinder, 2498cc, fuel-injection (carburetors in US).

POWER OUTPUT 152 bhp at 5500 rpm (1969–1973), 125 bhp at 5250 rpm (1973–1975), 104 bhp at 4500 rpm (US).

TRANSMISSION Manual four-speed with optional overdrive on third and top.

SUSPENSION Independent by coil springs all around; wishbones at front, swing-axles & semi-trailing arms at rear.

BRAKES *Front:* discs; *Rear:* drums.

MAXIMUM SPEED 119 mph (191 km/h, 150 bhp), 107 mph (172 km/h, US)

0–60 MPH (0–96 KM/H) 8.2 sec (150 bhp); 9.0 sec (125 bhp); 10.6 sec (104 bhp)

0–100 MPH (0–161 KM/H) 29 sec

A.F.C. 25 mpg (8.8 km/l)

TUCKER *Torpedo*

THERE'S NO OTHER POSTWAR CAR that's as dramatic or advanced as Preston Tucker's futuristic '48 Torpedo. With four-wheel independent suspension, rear-mounted Bell helicopter engine, pop-out safety windshield, and uncrushable passenger compartment, it was 20 years ahead of its time. "You'll step into a new automotive age when you drive your Tucker '48," bragged the ads. It was a promise that convinced an astonishing 300,000 people to place orders, but their dreams were never to be realized. Problems with the engine and Tuckermatic transmission, plus a serious cash-flow crisis, meant that only 51 Torpedos left the Chicago plant. Worse still, Tucker and five of his associates were indicted for fraud by the Securities Exchange Commission. Their acquittal came too late to save America's most eccentric car from an undignified end.

LOW PROFILE
One of the fastest cars on American roads, the Tucker had a low floor that gave it a huge aerodynamic advantage. The roof tapered in two directions to reduce lift forces, and the drag coefficient was as low as 0.30. The Torpedo's top speed was 120 mph (193 km/h), and an astonishing 30 mpg (10.6 km/l) was possible.

CUSHIONING
Front and rear seat cushions could be interchanged to spread wear and tear.

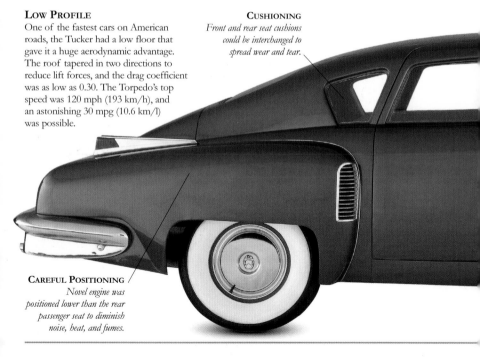

CAREFUL POSITIONING
Novel engine was positioned lower than the rear passenger seat to diminish noise, heat, and fumes.

ENGINE

The first of the Tucker engines was a monster 589cid aluminum flat-six that proved difficult to start and ran too hot. It was replaced by a 6ALV 335cid flat-six block, developed by Air-Cooled Motors of Syracuse. Perversely, Tucker later converted this unit to a water-cooled system.

SPECIFICATIONS

MODEL Tucker Torpedo (1948)
PRODUCTION 51 (total)
BODY STYLE Four-door sedan.
CONSTRUCTION Steel body and chassis.
ENGINE 335cid flat-six.
POWER OUTPUT 166 bhp.
TRANSMISSION Three-speed Tuckermatic automatic, four-speed manual.
SUSPENSION Four-wheel independent.
BRAKES Front and rear drums.
MAXIMUM SPEED 120 mph (193 km/h)
0–60 MPH (0–96 KM/H) 10.1 sec
A.F.C. 30 mpg (10.6 km/l)

INTERIOR DESIGN

Interior was designed by Audrey Moore, who had worked with Raymond Loewy on Studebakers.

LUGGAGE SPACE

With no engine upfront, luggage space was roomy.

NOSE DESIGN

Slippery front was designed to cleave the air.

AN INSTANT HIT
The public loved the Tucker not only for its comfort, power, and safety, but also because the styling was completely free from the usual prewar clichés. The prototype was ready in 60 days and more than 5,000 people attended the launch.

VENTS
*Vents were to reduce
the considerable
heat generated by
the engine.*

WIDE TRACK
The Torpedo was so different from anything else on four wheels that it was a complete sensation. It had the widest track of any car and had all-around independent suspension sprung by rubber-in-torsion units similar to those of Issigonis's Mini *(see pages 44–47).*

REAR LIGHT
*Rear light, like much
of the Tucker, was
bought in, and was a
prewar Dodge design.*

ENGINE
*Engine was place
crosswise on the
overhang between
the two
independently
sprung rear whee*

CYCLOPS LIGHT
Daring cyclops headlight swiveled with the front wheels.

TUCKER BADGE
The horn on the steering wheel lay flush for safety and was adorned with the Tucker family crest.

INTERIOR
Some say that Detroit conspired to destroy Tucker, but steering wheels on Torpedos were from the Lincoln Zephyr, given freely by Ford as a gesture of assistance. Although the interior was groaning with safety features, the Tucker sales team figured it was too austere.

BUMPER
Steerhorn bumper gave the car a dramatic frontal aspect.

UNIQUE AND EXCITING
The front was like no other American car, with a fixed circular headlight lens that pivoted with the steering and a front panel that blended artfully into the bumper and grille. Designed by former Auburn-Cord-Duesenberg stylist Alex Tremulis, the Tucker was so low that it only came up to a man's shoulder.

VOLKSWAGEN *Beetle Karmann*

BEETLE PURISTS MAY WAX lyrical about the first-of-breed purity of the original split-rear-window Bugs and the oval window versions of 1953 to 1957, but there is one Beetle that everybody wants—the Karmann-built Cabriolet. Its development followed that of the sedans through a bewildering series of modifications, but it always stood apart. With its top retracted into a bulging bustle, this Beetle was not only cheerful, but chic too, a classless cruiser at home equally on Beverly Hills boulevards, Cannes, and Main Street. The final incarnation of the Karmann convertible represents the ultimate development of the Beetle theme, with the peppiest engine and improved handling. It's strange to think that the disarming, unburstable Bug was once branded with the slogan of the Hitler Youth, "Strength through Joy." Today, modern retro Beetles have become suburban middle-class trinkets.

ROADSTER PLANS
Before Karmann chopped the lid off the Bug, there had been plans for a Beetle-based roadster. The prototypes inspired coachbuilders Joseph Hebmüller & Sons to build a short-lived roadster, but just 696 were built before a factory fire scuppered the project.

SURFMOBILE
Cabriolets like this California-registered car are a mainstay of surfing culture.

BRAKES
Front discs were introduced in 1966.

INTERIOR

The Beetle is still bare, its dash dominated by the one minimal instrument; on this model the speedo incorporates a fuel gauge. It also has a padded dash, replacing the original metal unit.

SPECIFICATIONS

MODEL VW Beetle Karmann Cabriolet (1972–1980)

PRODUCTION 331,847 (Karmann Cabriolets from 1949 to 1980).

BODY STYLE Four-seater cabriolet.

CONSTRUCTION Steel-bodied, separate chassis/body.

ENGINE Rear-mounted, air-cooled flat-four, 1584cc.

POWER OUTPUT 50 bhp at 4000 rpm.

TRANSMISSION Four-speed manual.

SUSPENSION *Front:* independent MacPherson strut; *Rear:* independent trailing arm and twin torsion bars.

BRAKES Front discs, rear drums.

MAXIMUM SPEED 82.4 mph (133 km/h)

0–60 MPH (0–96 KM/H) 18 sec

A.F.C. 24–30 mpg (8.5–10.6 km/l)

UNIT GROWTH

The Beetle's capacity grew from 1131cc to 1584cc; the engines have a deserved reputation as robust, rev-happy units.

KARMANN COACHBUILDER

In addition to the Beetle convertible, Karmann also built the Type 1 VW Karmann-Ghia, a two-seater based on Beetle running gear.

REAR LIGHTS
Many later design changes like these "elephant footprint" rear light clusters were driven by US regulations.

FRESH AIR
With the top raised, the Karmann cabriolet is a bit claustrophobic, but it comes into its own as a timeless top-down cruiser that is still a full four-seater. Rear vision with the top up is not much better than on early split-windowed and oval-windowed models.

ONE-MODEL POLICY
The one-model policy that VW adopted in its early years was successful while Beetle sales soared, but by 1967 Fiat had overtaken VW as Europe's biggest car manufacturer. It was not until 1974 that the Golf and Polo revived the company's fortunes.

ENGINE
You can always tell that a Beetle is on its way before it comes into sight thanks to the distinctive buzzing of the air-cooled, horizontally opposed four-cylinder engine.

WINDSHIELD
*Curved "panoramic"
windshield replaced the
flat window in 1972.*

INDICATORS
*First cars had
semaphores; then
indicators were
fender-mounted.*

VOLKSWAGEN *Golf GTi*

EVERY DECADE OR SO A really great car comes along. In the Seventies it was the Golf. Like the Beetle before it, the Golf was designed to make inroads into world markets; yet while the Beetle evolved into the perfect consumer product, the Golf was planne that way. The idea of a "hot" Golf was not part of the grand plan. It was the brainchild of a group of enthusiastic Volkswagen engineers who worked evenings an weekends, impressing VW's board so much that the GTi became an official project in May 1975. Despite its youth, the GTi is as much of a classic as any Ferrari. Its claim to fame is that it spawned a traffic jam of imitators and brought an affordable cockta of performance, handling, and reliability to the mass-market buyer. Few other cars have penetrated the suburban psyche as deeply as the original Golf GTi, and fewer still have had greatness thrust upon them at such an early age.

GTi ENHANCEMENTS
GTi suspension was lower and firmer than the standard Golf, with wider tires and wheels. Front disc brakes were ventilated, but keeping standard drums at the rear was a mistake— early Golfs were very disinclined to stop.

HATCHBACK
The Mk I Golf was the first of the Seventies' hatchbacks.

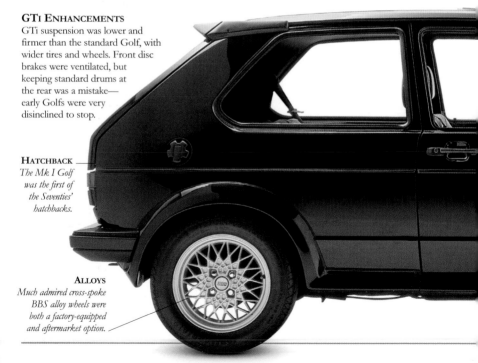

ALLOYS
Much admired cross-spoke BBS alloy wheels were both a factory-equipped and aftermarket option.

SPECIFICATIONS

MODEL Volkswagen Golf GTi Mk 1 (1976–83)

PRODUCTION 400,000

BODY STYLE Three-door five-seater hatchback.

CONSTRUCTION All steel/monocoque body.

ENGINES Four-cylinder 1588cc/1781cc.

POWER OUTPUT 110–112 bhp at 6100 rpm.

TRANSMISSION Four- or five-speed manual.

SUSPENSION *Front:* independent; *Rear:* semi-independent trailing arm.

BRAKES Front discs, rear drums.

MAXIMUM SPEED 111 mph (179 km/h)

0–60 MPH (0–96 KM/H) 8.7 sec

0–100 MPH (0–161 KM/H) 18.2 sec

A.F.C. 29 mpg (10.3 km/l)

SIMPLE FRONT
Factory spec Golfs were understated, with just a GTi badge and a thin red stripe around the grille.

ENGINE
Capable of 150,000 miles (240,000 km) in its stride, the 1588cc four-cylinder power unit breathed through Bosch K-Jetronic fuel injection.

Volvo *P1800*

There has never been a Volvo like the P1800, for this was a one-time flight of fancy by the sober Swedes, who already had a reputation for building sensible sedans. As a sports car the P1800 certainly looked stunning, every sensuous curve and lean line suggesting athletic prowess. But under that sharp exterior was most of the engineering of the Volvo Amazon, a worthy workhorse sedan. Consequently, the P1800 was no road-burner; it just about had the edge on the MGB *(see pages 372–73)*, but only in a straight line. Another competitor, the E-Type Jag *(see pages 306–09)*, was launched in 1961, the same year as the P1800 and at almost the same price, but there the comparison ends. The P1800 did have style, though, and its other virtues were pure Volvo—strength, durability, and reliability. These combined to create something quite singular in automotive idiom—a practical sports car.

Design Credits
Official Volvo history credits the award-winning design of the P1800 to Frua of Italy, but it was actually penned by young Swede Pelle Petterson, then a trainee at Ghia. The Italian influences are obvious in the final form.

Jensen's Signature
Early cars like this were built in Britain by Jensen.

Luggage Space
As you would expect, the sensible sports car had a decent-sized trunk.

SPECIFICATIONS

MODEL Volvo P1800 (1961–73)

PRODUCTION 47,707 (all models)

BODY STYLES Two-plus-two fixed-head coupe; sports wagon (P1800ES).

CONSTRUCTION Unitary steel body/chassis.

ENGINES 1778cc straight-four, overhead valves; 1985cc from 1968–73.

POWER OUTPUT 100 bhp at 5500 rpm (P1800); 124 bhp at 6000 rpm (P1800E, P1800 ES).

TRANSMISSION Four-speed manual with overdrive/optional automatic.

SUSPENSION *Front:* independent coil-sprung with wishbones; *Rear:* rigid axle, coil-sprung, Panhard rod.

BRAKES Front discs, rear drums.

MAXIMUM SPEED 115 mph (185 km/h) (P1800 E/ES)

0–60 MPH (0–96 KM/H) 9.7–13.2 sec

0–100 MPH (0–161 KM/H) 31.4–53 sec

A.F.C. 20–25 mpg (7–10 km/l)

ENGINE
Early cars had 1778cc four-cylinder units with twin SU carbs; the 1985cc unit came later, followed by electronic fuel injection. All versions are reliable, willing revvers.

SAFETY MEASURES
The P1800 had a padded dash and seat belts of Volvo's own design.

GEARING
Super-tough gearbox had excellent synchromesh.

WHEELS
Stylized fake spokes identify this as an early P1800.

WILLYS *Jeep MB*

AS ONE WAR CORRESPONDENT SAID, "It's as faithful as a dog, as strong as a mule, and as agile as a mountain goat." The flat-fendered Willys Jeep is one of the most instantly recognizable vehicles ever made. Any American TV or movie action hero who wasn't on a horse was in a Jeep. Even General Eisenhower was impressed, saying "the three tools that won us the war in Europe were the Dakota, the landing craft, and the Jeep." In 1940, the Defense Department sent out a tough spec for a military workhorse. Many companies took one look at the seemingly impossible specification and 49-day deadline and turned it down flat. The design that won the bid and made it into production and the history books was a mixture of the ideas and abilities of Ford, Bantam, and Willys-Overland. A stunning triumph of function over form, the Jeep not only won the war, but went on to become a cult off-roader that's still with us now. The Willys Jeep is surely the most original 4x4 by far.

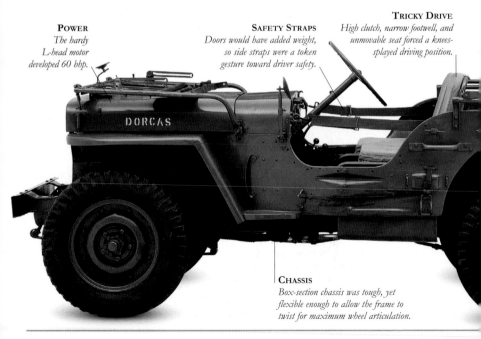

POWER
*The hardy
L-head motor
developed 60 bhp.*

SAFETY STRAPS
*Doors would have added weight,
so side straps were a token
gesture toward driver safety.*

TRICKY DRIVE
*High clutch, narrow footwell, and
unmovable seat forced a knees-
splayed driving position.*

CHASSIS
*Box-section chassis was tough, yet
flexible enough to allow the frame to
twist for maximum wheel articulation.*

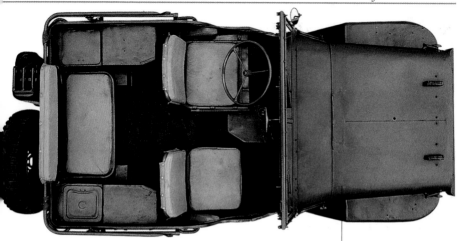

SUSPENSION
*Leaf springs and
hydraulic shocks gave a
surprisingly good ride.*

EXPOSED COLUMN
Driver safety wasn't a Jeep strong
point. Many GIs ended up
impaled on the steering column
even after low-speed impacts.

THIRSTY
*The Jeep may have
had competence, but it
also had a prodigious
thirst for fuel.*

LIFESPAN
*The Jeep was a brilliantly
simple solution to the
problem of mobility at war,
but the life expectancy of an
average vehicle was expected
to be less than a week!*

JEEP NAME
Jeeps were first called General Purpose
cars, then MA, and finally MB, but
nobody's sure of the origins of the
Jeep name. Some say it is a corruption
of GP, or General Purpose, others that
it was named after Eugene the Jeep, a
character in a 1936 Popeye cartoon.

SPECIFICATIONS

MODEL Willys Jeep MB (1943)
PRODUCTION 586,000 (during
World War II)
BODY STYLE Open utility vehicle.
CONSTRUCTION Steel body and chassis.
ENGINE 134cid straight-four.
POWER OUTPUT 60 bhp.
TRANSMISSION Three-speed manual,
four-wheel drive.
SUSPENSION Leaf springs front and rear.
BRAKES Front and rear drums.
MAXIMUM SPEED 65 mph (105 km/h)
0–60 MPH (0–96 KM/H) 22 sec
A.F.C. 16 mpg (5.7 km/l)

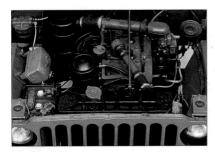

ENGINE

Power was from a Ford straight-four, which took the Jeep to around 65 mph (105 km/h), actually exceeding US Army driving regulations.

RAD CHANGES

Earlier Jeeps had a slatted radiator grille instead of the later pressed-steel bars, as here. The silhouette was low, but ground clearance high to allow driving in streams as deep as 21 in (53 cm). Weather protection was vestigial.

CLUTCH

Quick-release clutch disengaged engine fan for fording streams and rivers.

GEARBOX

The Warner three-speed manual box was supplemented by controls allowing the driver to select two or four-wheel drive in high or low ratios.

FRONT VIEW

The Jeep's hood was secured using quick-release sprung latches. The upper latch held the fold-down windshield. Those stark fenders and large all-terrain tires may look humble and functional, but the Jeep's claim to fame is that it spawned utility vehicles from Nissans and Isuzus to Discoverys and Range Rovers.

DORCAS

WIPERS
*Hand-operated
windshield wipers.*

GEAR LEVER
*First production
Jeep model, the
MA, had a
column change.*

SPARTAN INTERIOR
Only the generals fought the war in
comfort, and Jeep accommodation
was strictly no frills. Very early Jeeps
have no glove compartment.

EXTRAS
*Jeeps came with gas
can, shovel, and
long-handled ax.*

HEADLIGHT
The dual-purpose headlight
could be rotated back to
illuminate the engine bay,
which was very useful during
night-time maneuvers.

JOINT EFFORT
Willys and Ford Jeeps saw service in every theater
of war, and the two versions were almost identical.
By August 1945, when wartime production of the
Jeep ended, the two companies together had
manufactured over 600,000 Jeeps. The US Army
continued using Jeeps well into the Sixties.

INDEX

A

ACKNOWLEDGMENTS

ORLING KINDERSLEY WOULD LIKE TO THANK:
cky Lampon for additional editorial assistance;
haya Sajwan, Supriya Mahajan, Namita, and Neha
arma for design assistance; Shanker Prasad for
ditional DTP design assistance; Georgina Lowin for
cture research; Myriam Megharbi in the picture library;
corn Studios PLC; Action Vehicles of Shepperton
lm Studios; Sarah Ashun; Dave Babcock; Philip Blythe
r supplying number plates; Bob and Ricky from D.J.
otors; Andy Brown; Geoff Browne at *Classic Car
eekly*; Phillip Bush at Readers Digest, Australia for
pervising the supply of the Holden; Paul Charlton;
rry Clarke; *Classic American* magazine; Cobra Studios,
anchester; Coulsdon Mark; Cricket; Barry Cunlisse of
e AAC (NW); Al Deane; Michael Farrington; Derek
sher; Jenny Glanville and Kirstie Ashton Bell at
ough Studios; Rosie Good of the TR Owners Club;
dy Greenfield of the Classic Corvette Club (UK);
ter Grist of the Chrysler Corp. Club (UK); William
ill) Greenwood of the Cadillac Owners Club of Great
itain; Rockin' Roy Hunt; Kilian and Alistair Konig
Konig Car Transport for vehicle transportation
d invaluable help in sourcing cars; Dave King; Bill
cGarth; Ken McMahon at Pelican Graphics; Bill
edcalf; Ben, Dan, and Rob Milton; Geoff Mitchell; Mr
eVoe Moore, Jeff Moyes of AFN Ltd; Colin Murphy;
rry Newbury; Colin Nolson; Gary Ombler; John
rsler; Paul Osborn; Ben Pardon; Tony Paton; Derek
arson; Pooks motor bookshop and Cars and Stripes
c original advertising material and brochures; Tony
well at Powell Performance Cars; Antony Pozner at
endon Way Motors for helpful advice and supply of
ne cars; Kevin O' Rourke of Moto-technique; Dave
shby; Peter Rutt; Ian Shipp; David and Christine
nith; Ian Smith; George Solomonides for help with
urcing images; John Stark; Richard Stephenson; Steve
Trident Recovery; Straight Eight Ltd; Ashley Straw;
ve and Rita Sword of the AAC; Tallahasee Car
useum, Tallahasee, Florida; Gary Townsend; Marc
lpin (Belgian representative of the AAC); John Weeks
Europlate for number plate assistance; Rob Wells;
d Margaret McCormack for compiling the index.

DORLING KINDERSLEY WOULD LIKE TO THANK THE
FOLLOWING FOR ALLOWING THEIR CARS TO BE
PHOTOGRAPHED:
Page 12 courtesy of Anthony Morpeth; p. 16 A.J.
Pozner (Hendon Way Motors); p. 20 Louis Davidson;
p. 24 Richard Norris; p. 28 Valerie Pratt; p. 32 Brian
Smail; p. 36 Desmond J. Smail; p. 40 David and Jon
Maughan; p. 44 Tom Turkington (Hendon Way
Motors); p. 48 restored and owned by Julian Aubanel;
p. 52 courtesy of Austin-Healey Associates Ltd, Beech
Cottage, North Looe, Reigate Road, Ewell, Surrey,
KT17 3DH; p. 56 courtesy of Mr. Willem van Aalst;
p. 60 A.J. Pozner (Hendon Way Motors); p. 68 Terence
P.J. Halliday; p. 72 L & C BMW Tunbridge Wells; p. 78
The Rt. Hon. Greg Knight; p. 82 "57th Heaven" Steve
West's 1957 Buick Roadmaster; p. 86 Geoff Cook; p. 90
Tony Powell of Powell Performance Cars; p. 94 Tony
Powell; p. 98 Liam Kavanagh; p. 102 Stewart Homan,
Dream Cars; p. 106 Garry Darby, American 50's Car
Hire; p. 110 Tim Buller; p. 114 Alfie Orkin; p. 118
Dream Cars; p. 122 Mike and Margaret Collins; p. 124
Phil Townend; p. 126 Mark Surman; p. 130 Benjamin
Pollard of the Classic Corvette Club UK (vehicle
preparation courtesy of Corvette specialists D.A.R.T
Services, Kent, UK); p. 134 Colin Nolson; p. 138 car
owned and restored by Bill Leonard; p. 142 Rick and
Rachel Bufton; p. 146 Alex Gunn; p. 148 Tallahassee
Car Museum; p. 150 Mike Webb; p. 154 Colin Nolson;
p. 158 Geoff Mitchell; p. 162 Alex Greatwood; p. 166
Geoff Mitchell; p. 170 Classic Restorations; p. 174 on
loan from Le Tout Petit Musée/Nick Thompson,
director Sussex 2CV Ltd; p. 178 Classic Restorations;
p. 182 Derek E.J. Fisher; p. 186 Steve Rogers; p. 190
Daimler SP 250 owned by Claude Kearley; p. 194 Steve
Gamage; p. 196 Kevin Kay; p. 200 D. Howarth; p. 204
Nando Rossi; p. 208 Lewis Strong; p. 212 Neil Crozier;
p. 216 Gavin and Robert Garrow; p. 220 Charles
Booth; p. 224 owned and supplied by Straight Eight Ltd
(London); p. 233 A.J. Pozner (Hendon Way Motors);
p. 234 A.J. Pozner (Hendon Way Motors); p. 238 A.J.
Pozner (Hendon Way Motors); p. 243 Dr. Ismond
Rosen; p. 244 by kind permission of J.A.M. Meyer;

p. 254 Janet & Roger Westcott; p. 258 Bell & Colvill PLC, Epsom Road, West Horsley, Surrey KT24 6DG, UK; p. 262 Dream Cars; p. 266 Rockin' Roy Hunt – '50s aficionado; p. 270 M. Fenwick; p. 274 Teddy Turner Collection; p. 278 Max & Beverly Floyd; p. 282 Roy Hamilton; p. 286 Gordon Keeble by kind permission of Charles Giles; p. 292 David Selby; p. 294 Mike and Margaret Collins; p. 296 Jeff Hine; p. 304 c/o Hendon Way Motors; p. 306 owner Phil Hester; p. 310 John F. Edwins; p. 312 Tallahassee Car Museum; p. 316 John Skelton; p. 318 privately owned; p. 322 A.R.J. Dyas; p. 326 courtesy of Ian Fraser, restoration Omicron Engineering, Norwich; p. 330 courtesy of Martin Cliff; p. 336 Michael Farrington; p. 340 Geoff Tompkins; p. 344 owner Phillip Collier, rebuild by Daytune; p. 346 Alexander Fyshe; p. 350 Edwin J. Faulkner; p. 352 Irene Turner; p. 360 Mrs. Joan Williams; p. 366 courtesy of Chris Alderson; p. 370 John Venables; p. 372 John Watson, Abingdon-on-Thames; p. 374 Martin Garvey; p. 378 E.J. Warrilow saved this car from the scrapyard in 1974; restored by the owner in 1990, maintaining all original panels and mechanics; winner of many concourse trophies; p. 382 NSU Ro80 1972 David Hall; p. 384 Barrie Cunliffe; p. 388 Cared for and cruised in by Mark Phillips; p. 392 Peter Morey; p. 394 Panhard PL17 owned by Anthony T.C. Bond, Oxfordshire, editor of "Panoramique" (Panhard Club newsletter); p. 396 Nick O'Hara; p. 400 Maurice Harvey; p. 404 Alan Tansley; p. 408 courtesy of Peter Rutt; p. 412 Roger Wait; p. 416 owner Mr P.G.K. Lloyd; p. 420 c/o Hendon Way Motors; p. 424 Richard Tyzack's historic rally Alpine; p. 428 owned by Ian Shanks of Northamptonshire; p. 434 David C. Baughan; p. 436 Dream Cars; p. 438 Peter Matthews; p. 442 Lord Raynham of Norfolk; p. 444 E.A.W. Holden; p. 448 Brian Burgess; p. 452 Mr. DeVoe Moore, Tallahassee Car Museum, Tallahassee, Florida; p. 456 Nick Hughe & Tim Smith; p. 460 Roy E. Craig; p. 462 Kevin Price Volvo Enthusiasts' Club; p. 464 Peter Barber-Lomax.

PICTURE CREDITS

THE PUBLISHER WOULD LIKE TO THANK THE FOLLOWING FOR THEIR KIND PERMISSION TO REPRODUCE THEIR PHOTOGRAPHS:

t= top b= bottom c= center
l= left r= right a= above

COMMISSIONED PHOTOGRAPHY

Most pictures in this book are by *Matthew Ward,* with a significant contribution by *Andy Crawford.* Additional pictures are by:
Nick Goodall : pp. 19t, 358br, 447tr
Clive Kane : pp. 288–91
Dave King (US): pp. 148–49, 312–15, 452–55

AGENCY PHOTOGRAPHS

Aerospace Publishing Ltd: 64tl, 64–65bc, 65tl, 66cl, 66bl, 67br, 67–66tcr, 208tl, 208bc, 209tl, 210tc, 210clb, 211tc, 210–11b, 224bc, 225tc, 226tl, 226bl, 227tc, 227bc, 232tl, 232c, 232bc, 242tl, 242c, 242bc, 300tl, 300bc, 301tc, 302tl, 302–03bl, 303tc, 303bcr, 322–23b, 323tc, 324tl, 324cb, 325tr, 325b, 442bl, 442–43bc, 443tc.

Peter Newark's Pictures: 277tr.

Giles Chapman Library: 63t, 77t, 253t, 335t, 365t, 423t, 433t, 441t.

Magic Car Pics: 249t, 251t.

Poole Collection: 19tc.

Reader's Digest: 288tl, 288bc, 289tc, 289bc, 290tl, 290c, 290bl, 291br.

All other images © Dorling Kindersley
For further information see: www.dkimages.com